THE SILENT SEASON OF A

A Writer's Life (2006)
The Gay Talese Reader (2003)
The Bridge (revised and updated) (2003)
The Literature of Reality (with Barbara Lounsberry) (1996)
Unto the Sons (1992)
Thy Neighbor's Wife (1980)
Honor Thy Father (1971)
Fame and Obscurity (1970)
The Kingdom and the Power (1969)
The Overreachers (1965)
The Bridge (1964)
New York: A Serendipiter's Journey (1961)

THE SILENT SEASON OF A HERO

The Sports Writing of Gay Talese

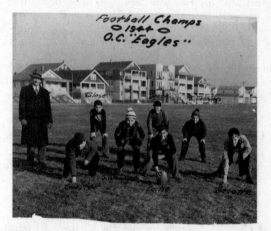

Edited by Michael Rosenwald

Walker & Company
New York

In the photo on the title page, the author appears third from the left.

The articles on which a portion of this book is based originally
appeared in the *New York Times*, and to the extent they are
reprinted here, they are reprinted with permission.

Published by Walker Publishing Company, Inc., New York

All papers used by Walker & Company are natural, recyclable products
made from wood grown in well-managed forests. The manufacturing
processes conform to the environmental regulations
of the country of origin.

Library of Congress Cataloging-in-Publication Data

The silent season of a hero : the sports writing of Gay Talese / edited
by Michael Rosenwald.—1st U.S. ed.
p.   cm.
Includes bibliographical references.
ISBN 978-0-8027-7753-9
1. Talese, Gay.   2. Sportswriters—United States.   3. Journalists—
United States.   4. Sports—United States.   I. Rosenwald, Michael.
II. Title.
GV742.42.T38S55 2010
070.4'49796—dc22
2010024507

Visit Walker & Company's Web site at www.walkerbooks.com

First U.S. edition 2010

1 3 5 7 9 10 8 6 4 2

Typeset by Westchester Book Group
Printed in the United States of America by Worldcolor Fairfield

CONTENTS

CONTENTS

CONTENTS

INTRODUCTION
Gay Talese

The jockey came to the doorway of the dining room, then after a moment stepped to one side and stood motionless, with his back to the wall. The room was crowded, as this was the third day of the season and all the hotels in the town were full . . .

He examined the room until at last his eyes reached a table in a corner diagonally across from him, at which three men were sitting . . . a trainer, a bookie, and a rich man. The trainer was Sylvester—a large, loosely built fellow with a flushed nose and slow blue eyes.

It was Sylvester who first saw the jockey . . .

Sylvester turned to the rich man. "If he eats a lamb chop, you can see the shape of it in his stomach a hour afterward. He can't sweat things out of him any more . . ."

—Extracted from "The Jockey," a short story first published in the *New Yorker* on August 23, 1941 and written by Carson McCullers when she was twenty-four years old.

WHEN I WAS twenty-four years old in 1956, and was working as a feature writer in the sports department of the *New York Times*, I read "The Jockey" for the first time in a paperback anthology, and as I read and reread that memorable sentence—"If he eats a lamb chop, you can see the shape of it in his stomach afterward"—I kept wondering how Carson McCullers had come to write it. Had she once met an aging and food-craving jockey whose taut and tiny stomach was imprinted with the shape of a lamb chop? Did she just dream up the image? Did some horse trainer or jockey describe it to her? From reading articles about her in the press—she was quite famous as a young woman, having published at twenty-three a best-selling first novel, *The Heart is a Lonely Hunter*—I knew that when she was twenty-four she was living near a race track in upstate New York while enrolled as a writer-in-residence at the Yaddo artists' retreat; and I assumed that during this time she had mingled with the racing crowd and had gathered the material out of which would come "The Jockey"—although nothing that I had read about her confirmed this. All I knew was that Carson McCullers suffered a stroke before her story appeared in the *New Yorker*, and that within a few years she experienced two more strokes that partly paralyzed her and caused her to write thereafter, until a final stroke finished her at fifty, with one finger on a typewriter—leaving behind a body of work that included five novels, two plays, twenty stories, and that single line about the lamb chop that to me represented a peculiarly interesting and original way of creating in a few words a lasting impression.

As a young writer I never aspired to follow Ms. McCullers into fiction, even though she and most of the other writers that appealed to me used their imaginations to tell their stories. They fabricated reality. They made up names and provided their characters with words, scenes, and situations. They fantasized, mythologized, and created mysteries and sometimes magic with their prose. When I was in college studying journalism I spent my leisure time reading novels and short stories while wondering how I might best borrow the tools of a fiction writer— scene-setting, dialogue, drama, conflict—and apply these to the nonfiction pieces I hoped to contribute someday to a major newspaper or magazine. There were so many fine fiction writers, it seemed to me, and not enough nonfiction writers who had mastered the art of storytelling, and so it was my goal to become one of these.

But I wanted to write short stories using *real* names, to describe situations that had truly occurred and were factually verifiable. I wanted to be there in person, to observe situations with my own eyes, and to describe what I saw in a literary manner worthy of those writers I admired and whose special sentences and word choices I often underlined on the page, sometimes adding in the margin a complimentary comment or perhaps a question of my own about the usage.

After first reading "The Jockey," I underlined Carson Mc-Cullers's description of the horse trainer Sylvester—"a large, loosely built fellow with a flushed nose and slow blue eyes." *Slow* blue eyes? I wondered: What does she mean by *slow*? Maybe a typo for "sloe-eyed," I thought. But no, I decided after consulting a dictionary, she must be referring to the fifth definition listed there: "*slow*—sluggish, inactive . . ." Yes. Later she described how the jockey entered the race track's restaurant and "scrutinized the room with pinched, crêpe eyes . . ." To the dictionary again: "crêpe—a light, soft thin fabric of silk, or another fiber, with a crinkled surface." Ah, *pinched, crêpe* eyes—yes. And that lamb chop: At first I doubted the possibility of anyone being able to see its shape on the jockey's stomach, and so one day in 1958 when I was given an assignment by the sports editor to interview an ex-jockey named Harry Roble—who had once been the top jockey in the United States—I decided to question him about the lamb chop. I began by describing Ms. McCullers's story to him (he had never heard of it); but after I read him the line I loved, he nodded and said, "Yes, that's possible," adding, "I never liked lamb chops, but I'd sometimes sneak in a steak afterwards I could feel the damn steak pressed against my skin. In those days, when I was weighing 98 pounds and struggling to keep it at that, I'd even put on two pounds with each bowl of soup."

In my profile on the ex-jockey, which appeared in the *Times*'s sports page on July 20th of 1958, I wrote this lead (privately dedicating it to Carson McCullers):

> Harry Roble was one of those jockeys who gained two pounds after every bowl of soup and, if he ate a steak, you could sometimes see its lumpy outline lodged in his stomach.

Among other fiction writers who influenced me during those days were Ernest Hemingway, F. Scott Fitzgerald, John O'Hara, and Irwin Shaw, the latter two being regular contributors to the *New Yorker*, which I began reading shortly after I was hired as a copyboy on the *Times* in the summer of 1953 following my graduation in June from the University of Alabama. At Alabama I'd been the sports editor of the campus newspaper, the *Crimson-White*, and I also wrote a column called "Sports Gay-zing" that at times tried to emulate such well-known columnists as Red Smith, Jimmy Cannon, and Dan Parker. At the same time I was drawn more to the authors of fictional stories in magazines, especially when their stories were set within the atmosphere of sporting events: Hemingway on bull fighting and fishing, O'Hara on the esoteric game of court tennis, Irwin Shaw on football, and F. Scott Fitzgerald on a status-conscious caddy who carried bags at a club in Minnesota, where Fitzgerald grew up.

Fitzgerald's story "Winter Dreams" was my all-time favorite. In the opening section it described the caddy skiing over the snow-covered hills of the country club feeling offended that "the links should lie in enforced fallowness," but then in April the members reappeared to play golf with red and black balls that were easier to see than white ones when hit into patches of snow along the fairways and the rough—and among the sharp-eyed caddies who most quickly spotted the balls was Fitzgerald's young hero Dexter Green.

As a schoolboy I also worked at times as a caddy, doing so at a club across the bay from my hometown in Ocean City, N.J.; and like Dexter Green, I always closely followed the direction of the ball after the golfer had hit it, and rarely did I fail to find it no matter where it had landed. Indeed, my capacity to retrieve golf balls would help me decades later while researching a piece for *Esquire* on Joe DiMaggio, which would be published in July of 1956, fifteen years after he had retired from baseball.

I had first been introduced to DiMaggio in 1965 at an "Old Timers" game at Yankee Stadium by a *New York Times* photographer we both knew; and during our friendly chat in the locker room DiMaggio indicated that he would be willing to see me whenever I happened to be in his hometown of San Francisco. Months later I notified him in a letter that I was coming, but on entering the restaurant he owned on Fisherman's Wharf I was rebuffed in a way that astonished me but that also provided me with my article's opening scene, one in which I was ejected from the premises by Joe DiMaggio himself.

The fact that I was able to become reacquainted with DiMaggio a few days later was the result of a request that I had made through one of DiMaggio's friends and golfing partners that I be allowed to follow their foursome through one eighteen-hole round at a club in the outskirts of San Francisco. During the golfing session, DiMaggio, who hated to lose golf balls, lost three of them. I found them. After that DiMaggio's attitude toward me improved noticeably. I was invited to other matches and to join him in the evening at social events as well as to interview him in his home, and finally to accompany him on a flight to the Yankees' spring training camp in Fort Lauderdale, Florida, where he served as a batting instructor.

Having been forewarned by one of DiMaggio's friends, I never questioned him directly about his private life with the late Marilyn Monroe, whose break-up of their marriage was said to have caused him much grief and frustration. But my approach to the piece was never intended to deal with the reality of the DiMaggio-Monroe relationship but rather with DiMaggio's sense of loneliness and longing for a woman he had idealized and had lost, and who, following her death, had left him with little else but to mourn her. As I mentioned in the piece, he ordered that fresh flowers be placed on her grave "forever."

What I wrote about DiMaggio was laden with nostalgia, which is true as well of Fitzgerald's story about Dexter Green—who, after his caddying days were over and he had fulfilled his ambition to become very rich, was playing golf one day with other affluent men when he saw, pitching a ball into a sand pit on the other side of the green, a young woman whom he had first seen a decade or so earlier when she had been taking lessons as an eleven-year-old and he was a caddy of fourteen. Her name was Judy Jones, and now in the story Dexter Green pauses to appreciate the reappearance of her in his life:

She wore a blue gingham dress, rimmed at the throat and shoulders with a white edging that accentuated her tan. The quality of exaggeration, of thinness, which had made her passionate eyes and down-turned mouth absurd at eleven, was gone now. She was arrestingly beautiful.

Of course Dexter Green fell in love with her, and while this would in time proceed to an exciting affair it was one that she impulsively terminated as her attentions were drawn to another man, and then another. Dexter Green soon moved from the Midwest to Wall Street and added to his fortune, but he was finally forced to conclude, as Fitzgerald had phrased it, that Judy Jones:

> . . . was not a girl who could be "won" in the kinetic sense . . . She was entertained only by the gratification of her desires and by the direct exercise of her own charm. Perhaps from so much youthful love, so many youthful lovers, she had come, in self-defense, to nourish herself wholly from within.

I thought that this could have been written about Marilyn Monroe; and, in fact, as Fitzgerald's biographers have pointed out, the fictional Judy Jones was based on a real woman whom Fitzgerald himself had once ardently courted—a lovely and elusive Midwestern socialite named Ginevra King. It is also true, I believe, that there was a bit of Dexter Green's spirit in Joe DiMaggio and me and in many of the men I have encountered and befriended since I first came to New York in 1953 as a copyboy. I then learned a month later, much to my despair and in spite of my best efforts to get her to change her mind, that the first love of my life—*my* Judy Jones in Alabama—had left me for someone else. Although a half-century has since passed and I have never seen her again, I have—like Dexter Green in "Winter Dreams"—regularly kept up with her through the comments and observations of mutual friends who occasionally visit me in New York. Whenever she is mentioned, I cease thinking about other things and listen. And after I had been promoted from copyboy to reporter and had published a piece about caddies in the June 12, 1960 issue of the *New York Times Magazine*, my lead began with Fitzgerald's description of what a wealthy Dexter Green was thinking as he and his golfing partners advances along the fairway:

> . . . he found himself glancing at the four caddies who trailed them, trying to catch a glance or gesture that could remind him of himself, that would lessen the gap which lay between his present and his past . . .

Another fiction writer who influenced my early journalism was Irwin Shaw, who, before he began publishing such best selling novels as *The Young Lions*, *Rich Man*, *Poor Man*, and *The Troubled Air*, and also more than eighty stories in various magazines, had been a football player at Brooklyn College. He brought his knowledge of the game to much of what he had created with his prose. He once told a class he was teaching: "Writing is an intellectual contact sport, similar in some respects to football. The effort required can be exhausting, the goal unreached, and you are hurt on almost every play; but that doesn't deprive a man or a boy from getting peculiar pleasures form the game."

From reading his fiction I saw greater possibilities from myself as a writer of nonfiction, as a scene-setter, a dialogue writer, a reporter who could recount true-to-life tales *more fully and interestingly* by deviating from the then prevailing formulaic

code of 5-W journalism (who-what-when-where-why) and em-
ploying the story-telling techniques of people like Irwin Shaw.
While my efforts were often rejected or rewritten by my editors (after I had reviewed packages of my old clippings in the
Times's morgue in 1959 and had underlined certain words and
sentences and had scribbled next to them my complaint: "I
didn't write this!," the morgue's director inserted a note of his
own: "GT: Modesty will get you no where. Mutillating morgue clippings is worse than a Federal offense!") I did manage,
through some polite persuading on my part and the good will
of my superiors, to get into the paper word-for-word much of
what I wrote.

For example in 1958 when I was sent to cover the spring training activities of the San Francisco Giants baseball team I devoted
an entire piece to the wearability of the players' uniforms, point-
ing out that after one season the uniforms become "too weary
for major league play and are sent down to the minors." In the
same year I wrote a nineteen-paragraph profile about a young
prize fighter named Jose Torres without mentioning his name
until the last paragraph. Similarly in 1958 I covered a college
baseball game between New York University and Wagner College that was held in freezing early-spring weather in front of
only eighteen spectators. I described the game through the per-
spective of the spectators, focusing my attentions, for example,
on a nineteen-year-old hazel-eyed brunette sophomore named
Gloria Maurikis who had shivered through the game out of affection from the N.Y.U. third baseman, Dick Reilly, whom she
had met five months before in Sociology I, a required course. The
N.Y.U. team was leading 3–0 going into the seventh inning, and
as I wrote in the last paragraph: "The score remained unchanged
until Reilly's double in the seventh scored two more and sent
Gloria home."

Writing about a young woman sitting in the bleachers watching a sporting event was perhaps an idea I'd appropriated, without consciously realizing it, through my familiarity with many of Irwin Shaw's romantic scenes involving athletes. There are many such scenes in his story "The Eighty-Yard Run." The two main characters are named Christian Darling, a handsome substitute halfback on a college team in the Midwest, and his wealthy girlfriend Louise, who is described in the story as the lovely daughter of an ink manufacturer. On the sunny afternoon after Christian Darling had run for eighty yards in a practice session, Louise is waiting for him outside the stadium in her car with the top down; and, as he approaches, she opens the door and asks:

"Were you good today?"

"Pretty good," he said. He climbed in, sank luxuriously into the soft leather, stretched his legs far out. He smiled, thinking of the eighty yards. "Pretty damn good."

But although Christian Darling would be promoted to the starting team thanks to his performance in practice, he would never again experience the exhilaration he had felt on that particular afternoon; or, as it was elaborated upon in the story:

... the longest run he'd ever made was thirty-five yards, and that in a game that was already won, and then that kid had come up from the third team, Diederich, a blank-faced German kid from Wisconsin, who ran like a bull, ripping lines to pieces Saturday after Saturday, plowing through, never getting hurt, never changing his expression ...

Darling was a good blocker and he spent his Saturday afternoons working on the big Swedes and Polacks who played

tackle and end for Michigan, Illinois, Purdue, hurling into huge
pile-ups . . . to open holes for Diederich coming through like a
locomotive behind him. Still, it wasn't so bad. Everybody liked
him and he did his job and he was pointed out on the campus . . .
and [Louise] drove him around in her car keeping the top down
because she was proud of him and wanted to show everybody
that she was Christian Darling's girl . . .

The couple got married after graduation in the mid-1920s and
moved to New York, where Louise's father underwrote the
cost of their apartment on Beekman Place and established an
East Coast office with three hundred ink-buying accounts for
his son-in-law to supervise. The young couple lived well, attended Broadway shows, visited speakeasies, and made many
new friends (some of whom referred favorably to the fact that
Darling had once played in the backfield with the great
Diederich); and while Louise remained enamored of her husband, who kept in shape playing squash three times a week,
she also invested much time going alone to "art galleries and
the matinees of the more serious plays that Darling didn't like
to sit through."

Then after the Depression, during which Louise's father lost
all his money and committed suicide, she got a job with a
woman's fashion magazine and obtained a less expensive apartment for herself and Darling downtown, where he idled away
the hours for months and years at a time while she gradually
advanced as an editor and connoisseur of avant-garde art, poetry, playwriting, and fashion while associating more and more
with individuals who cared little about football. When her
husband finally got a fulltime job in his mid-thirties it was as a
representative of a men's clothing firm that was in competition
with Brooks Brothers and that expected Darling to travel from

campus to campus with his *"broad shoulders and well-kept waist . . . his carefully brushed hair and his honest, wrinkle-less face"* to glad-hand potential customers and prompt them to think: *There's a university man.* The executive who had hired Darling admitted that he had done a background check on him and was pleased to learn that he was favorably remembered at his alma mater and had been Diederich's teammate.

Darling nodded. "Whatever happened to him?"

"He is walking around in a cast for seven years now. An iron brace. He played professional football and they broke his neck for him.

Darling smiled. That, at least, had turned out well.

Irwin Shaw ends his story with a scene of Darling revisiting his old campus and strolling alone onto the grassy field of the stadium where, fifteen years before, he had gone eighty yards.

. . . The high point, an eighty-yard run in practice, and a girl's kiss and everything after that a decline. Darling laughed.

. . . He looked around him. This was the spot . . . the high point. Darling put up his hands, felt all over again the flat slap of the ball. He shook his hips . . . ran easily, gaining speed, for ten yards, holding the ball lightly in his two hands . . . his shoes drumming heavily . . .

It was only after he had sped over the goal line and slowed to a trot that he saw the boy and girl sitting together on the turf, looking at him wonderingly.

He stopped short, dropping his arms. "I . . ." he said, gasping a little, though his condition was fine and the run hadn't winded him. "I—once I played here."

The boy and the girl said nothing. Darling laughed embarrassedly, looked hard at them sitting there, close to each other, shrugged, turned and went toward his hotel, the sweat breaking out on his face and running down into his collar.

When I first finished reading "The Eighty-Yard Run" I was in tears, thinking of how sad the story was, and how true it probably was, although I knew very little at this point in my career about athletes growing older. As a junior writer in the *Times*'s sports department in the mid-1950s, and before that as a contributor to the sports sections of my college paper and my hometown weekly, I had mainly interviewed athletes who were about my age. But as I approached my thirties in the early 1960s, however, and concentrated less on daily journalism than magazine writing—which allowed me more space and time, especially in the monthly pages of *Esquire*—I was better able to pursue my interest in profiling people whose up-and-down experiences broadened my capacity for storytelling and writing scenes that shifted between the past and the present.

Boxers held special appeal for me, and this book describes the lives of three boxers in periods following their reigns as heavyweight champions: There is Muhammad Ali entering middle age while battling the effects of Parkinson's syndrome, and Floyd Patterson seeking to obscure his identity and his sense of humiliation after each poor performance in the ring by wearing false whiskers and a mustache while walking in the streets, and the forty-eight-year-old ex-champ Joe Louis trying to find marital contentment with his third wife while following a daily routine that consisted mainly of watching television and playing golf. I interviewed Louis in 1962 during one of his visits to New York, and, after I had accompanied him on a flight back to his home in Los Angeles, my story began:

"Hi, sweetheart!" Joe Louis called to his wife, spotting her waiting for him at the Los Angeles airport.

She smiled, walked toward him, and was about to stretch up on her toes and kiss him—but suddenly stopped.

"Joe," she said, "where's your tie?"

"Aw, sweetie," he said, shrugging, "I stayed out all night in New York and didn't have time—"

"All night!" she cut in. "When you're out here all you do is sleep, sleep, sleep."

"Sweetie," Joe Louis said, with a tired grin, "I'm an ole man."

"Yes," she agreed, "but when you go to New York, you try to be young again."

They walked slowly through the airport lobby toward their car, being followed by a redcap with Joe's luggage . . .

Tom Wolfe read this article in *Esquire* in 1962—it was entitled "Joe Louis: The King as a Middle-Aged Man"—and celebrated it as a groundbreaking example of what he called "The New Journalism." But I was not entirely happy to be identified as a founder of the so-called New Journalism because I never though that what I was doing was particularly "new." Its foundation in my case was old-fashioned reporting, lots of leg work, combined with much patience and polite persistence; and if anyone was to be credited for giving shape and direction to my writing style it was those fiction writers I have already quoted from at length earlier in this space—Carson McCullers, F. Scott Fitzgerald, and Irwin Shaw.

In the final paragraph of my 1966 piece in *Esquire* on Joe DiMaggio—the title of which, "The Silent Season of a Hero," is repeated on the cover of this book—I describe how a number of reporters had gathered behind the batting cage at the Yankees' spring training camp in Fort Lauderdale, Florida, watching as the fifty-one-year-old Joe DiMaggio responded to a batting-practice pitcher, Vern Benson, who had just called out to him:

"Joe, wanna hit some?"
"No chance," DiMaggio said.
"Com'on Joe," Benson said.

The reporters waited silently. Then DiMaggio walked slowly into the cage and picked up Mantle's bat. He took his position at the plate, but obviously it was not the classic DiMaggio stance; he was holding the bat about two inches from the knob, his feet were not so far apart, and, when DiMaggio took a cut at Benson's first pitch, fouling it, there was none of that ferocious follow through, the blurred bat did not come shipping all the way around, the No.5 was not stretched full across his broad back.

DiMaggio fouled Benson's second pitch, then he connected solidly with the third, the fourth, the fifth. He was just meeting the ball easily, however, not smashing it, and Benson called out, "I didn't know you were a choke hitter, Joe."

"I am now," DiMaggio said, getting ready for another pitch. He hit three more squarely enough, and then he swung again and there was a hollow sound.

"Ohhh," DiMaggio yelled, dropping his bat, his fingers stung. "I was waiting for that one." He left the batting cage rubbing his hands together. The reporters watched him. Nobody said anything. Then DiMaggio said to one of them, not in anger nor in sadness, but merely as a simply stated fact, "There was a time when you couldn't get me out of there."

When I heard DiMaggio say that, as I stood next to some of the reporters, I thought again of the final paragraph of Irwin

Shaw's "The Eighty-Yard Run," in which the former halfback, Christian Darling, returns to the stadium and retraces his steps of fifteen years before, and . . .

> It was only after he had sped over the goal line and slowed to a trot that he saw the boy and girl sitting together on the turf, looking at him wonderingly. He stopped short, dropping his arms.
>
> "I . . ." he said, gasping a little, though his condition was fine and the run hadn't winded him. "I—once played here."

In closing I would like to thank two individuals who contributed much to the existence of this book: its publisher, George Gibson, whose idea it was to collect my sports pieces, and Mike Rosenwald of the *Washington Post*, who selected them and whose comments about them appear on the following pages.

SPORTS GAY-ZING

GAY TALESE GREW up in Ocean City, N.J., a seaside resort town a couple of hours by car from New York City. His father was a tailor and his mother sold dresses, and they doted on their customers at their small shop, Talese Town Shop, located just underneath the family's apartment. Talese was an outsider in school, not unlike his parents, who were Catholic Italian-Americans making their lives in an old Protestant town. While his classmates dressed in mackinaw jackets, Talese wore handsome fitted clothes—jacket and tie, always—that his father had stitched together at the shop. Decades later, at a class reunion, Talese remembers classmates told him that they had found him "aloof" and "quirky" and "in another world." Talese got lousy grades. He even flunked English. "I really had nothing going on," he felt.

His outlook changed one day when Lorin Angevine, the editor of the weekly town newspaper the *Sentinel-Ledger* and a regular customer at the store, suggested to Talese's father that his wayward son should submit articles to the paper. Talese had become interested in short stories after discovering a

Maupassant collection in his house, and that led to him penning articles here and there for the high school paper. He enjoyed seeing his byline in print, so he went to see Angevine, who offered him a column called "High School Highlights" at a salary of ten cents per column inch. "The first break I had in life was working for the town weekly because it gave me an excuse for a career future," Talese says. "I didn't have a career future. I wasn't going to be a tailor because the tailoring business was dying."

Talese, an outsider to his school's social scene, attended dances as a reporter rather than a young man with a date, chronicling who wore what and who strolled in on the arm of the football captain. Though he could hit a baseball his contributions to the town's sporting scene came primarily at his typewriter. He wrote a popular column called "Sportopics." Looking at these early efforts there are hints of Talese's lifelong obsession, and compassion, for outsiders and losers. "Short Shots in Sundry Sections," from Dec. 23 1948, is about a six-foot seven-inch freshman basketball player taking the court for the first time. Clueless about the game, but towering over the other players, his coach instructs the awkward giant to stand under the basket and wait for teammates to toss him the ball. "He missed lots of passes and didn't score, but he's still learning," Talese wrote, "and willing."

Talese was rejected by every college in the region. A customer of his father's who graduated from the University of Alabama made a few phone calls to the admissions office in Tuscaloosa, and Talese was accepted there a few weeks later, not even knowing he had applied. On the train ride down, Talese read a novel by Irwin Shaw, one of his favorite writers. Though he wasn't elected sports editor of the *Crimson-White* until his junior year, as a journalism major he immediately resisted his teachers' efforts to drill into his writing the who-what-when-where-why formula of daily journalism by incorporating into his stories the tools of a fiction writer—scene, characters, dialogue, narrative.

In his feature stories for the *Crimson-White* and later in his column "Sports Gay-zing," Talese cared little about final scores and more about the characters playing the games. The column, he once wrote, "was inspired to the point of plagiarism by the bittersweet romanticism of Irwin Shaw's short stories in the *New Yorker* and Red Smith's lyrical musings on athleticism in the *New York Herald-Tribune*." As a rule, losers were always more attractive subjects than winners, and in these portraits the now singular Talese voice—deft, precise, gentle, sometimes formal, sometimes witty—begins appearing. In a story about a devastating football team loss, Talese described the players in the locker room as "dressed in shorts, or in towels, or in nothing." About the first football practice one season, Talese wrote: "Under hail, a cold wind, a 30-degree temperature Saturday afternoon, Coach Harold (Red) Drew gently tooted the whistle at 3:30 P.M. and 80 huge hunks of Alabama scholarships began to smash and lash at one another." Talese graduated in 1953, returning north and landing a copyboy job at the *New York Times*.

MR

SHORT SHOTS IN
SUNDRY SECTIONS
Ocean City Sentinel-Ledger, 1948

YOU MAY HAVE seen that tall awkward kid on the basketball court Friday night, in the freshman game which preceded the Millville affair. You may have noticed the ribbing he took from the crowd. It was obvious he didn't know much about basketball wasn't it? But then who does when he plays it for the first time?

The tall boy is Leslie Kelley, a 6-foot, 7-inch freshman from offshore. John Carey, freshman coach, says he (Kelley) hasn't finished growing yet by any means. Friday evening marked the first time he had ever been on a basketball court during a game. He didn't do anything but hang under the offensive basket as Coach Carey had instructed him to do, waiting for his teammates to throw it to him so he could drop it through.

He missed lots of passes and didn't score, but he's still learning, and willing. You just have to give him lots of credit for having the stamina to stay out there on the floor, especially when the spectators are having a big time watching you flub-up.

Yes, he is awkward now, but he's young, and who knows! He, like anyone else, can become a basketball player. A 6-foot,

7-inch freshman, who may be a 7-foot senior, could be mighty valuable to any team when taught how to play.

You know, Bob Kurland, styled "Foothills" in his younger days, wasn't exactly a picture of grace and coordination, but practice and patience made him a court star.

No, we didn't say Kelley would ever be a Bob Kurland!

If you think that Joe Verdeur, the invincible breast stroker, was born in a swimming pool, as an Infant Prodigy of the water, this will prove you to be no less than 100 percent wrong.

Verdeur, believe it or not, was so afraid of the water that he didn't go near a pool until he was 15. (There's something for you, Ripley!)

He turned down Yale's offer in favor of little LaSalle so he could stay home and help support his widowed mother.

Chuck (The Clutch) Bednarik may be called America's foremost member of the banquet league. The Penn center has been attending football dinners and grid gatherings since the season ended for Penn.

This All-American can really eat too! Last Wednesday he only had two dinners and three helpings of dessert. (He wasn't very hungry.)

Foul shooting has failed to improve a whole lot for the Careymen. The last two games (Pleasantville and Millville) saw only a slight improvement—and a very slight one it was.

In these two games, they converted only 12 out of 34. Added to the season's average, the local high school five has an average of less than one-third. They have made good on 21 out of 66 attempts.

* * *

The Somers Point Chiefs, under the sponsorship of Frank De-Feo, are undefeated in four games. In their first year under DeFeo's wing, the Chiefs have been doing right well for themselves. Jack Gerety is their manager, while Jack Gerety and Bill Carrol are pacing the offense so far.

Two nice trophies arrived at the high school on Monday. They are for the varsity and junior varsity football squads, both of which have taken Cape May County.

It's going to be gold footballs for the champions this year. Seventeen varsity football point winners, plus the manager, coaches, and Dr. Howard Hudson, team physician, will be given these gold footballs for taking South Jersey. The footballs will each have the name of the player, position, etc. inscribed on it.

Intramurals league competition is going right along. Basketball will start when the students get back to school, as will swimming. Soccer has just been completed and volleyball is almost completed.

To date in the senior league, team X, captained by Joe Avis, is leading the league with 18 points. X has placed in all sports so far. It finished in a tie for fourth for football, ended second in soccer, is among the leaders in volleyball, and took tennis. Team U, captained by Bill Redrow, is in second place with 15 points.

The high school junior varsity is still unbeaten, with a victory string of four. It has beaten Egg Harbor, 49–22; Pleasantille, 51–33; Millville, 39–21; and Penn Charter, 26–25.

* * *

Franny Townsend, Bill Corson, John Haines, all former varsity players with the Careymen, are now on their prep and college teams.

Townsend, who led the local dribblers in scoring last year, is on the varsity squad at Pennington prep. Haines has made the squad at Springfield, while Corson is on Mercersberg's squad.

TALKING BASKETBALL
WITH ANGELO MUSI

Ocean City Sentinel-Ledger, 1949

MARTY GLICKMAN, THE Madison Sq. Garden basketball announcer, was broadcasting the Warriors-Knickerbockers professional BAA basketball game: "The Warriors come up quickly into offensive zone. Musi, with the ball, sets . . . shoots . . . He hits! Like Nedick's Fresh Fruit Orange Drink!" Now whether the little, eagle-eyed ex-shooter of the Philadelphia Warriors is as good—or better—than the mentioned beverage is beside the point, but just ask any Warrior adherent during the court season and you'll find out that the smallest player in the Basketball Association of America is definitely a Big Man in the Philadelphia attack. His field goals that click from the outside with remarkable accuracy have sent arena customers home talking and amazed over "Little No. 5" and asking one another what makes that guy tick.

I attempted to find out a little more about Mr. Musi in a pleasant interview at his 17th st. and Asbury av. apartment, Saturday. I found Angelo to be extremely likable, with a pleasing personality, modest, and intelligent. He is devoted to his pretty wife and two-year-old son and seems to enjoy nothing better in life than just to sit back and relax at home with them.

"How about the Warriors this season?" I asked.

"I can't tell yet," he said. "The Warriors' only signed regular is George Senesky. The new league will be tough this year with all 15 teams strong. Vern Gardener, from Utah, will help us a lot."

The Warriors will begin training October 1, in Hershey. As a rule, the professional players begin getting their eyes on the basket late in August. Angelo will do lots of shooting once or twice each week from now on until October.

Musi went to Overbrook High School, and it was there that he spent many long hours with his set-shooting. He later attended Brown Prep from where he went to Temple in 1938. He made the varsity in his first year. He also was a good baseball player—good enough to be appointed captain of the Temple nine in his junior year, while playing second base. After graduation at Temple (he majored in accounting) he played two years of professional basketball with Wilmington of the American League. He was a key man with this outfit as he sparked Wilmington to the crown, beating out Eddie Gottlieb's (the present coach of the Warriors) Spahs in a close race.

In November of '46 he came to Philadelphia in the Basketball Association of America's initial season.

Like all pro players and the fans, Angelo is an admirer of the famous Joe Fulks, his teammate. He thinks Joe is destined to go down in basketball history as one of its greatest performers.

I asked him who was the toughest player to guard in the B.A.A. "George Mikan, I guess," he replied. "Because of his height he's awful hard for any guard to handle."

When asked which team in the league was the hardest for

the Warriors to top, Fort Wayne was the reply. The Warriors did not beat Fort Wayne all last season.

Angelo actually isn't as short as he looks on a professional basketball floor. He is 5 feet, 9 inches, but when he's seen with nine other skyscrapers, he does seem to be standing in a hole.

"What group of spectators in the B.A.A. were the toughest on the visiting teams last year?" I questioned.

"Well, I think those St. Louis fans were the hardest on the visitors," he said. "Our own Philadelphia fans, though, are pretty tough on the opposition."

When asked about the finest floor to play on, he said "The Arena in Philadelphia is very good. The Boston Garden is another."

The Warriors travel to other league cities by plane, except to New York, Baltimore and Washington, to which they go by train.

I was interested in knowing if there are any "showmen" on the Philadelphia team.

"No, not any more," he said, "but we used to have a fellow named Petey Rosenberg. He was quite a comic. He's in retirement now. Most of the players are pretty natural."

"Is there any moment, of basketball glory that you will remember above all others?" I asked.

"Well, let's see," he pondered. "There was my freshman year at Temple. We were playing Wyoming Seminary. I played only half a game, but I scored 80 points. I was really hot that night. I can remember in the Toronto Maple Leaf game, in the first year of the B.A.A. when I made 13 field goals."

When asked to compare basketball today with the old days (the Boston Celtics era) he replied, "Well basketball today is faster and has more spectator appeal. Never could they have drawn 15,000 people on one night in those days."

"Mr. Outside" of the Warriors likes Ocean City very much. He commented on the fine basketball team that Ocean City High had during the past season.

When in our little talk I found I had no more questions, I left the Musis, after being asked to stop around again.

When the interview was over, Angelo started to play with little Tommy again, something he enjoys as much (perhaps more) as clicking with set shots from the red line or half court in the Arena—those beautiful shots that swish to pile up precious points to a Warrior win while the Philly fans shout: "Viva Angleo!"

Here's Angelo Musi's All-B.A.A. team.

Joe Fulks. . . . . .Philadelphia
George Mikan . . . . .Minneapolis
Max Zaslofsky . . . . .Chicago
Bob Davies . . . . .Rochester
Bob Ferrick. . . . . .Washington

THE LOCKER ROOM
Crimson-White, 1952

ATLANTA—STEAM COMING from the showers gave the Alabama dressing room an obscure shade of grey as a disappointed Crimson Tide team, playing its greatest game of the season, remorsed in a heart-breaking 7–3 defeat to unbeaten Georgia Tech Saturday.

Outside the sun was setting on Grant Field which had been the scene of a bone-busting, nerve-wrecking football battle. It had been a scene filled with wild, thrilling play. It was attended by 40,000 shirt-sleeved gridiron enthusiasts and it had millions of TV-lookers tense & spellbound every moment and limp at the finish.

But now, behind the closed door of the Alabama dressing room, the sterling struggle was over. Things were quiet.

"We were that close there in the first quarter," quarterback Clell Hobson said sadly, as he slumped back on the locker bench and held his hands a foot apart. "Only one foot from the Georgia Tech goal line—so close I could smell the Orange Bowl blossoms!"

Near the door of the dressing room Coach Harold (Red) Drew, with his brown hat tilted slightly and his green sports shirt open at the neck, talked to newsmen. He didn't feel like talking but he talked anyway.

"Of course I thought we were going to score," Drew answered one journalist who asked if the past-period offside penalty inside the 20-yard-line killed Bama's winning threat. "I always think we are going to score when we move inside the 20-yard-line . . . Do I think their defense was good? well, it beat me, din't it? What else could I think?"

Alabama players, dressed in shorts, or in towels, or in nothing, talked with some understandable bitterness & great disappointment.

"We shoulda won, Punchy, we shoulda won," guard Bob Wilga was telling his mate Ralph Carrigan, the ace Tide linebacker.

"We just have to GET Maryland next week," Carrigan answered.

"If we could ONLY play them again," added end Hyrle Ivy, slowly shaking his head.

In the corner an Atlanta newsman was talking to halfback Bobby Marlow who took the defeat badly and did very little talking. Marlow's father was off to the side holding Bobby's jacket.

"Did you really expect to find such a good Tech line, Bobby?" the reporter asked as he put his arm around Marlow's bare shoulder.

"Yes."

"Er . . . were you a little bit . . . er . . . surprised, Bobby, at the way Alabama came through and almost won?"

"No." Bobby answered.

"Did you think Alabama was going to score in the final period?"

"Yes," Bobby said.

The reporter moved on and quoted Marlow as saying: "Georgia Tech is good defensively, but not as hard-hitting as the team of last year."

End coach Malcolm Laney leaned against the equipment trunk in the hot locker room and said with sincerity: "A finer Bama spirit and team play and a stronger desire to win I have never seen. Our boys were great today."

Big & rough All-America Tech linebacker George Morris came in the dressing room later and told Tide players: "You people played the greatest game we have seen in two years. It was the toughest game we had since you came and beat the hell out of us here two years ago."

Some of the players walked around aimlessly. Others quickly dressed and met parents and friends who were awaiting them outside. Someone brought in late word that Ole Miss had just KOed unbeaten Maryland in Oxford, Miss., 21–14. This was NOT what the Bama players wanted to hear. It meant that now the powerful SEC had three teams in post-season Bowl games (Ole Miss, Tech, & Tenn). Where did this all leave Bama's Bowl chances? Would the Orange Bowl committee select a fourth SEC team? This big question was unanswered as this went to press.

"If the Orange Bowl committee would only wait!" Jess Richardson said. "If we could only beat Maryland—we'd have a chance!"

Forty-eight players boarded the planes at the Atlanta airport and flew back to Tuscaloosa quietly, thinking about all the "IFs" involved in this 1952 Bama-Tech battle . . . "IF Marlow had scored . . ." . . . "IF Dick Pretz had been stopped from scoring for Tech . . ." . . . "IF Hobson's last pass on the five yard line was complete . . ." . . . "IF the Bama 15-yard penalty had not been . . ." . . . "IF-IF-IF!" . . . They'll be talking "IFs" all week.

But it was a hell of a ball game Saturday in sunny Atlanta.

AN AFTERNOON ON
THE FOOTBALL FIELD

Crimson-White, 1953

UNDER HAIL, A cold wind, a 30-degree temperature
Saturday afternoon, Coach Harold (Red) Drew gently
tooted the whistle at 3:30 p. m. and 80 huge hunks of Alabama football scholarships began to smash and lash at one
another. Saturday marked the first genuine scrimmage session
of the 20-day spring drill period. The sidelines were flanked
with curious Tuscaloosa and University football fans, interested in getting a premature peek-a-boo at next fall's Crimson
Tide eleven.

Wearing a green pitcher's warm-up jacket, a blue baseball
cap, and a ruddy grin, Drew meant business on this bitter afternoon. For two successive days last week rain had held down
practice, made the field a mass of mud, and training was behind schedule.

"We've got lots of work to do," Drew warned. The team
filed out of the gymnasium locker room, trotted across the
street, past the glances of Adams-Parker co-eds, and onto
Thomas Field.

*   *   *

As football practice began Saturday, one thing was certain. The Alabama coaching staff was in good voice.

"Aw, hell, Banes," yelled Drew at Montgomery freshman halfback Robert Barnes, who was stopped and cut down by guard Bob Wilga's massive arm. "You'd fall over a blade of grass!"

The squad was divided up into four teams, all wearing different colored shirts. There were the "Reds," the "Whites," the "Yellows," and the "Greens."

The afternoon wore on, the tempo of the scrimmage became doubled, the tackles were twice as vicious, and the coaches seemed to scream twice as loud.

Bart Starr, quarterback, was crouched behind the center in the T-formation and called signals. Opposing linemen dug in, ready to smash heads. The ball was snapped. Starr drifted back, faked a hand-off to halfback Bobby Luna and handed to flashy Corky Tharp. Tharp was hit solidly by a fat defensive tackle, tripped and dumped in the mud.

"Stay up! Stay up! Tharp," Drew shouted. "You're no good on the ground!"

"Com'on Corky. Com'on Corky." hollered the fatherly backfield coach Happy Campbell.

"You ends WEREN'T blocking," the gentle end coach Malcolm Laney chimed in, looking pathetically at the tall end sprawled on the wet ground.

Veteran line chief, Hank Crisp, shook his head in disgust. Momentarily he hesitated, then looking at two prostrate linemen sternly, he yelled: "THIS AIN'T NO KID'S GAME! After practice you take 10 laps around the field. YEAH, Y-O-U!!"

Just as the scrimmage got more jarring, so did tempers become hot. Gigantic tackle Billy Shipp, 6-foot, 4-inch 255-pounder from Mobile, got into a brief scrap with defensive toughboy Ralph Carrigan and it seemed like the two would stage a few rounds of sparring.

Three team mates jumped on the tackle and held him back from Carrigan. The latter had his left arm crooked and fist doubled for a quick knock-out (just in case).

(The dialogue here is discreetly omitted.)

(P. S.—The two are now friends again.)

Later in the scrimmage, center John Snoderly, sophomore from Montgomery, was banged so hard in one line scramble that he was out cold and had to be carried off the field on a stretcher. He spent the night in the hospital but was back Sunday without concussion. He will be back at work today.

After two hours of scrimmage Drew tooted the whistle. It was getting colder. Scrimmage was over.

Who says football players have it soft?

THE .200 HITTER

IN JANUARY OF 1956, Lt. Gay J. Talese, stationed at the Public Information Office of the Army in Fort Knox, received a letter from *New York Times* sports editor Raymond J. Kelly promising that when he finished his Army service "you will come back to the Sports Department as a reporter on trial." Talese had done well as a copy boy at the *Times* after graduating from the University of Alabama, and he had impressed his superiors with his writing before the Army commissioned him. "I have no doubts of your success," the letter continued. "You are a first-rate writer, and I hope that in time you will become one of the best men on my staff. Meanwhile, keep yourself informed on sports news."

Upon arriving for duty as a sportswriter, Talese took his notebook in the opposite direction of news. He avoided assignments that had the possibility of landing on page one, where he knew that news dominated the story. Talese wanted to form his own stories—to write short stories that happened to be true about unknown characters being ignored in the press and by the great nonfiction writers of the day.

He found subjects like Ruby Goldstein, a boxing referee who was the "most lonely guy in boxing," cutting off all his friends in the fight game to maintain his integrity, and a troupe of midget wrestlers who rode to work in a Cadillac that "comfortably seats eight midgets and a driver." Talese constructed his factual short stories with the formal yet whimsical voice that has come to define his work. Roller derby star Gerry Murray was "a curvesome woman pushing 40 with the gentility of a waterfront bouncer." About Mike Gillian, a horseshoe maker, Talese wrote: "Many of the prize animals that have been running around Madison Square Garden this week have been purchasing Gillian's footwear for years."

Though Talese often says that Fitzgerald and Shaw and O'Hara were his inspiration, another person should be added to the list—Gilbert Millstein, a name almost nobody recognizes. Millstein was an editor in the Sunday department of the *Times*. He also wrote quite a bit, and Talese loved his formal style, especially his leads that stretched on for paragraphs. "I would tell him how great he was," Talese says. "I became a little pet of his." Millstein edited many of Talese's pieces for the *Times*'s Sunday magazine. "I remember once reading about Hemingway and how he kept doing the sentences over to try to tighten them up, meaning that everything was so essential you couldn't move it in and out without everything falling apart and I saw Milstein actually doing that on a piece of mine," Talese remembers. "He cut some words and he tightened everything. God, this is wonderful, I thought."

With Millstein's encouragement, Talese began taking bigger risks with his stories. He wasn't always successful at convincing his editors, and he came to call himself a .200 hitter—like a baseball player who got a hit 2 of out 10 times at bat. But when he succeeded in his risk-taking, Talese's stories were like nothing else published in the *Times*. One story that particularly stood out appeared on Oct. 12 1958. In "Portrait of a Young Prize Fighter," Talese's profile about Jose Torres, he does not reveal the fighter's name until the last paragraph. "At 22," Talese wrote, "the prize fighter has sad, dark eyes. He has jagged, small facial scars and a flattened nose that has been hit by obscure amateurs he has already forgotten." His story about Torres—and those about the horseshoe maker, the roller derby woman, and many others—were so different that many reporters thought he was making them up. Instead, he was simply looking where those other reporters weren't—in the corners, in the shadows.

MR

THE LONELIEST GUY IN BOXING

New York Times, 1957

WHEN RUBY GOLDSTEIN was a lightweight prizefighter a generation or so ago, he was the golden boy of the Lower East Side, and some people called him the Jewel of the Ghetto and the Paderewski of the Mitts. If he had only been able to take a punch as well as give one, then perhaps he would have become a champion, but sometimes it seemed that his jaw was made of Dresden china. When he was hit by Ace Hudkins in 1926, somebody said Ruby Goldstein went down "like a guy falling off a building." The punch changed the course of his whole life. He faded as a fighter and, some years later, he became a referee. Today, Ruby Goldstein is regarded as the best referee in boxing. Whenever he works, thousands of fight fans are watching him in the ring and on television. Yet, his job as the ring's third man has made Ruby Goldstein possibly the most lonely guy in boxing.

For fourteen years, he has shied away from a lot of people. He rarely talks to his old boxing acquaintances any more and he has been known to cross streets, switch subways and leave restaurants to avoid his friends. It has been over ten years since he walked on Forty-ninth Street between Broadway and Eighth Avenue—a block traditionally populated by the fight mob. Before a big fight some years ago, a sports-writer saw Goldstein with his hat brim down low walking quickly toward the press gate holding a handkerchief to his face as if stifling a cough.

"I just can't take chances," Ruby explains earnestly but not defensively. "As a referee, I don't want to hobnob with boxing people. It's better for me and better for boxing that way." Because he feels this is the best way for him to maintain his reputation as a scrupulously honest referee, his life has become a lonely, never-ending routine of dodging people, especially bookmakers; slipping around corners and moving carefully through large crowds.

Even while standing in the center of the ring before a bout, surrounded by thousands of spectators, Goldstein feels alone. He is joined by the fighters and they bend slightly toward him as he begins to give the instructions, but even the fighters cease to be individuals to a referee. Goldstein has read in the newspapers that one of the fighters is a clean-living, likable chap and the other one is sly and low, but Goldstein forgets all this now and forgets their names to say, for the umpteenth time, "Now, you're both familiar with the rules . . . I want no holding and hitting . . . and when I say break, I want ya to break . . . shake hands now . . ."

The speech is pointless. Who listens to it? The fighters never do. During his fourteen years as a professional referee, Ruby has often become vaguely amused as he makes his speech and watches the fighters pay no attention to him. They are looking down, or looking at their manager, or looking out into the grandstand trying to count the house, or they are peering into the ring lights counting the moths.

The fight begins and the rounds seem to go quickly to Ruby. And then the fight is over.

The decisions of the referee and the two judges are announced. Ruby climbs out of the ring and walks into the dressing room. If the two judges are there, he might exchange greetings, but they never have much to say and they never discuss the fight afterward with each other.

But Goldstein will never forget Dec. 5, 1947. That was the night Jersey Joe Walcott, a 10-to-1 underdog, twice dropped the heavyweight champion, Joe Louis. Goldstein voted for Walcott seven rounds to six with two even. The judges both voted for Louis. "As I changed my clothes in the dressing room that night the judges said nothing to me," Ruby recalled. "And I said nothing to them. There was this mad silence. Then I left and drove home."

By the time he reaches Brooklyn, his wife, May, and Herbert, his 13-year-old son, usually are asleep, but Ruby never can sleep after a fight. The only reason he can sleep before one is that he never knows a day ahead of time that he will referee. The State Athletic Commission usually does not notify the referee until the afternoon of a fight and nobody knows right now who will referee the middleweight title fight a week from tomorrow night at Yankee Stadium between Sugar Ray Robinson and Carmen Basilio. But Ruby will wait around the house that afternoon just in case his telephone rings.

"I especially can't sleep after a fight if the decision was close and I was booed," he said. When a referee is booed, he is always surprised. "You can't understand it. 'I voted right, I saw it right, but why did the people boo me?,' you keep asking yourself. So you stay up all night. You wait for the morning newspapers to see what the sportswriters have to say about the fight. You cross your fingers and hope they'll have seen the fight your way. I guess play producers on Broadway feel the same way after opening night as they wait to read what the critics have written. You can't go to bed until you know."

It is during these quiet hours that Ruby re-lives every fight.

When he is in the ring, he stands very close to the fighters— sometimes he is only a foot away from them—but he has never been hit. He is still, at 51, graceful and swift and he feints, covers and dodges punches in the ring as if he were fighting again. From his close-up view, he can look up into the fighters' eyes, and if he is looking at a beaten fighter, he can read the look of defeat in the man's eyes.

"It is a queer, hurt expression," Goldstein says, "and you know it is only a little while until he'll go down. You also notice his mouth is hanging open slightly because of all the punishment he's taken there. The beaten fighter is breathing hard and when you try to break him away from his opponent, the beaten fighter tries to resist you. He holds on. He is trying to get every second he can in the clinch so he won't get hit again. You ask the beaten fighter how he is and he is afraid you're going to stop the fight, so he answers boldly and gets mad at you and says 'I'm okay, I'm okay,' and that's when you know he is not so sure.

"And when the big punch comes, and the beaten fighter begins to fall, you can, if you watch closely, tell if he will get up again—even if he has not yet hit the floor. If a guy is going to get up, he begins to prepare himself for getting up even before he lands. He turns his hand and leg in a certain way so he'll be in a getting-up position. But when you see the body that just crumbles and pours onto the floor, you know it is not going to get up. When I saw Rocky Marciano knock Joe Louis through the ropes in 1951, I stopped the count at 4. I knew Joe was not going to get up."

As they swing at each other in the ring, the fighters sometimes talk, or even curse one another and Ruby tries to stop this immediately lest it be picked up and heard on radio and television. During the heavyweight title bout on July 31 at the Polo Grounds, Tommy (Hurricane) Jackson kept saying to Floyd Patterson, "Com' on fight, you bum," until Ruby warned him.

Outside the ring, Ruby hears the voices of the crowd offering assorted comments—"Stop the fight, Ruby," "Low blow," "Molder the bum," "Kill 'im," "I hope youse bot' get knocked out." Ruby pays no attention to what the customers say, since he knows that the fans who most often yell "Low blow!" usually have a bet on the fighter who is getting hit. He also pays no attention to the vituperative letters he sometimes receives from television fans who say, "What's the matter with you— you blind? DeMarco was hitting low all night." Goldstein says that only one low blow in a million is deliberate and it is nearly impossible to see a low blow from a television screen.

It is an extremely rare occasion when Ruby Goldstein thinks he is refereeing a "fixed" fight, but he did suspect one such fight several years ago at Madison Square Garden. During this match, a fighter Ruby knew to be an accurate puncher was consistently missing his mark. Goldstein watched the fighter carefully for a round or two, then in the fourth he went to the fighter's corner and said. "Look, you, I got a sneaky suspicion you got the handcuffs on. Well, get 'em off. If you don't, you'll be barred all over the country." Goldstein said the fighter showed marked improvement after that and won the fight easily. "If a fight were fixed," he said, "I'm sure I'd smell it."

Most experts and sportswriters generally agree that Goldstein's ring judgment is infallible. During the recent heavyweight fight at the Polo Grounds, Goldstein stepped between Patterson and Hurricane Jackson in the tenth round of the fifteen-rounder because Floyd's punches were anesthetizing Jackson. Although Jackson was on his feet when the fight was stopped, Ruby saw no reason for the challenger to get massacred. But there was a blast of disapproval from the customers. The hapless Hurricane also screamed in protest. Yet, the next day's newspapers were in unanimous agreement with the decision and one New York paper carried the headline, "Rah for Ruby!"

Goldstein's verdicts have even been acclaimed by television critics. In 1952, Ruby became "the true answer to the viewer's prayers" because he stopped a horribly dull fight (sometimes called a "no hitter") in the seventh round and relieved from boredom thousands of well-shaven, beer-guzzling fans. Even when Ruby voted against Joe Louis in the first fight with Walcott, Louis was quoted as saying afterward, "If Ruby call it that way, that's the way Ruby see it."

Ruby Goldstein is a mildly nervous man standing five feet eight and one-half inches tall, with sparse, dark-brown hair, irregular teeth, a soft voice and a nose that is flattened because somebody smashed it in during his second amateur fight three decades ago. Ruby looks like Peter Lorre.

He was born in a small, three-room apartment at 409 Cherry Street which rented for $7 a month and housed his widowed mother, two sisters and brother. Ruby was a peaceful boy, avoided most street fights and, in the summertime, to help ease the cramped living quarters, he would sleep on the fire escape—a common practice on the Lower East Side then—or even on the roof. He had to get up early when he slept on the roof, however, because once the sun came up it would melt the tar and ruin the blanket. Most of all, he enjoyed playing punchball in the evenings after supper. The "diamond" was a chalk-marked street with chalk bases and home plate was usually the manhole cover.

It is understandable that Ruby would be lured into prizefighting, because many superb fighters had come from his neighborhood, including the late Benny Leonard, who was Ruby's idol. Beginning his professional career in 1925, Ruby had a string of twenty-three consecutive victories until he ran into Ace Hudkins (the Nebraska Wildcat) on June 25, 1926. When Ruby was floored in the fourth round, the East Side went into mourning.

In all, Ruby Goldstein had fifty-three fights and lost only five (all by knockouts) and he retired in 1932 to enter the darkest period of his life. In 1933, he was broke. By his own description, he was a "hanger-on" along Forty-ninth Street, picked up odd jobs at the Eighth Avenue gymnasiums, made a comeback, retired again, trained a few fighters and even was part of the retinue of Billy Conn. He does not know where his money went—although he did lose much of it during the crash—but in 1934 "I was lucky I was eating."

The best thing that ever happened to him was the Army. He enlisted in 1942 and, while at Fort Hamilton, he was asked to referee a fight and that is how he got started. Later, he was assigned to accompany Joe Louis on a three-month tour of the Aleutians. Louis and Goldstein became close friends and the sportswriters recalled this in 1947 when Goldstein voted against Louis in the famous fight with Walcott. Goldstein admits that the vote for Walcott made him famous and he received congratulations from all over the nation and says he was asked to become an honorary member of every organization with the exception of the Ku Klux Klan.

Goldstein has no idea how many fights he has worked, but says he has handled twenty-five championship bouts, the most sensational of them being the Sept. 27, 1946, Tony Zale—Rocky Graziano slugging match which finally ended in the sixth when Zale knocked Rocky down for good. Ruby makes about $75 for an indoor fight, $200 for an outdoor fight and averages about $1,000 a year. He makes considerably more as a sales representative (or "missionary man") for a distiller, takes an occasional drink and smokes ten cigars a day, all of them plastic-tipped. His whisky job occasionally involves traveling and it is a rare thing, he says, when he does not receive an invitation from the hotel beauty parlor addressed to "Miss" Ruby Goldstein.

But Goldstein is recognized surprisingly often as he travels about and is constantly amazed that people remember his face, both as a boxer and as a referee. He was once out in Seattle, when a man approached him and asked: "Aren't you Ruby Goldstein, the fighter?" Ruby hesitated, then said he was. "Are you the same Ruby Goldstein who was knocked down in 1926 by Ace Hudkins?" This time Ruby hesitated for a longer time, but finally he said yes, and quickly added: "But if you're looking for a refund it's too late!"

N.Y.U. WINS DESPITE
2-WAY FREEZE

New York Times, 1958

NEW YORK UNIVERSITY'S baseball players were scrupulously avoided yesterday by their friends at Ohio Field, where Wagner College was defeated, thoroughly but silently, 5—0.

N. Y. U. has 31,068 students and is the third largest university in the nation. But only eighteen fans showed up for the game. Only one sat through it. And he was not a student.

He was a Consolidated Edison engineer named Joe Fernandez, who does not particularly like baseball or even N. Y. U. Fernandez quit work early yesterday to watch his nephew, Tony Diaz, a catcher. But Diaz did not get into the ball game.

For a while Fernandez had company in the bleachers. There were three mailmen there, some upper classmen and two freshmen, one of whom had a thermos bottle that contained scotch. Gloria Maurikis, a sophomore, also was in attendance.

Gloria, a hazel-eyed brunette of 19, was there to watch Dick Reilly, N. Y. U.'s third baseman, whom she met five months ago in Sociology I, a required course. Like everybody else, Gloria shivered in the 40-degree temperature and by the seventh inning, after Reilly had doubled to right, scoring two runners, Gloria was gone.

The wind blew in from left-center field, over the Zeta Psi fraternity house into the faces of the hitters, catcher and mailmen standing, hands in pockets, behind homeplate.

When he was not pitching, N. Y. U.'s right-hander, Art Steeb, bundled himself in an Army blanket. Wagner's bench-warmers were equipped with heavy mackinaws, their bowed heads covered with hoods, making them look from the rear like praying monks.

The outfielders, who were largely inactive, had their ungloved hands in their hip pockets.

N. Y. U.'s coach, Bill McCarthy, starting his thirty-seventh season, said this was not the coldest opening day; he remembers when N. Y. U. played Dartmouth in the snow in the mid-Thirties.

Unnoticed in left field by Gloria, McCarthy and the mailmen sat Sal Carillo, a freshman, who was drafted to tend the green scoreboard.

"I was sitting down on the bench before the game and the manager says, 'You wanna make $3?'" he explained. "I said, 'sure.' So they sent me out here."

Carillo, 18, had received seven tin-plated 1's; five 2's and sixteen 0's, among other scattered numerals. Since the game was scoreless for four and one-half innings, Carillo anticipated a 0-0 game and feared he would not have enough zeros.

But in the bottom of the fifth, Al Wise singled for N. Y. U. and Sy Faitell, a left-hander, smashed a homer 375 feet into the wind over the fence toward Gould Hall, a dormitory. That put the Violet Vikings ahead, 2—0.

The score remained unchanged until Reilly's double in the seventh scored two more and sent Gloria home.

JUDY IS MANY THINGS, MOSTLY FRANK

New York Times, 1958

SINCE SPORTS HEROES have traditionally attributed their success to such things as clean-living and breakfast cereal, it is refreshing, for a change, to talk to Judy Frank, a golf champion, who says she keeps late hours, smokes excessively and takes a drink from time to time.

If the things she says sound a trifle exaggerated, it is only because Miss Frank for years has been saying and doing things that would attract attention or shock people. At the age of 8, while other little girls were playing "house," Judy was playing shortstop on the boys' neighborhood baseball team; quarterback on the football team; and, on the side, she hijacked skate keys.

The women who lived in the Baker Field neighborhood disliked Judy almost as intensely as she disliked them. When Judy would skip by their window sills, they'd crane their necks and snap out after her, "There goes Judy Frank, the tomboy, the tomboy." Judy would straighten up, point her nose skyward and ignore them.

*   *   *

"These women used to upset me," Miss Frank admitted the other day at the Old Oak Country Club, where she is a member. "But I never knew what was the matter. I only know that since I was 8 years old I wanted to be famous. I remember once, while walking with my mother to Bloomingdale's, I stopped her and said, very dramatically, 'Mother, I'd like to tell you something. And I want you to remember this. I'm going to be famous.'"

Encouraged by her father, a lawyer, Judy took up golf at 11. Within five years, she was shooting in the 80s, driving a ball 200 yards and beating her father by 15 strokes. Now, at 23, she has won the women's Metropolitan title the past three years and she has become, almost without question, the grande dame of golf in New York.

While success has not spoiled Judy Frank, it also has not changed her. She is still the beguiling, unconventional girl she was fifteen years ago and many women still can not stand her. "Judy is too cocky," said one female gossip. "Judy Frank thinks nobody can beat her," complained another woman Judy beat.

In all honesty, Judy Frank does not seem cocky; rather, she is brimming over with confidence. Should a sportswriter ask Judy before a tournament, "Who's going to win?" Judy will reply, quite frankly, "I'll probably win."

This week, for instance, she believes she will probably win the Tri-County championship at Old Greenwich. Next week in Cooperstown, N. Y., she says she'll probably win the New York State women's championship.

Although some women golfers find this super confidence a bit distracting, Miss Frank's claqueurs—and there are many—think it's delightful. At the Old Oaks Country Club in Purchase, the women "adore" her and call her "dahling." The men there pay as much attention to Judy Frank as they would to Lady Godiva.

Miss Frank is 128 pounds, 5 feet 5 inches, with sunny, blonde hair and eyes that are sometimes blue, sometimes green. A Barnard graduate, she now lives alone in an East Side apartment with a hi-fi set and shelves of hardcover books, most of which she got at a 60 per cent discount last year when she worked as the secretary to the secretary of Alfred A. Knopf.

Around 2 A.M., after a date, she sometimes takes walks alone over the Fifty-ninth Street bridge. Since the girls she knew are now mostly married or boring, or married *and* boring, her social life generally revolves around golf, or the men who play it, or at it.

She awakens around 10 A.M., reads the newspaper, then heads for a Second Avenue parking lot to her automobile, a long, white hardtop in the back seat of which are strewn old golf balls, tees, yellow pencils and one dirty sweat sock.

The other day, while driving up the East Side drive to Old Oaks, Miss Frank said, casually, that she is unemployed, and if she doesn't soon find a job she will probably pawn the hundred prizes and golf trophies she has won since 1949.

At 11 A.M. she was on the first hole of the Old Oaks course, about to tee off with an older woman and two older men. The woman plopped her drive, like an infield pop-up, 50 yards away. Then Judy teed off on the men's tee, which is farther back than the women's tee.

"Judy, darling," said one man, trying to seem avuncular, "there's no faster way to lose a man than to tee off on men's tees."

"Yes, Judy," said the woman. "You're a woman first—remember, you're a woman first."

Judy smiled, ignoring both of them. Then she crashed a line drive 225 yards down the middle. Weakened, the men approached the tee. One of them hooked into the rough, the other sliced into the woods and frowned.

When last seen, Judy Frank was in the woods, seemingly gracious, trying to help everybody locate their lost golf balls. The man who sliced still was frowning.

IT'S A WONDERFUL
WHIRL TO GERRY

New York Times, 1958

GERRY MURRAY, A curvesome woman pushing 40 with the gentility of a waterfront bouncer, elbowed and bumped the New York Chiefs to a 21–17 triumph over the Chicago Westerns in the opening of the roller derby season at the Ninth Regiment Armory last night.

Outside the skating oval, Miss Murray is a charming person with disquieting good looks. But on skates, she is a female terror, swishing around the track at thirty-five miles an hour, hipping her opponents and zigzagging recklessly, her red hair, tied in a ribbon, winging along behind her.

For twenty years she has skated in competition, but undaunted by time, she was at her best last night. She scored 6 points and, to the delight of 2,380 partisans, displayed marked bad manners.

The roller derby is an uncomplicated, madcap contest in which men and women play under the same rules. The competition takes place on a banked, oval track. Each team has sixteen players—eight men, eight women.

*   *   *

Five skaters from each team are on the track at the same time, with the men and women skating in alternate periods. To score, a player must circle the entire field and then pass a member of the opposing team.

When one player is trying to pass, the others try to discourage him by elbowing, shoving, and uttering unkind remarks to him.

Fans with a penchant for games of elbowing and hipping are dedicated to this noble sport that had a meteoric rise nearly a decade ago with the help of television.

That's why they have a warm spot for Miss Murray. Last night she was clearly the star among the women. Even her 17-year-old son, Mike, whom she has tutored on skates since he was 2, saw action with the Chiefs. She is married to Gene Gammon, another skater for the Chiefs, whom she affectionately refers to as "Number 22."

"I skate because there's action," she says. "As a girl back in Iowa I played with the boys and I never read cookbooks. I played softball with the boys, and I guess I was a tomboy."

Because of her dramatic appeal, more than half of last night's audience were young girls, between 16 and 19, many of them pony-tailed and noisy.

"We like this game for the speed," said Pat Cotter, 20, of Queens.

"There's action," explained Terry Scarpati, 20.

"This is one sport where women feel needed," said Pat Dillon, a television actress who is the wife of James A. Farley Jr., the owner of the Chiefs.

PORTRAIT OF A YOUNG
PRIZE FIGHTER
New York Times, 1958

NEARLY EVERY DAY the young prize fighter is told to get lots of rest, avoid smoking, watch his diet, shun women and stay in shape so that, if he is knocked down, he will have the strength to get up and get hit again.

At 22, the prize fighter has sad, dark eyes. He has jagged, small facial scars and a flattened nose that has been hit by obscure amateurs he has already forgotten.

He has had six professional fights as a middleweight. Nobody has beaten him. In the closet of his $11-a-week furnished room at 340 Union Street, Brooklyn, he has eight suits, a dozen silk shirts and fourteen pairs of shoes. He also has a girl named Ramona. Both were born in Puerto Rico.

Each week Ramona, who is also 22, and her mother come to clean the fighter's room. The mother complains that it is always dirty, that he never picks up his socks, that he has too many shoes. Soon he says he will marry Ramona and will move to Manhattan, close to Stillman's Gymnasium, far from the mother.

* * *

While the fighter says he is at constant odds with the mother, he never argues with the manager, Cus D'Amato, who also manages the heavyweight champion, Floyd Patterson.

"Cus, he is like a second father to me," said the young prize-fighter yesterday in a small room on Eighth Avenue.

D'Amato, a square-shouldered man in a dark blue suit, smiled, and asked, "Have you ever disapproved of anything I've done for you?"

"No," said the fighter.

"Haven't I always welcomed suggestions from you?"

"Yes," said the fighter.

D'Amato smiled again, and went on to say, "I consider this boy extraordinary. This boy will build up boxing in New York. He will be the hero of the Puerto Rican people, and he will aid the juvenile delinquency problem."

"This boy can also draw a crowd," said Teddy Brenner, the boxing promoter. "When he beat Otis Woodward on Sept. 29 at St. Nicks we had a gate of $7,200—our largest in ten years."

As the men talked, the prize fighter sat quietly in a chair listening. Then he got up and went down a flight of stairs to Fifty-first Street and headed for Stillman's Gymnasium.

Puerto Ricans, recognizing the fighter, waved at him, and some followed him into the gymnasium to watch him spar. The fighter is a quick, clever puncher standing 5 feet 10 inches. His chest muscles twitched this way and that as he moved around the ring, jabbing at a sparring partner, without malice.

From ringside some of the Puerto Ricans yelled, "Pega duro, pega duro!" (Hit hard, hit hard!)

A half-hour later he was in a locker room, a towel over his neck, talking about how he hated the Army, how he liked fighting on the Olympic team in 1956, and how, earlier this year, he made headlines all over the country by supposedly knocking down Floyd Patterson in a sparring session in California before Patterson's title fight with Roy Harris.

"He was a little off balance," the young fighter said. "So when I hit Patterson he went down. I also boxed at Greenwood Lake with Sugar Ray Robinson. I think I hurt him once."

For his first five professional fights, the fighter was paid an average of $250 each, but on Sept. 29, when he lured Puerto Ricans into St. Nicholas Arena, he was able to clear $1,500. He sent $300 to his father in Playa Ponce, P. R., and banked the rest.

By 3 P.M. he was starting up the engine of his 1952 gray Plymouth, parked on Fifty-first Street, about to leave for Brooklyn, where he would take a nap. He will relax today, but tomorrow night, at St. Nicks, he will have his seventh professional fight, this one against a Philadelphian named Kid Anslem.

The young prize fighter believes he will knock out Anslem. He also believes that, with time, he will win the middleweight championship of the world.

This young prize fighter's name happens to be José Torres. But he actually thinks, talks and dreams like dozens of other inexperienced professionals who train each day in Stillman's, bang each other around between television commercials, and seem to agree that despite all the punching, boxing still beats working for a living.

GARDEN HORSESHOER
WORKS FAST

New York Times, 1958

MIKE GILLAN, THE Capezio of horseshoe makers, is an imperturbable gentleman of 64 who has spent most of his life trying to please some of the costliest, snootiest, most-pampered beasts in suburbia.

He has been eminently successful, as he will be the first to testify. None of his tailor-made shoes has ever been returned. Many of the prize animals that have been running around Madison Square Garden this week have been purchasing Gillan's footwear for years.

"The secret of my success is simple," he said yesterday, while banging one of his $25-a-pair specials onto a big female. "All you need to excel in this job is a strong back and a weak mind."

Gillan, who was born in Ireland's County Cavan, and whose dry wit and sheepish grin seem fashioned after Barry Fitzgerald's, is patronized by about 175 horses, most of them hunters or show-offs who live on Long Island.

He says it takes a horse anywhere from one to three months

to wear out one of his products. To replace them he charges $10, $25, or $50 a pair—or more, "if I can get it." (His price is from $3-to-$5 for adjusting a shoe.)

His shop is located on Split Rock Road in Syosset, L. I., but he always conducts his private fittings at the stable of the horse. Among his satisfied animals, says he, have been horses owned by Jock Whitney and Marshall Field.

Spectators at the horse show this week have not been aware of Mike Gillan, but he has been sitting on the sidelines from 10 A.M. until 11 P.M. to hear any complaints. He got one on Wednesday night when one horse tossed off a Gillan shoe. It was then (and only then) that Gillan strode onto the arena floor, a swaggering little man in a leather apron, to fix things up.

According to the rules, he receives seven minutes to fix it. More than that and the beast is disqualified. As usual Gillan came through within the time limit.

He has been the official shoer for each of the last six Garden shows, and invariably one or two horses will flip a shoe, and invariably Gillan is back in action, and then off again into obscurity.

For forty-two years he has been fitting horseshoes. He started in New York in 1916 with milk-wagon horses, switched to cavalry horses during World War I, and has been with show horses ever since. He says he makes plenty of money. A widower, he lives alone in an eight-room house in Jackson Heights, Queens. During his idle moments at the Garden he slouches back and reads tabloids or magazines. Horse shows bore him.

LAST OF BARE-KNUCKLE FIGHTERS STILL SPRY AT 93

New York Times, 1958

SOME OLD MEN will attribute their longevity to anything from clean living to shredded marijuana, but Billy Ray accredits his long life to street fighting, prize fighting and women.

Billy Ray, a prize fighter when Harrison was president, was so tough that when boxing gloves became popular, in the Eighteen Eighties, he retired. The game was getting too soft. He is now pushing 94. Everybody who ever hit him is dead. Billy Ray is the last of the bare-knuckle fighters.

Aside from the fact that he has no teeth and hears poorly, he still is a noisy, ruddy, spry 122-pounder. At that weight he won 130 of 150 bare-knuckle fights more than seventy years ago. Rarely does he get to bed before 2 A.M.

He has been married seven times. His last wife died seventeen years ago, while he was working as a bouncer in a saloon. During his post-ring days he owned fifteen saloons, most of them in Brooklyn, where he has long been a clamorously prominent resident.

*　　*　　*

THE SILENT SEASON OF A HERO

His comments on life are, if nothing else, succinct.

On coffee: "It'll kill you."

His cure for heart trouble: "Two shots of whisky daily."

On modern boxers: "They don't know nothing."

On boxing: "Most of it is fixed."

Billy Ray, born on the Lower East Side on Feb. 21, 1865, began fighting for money in his mid-teens. He fought on barges, in saloons, and on the third floor of Pete's Hall, across from Calvary Cemetery in Queens. On the second floor Pete held cockfights. In the basement Pete featured dogfights.

"The gravediggers would also watch us fight," Ray said yesterday, "and after each fight we fighters would go around with a basket. Half the money you got was bad. Gravediggers'd give you iron nickels." While he never became champion, he thrice fought draws with the bantamweight king, George Dixon.

When recalling his prime, the old man closes his eyes a bit and rambles: ". . . Lillian Russell . . . beautiful. . . . Only cost a dime for a haircut in the Eighties. . . . They threw Florence Burns out of the Sheepshead Bay race track for smoking. . . . Irish women would smoke clay pipes at wakes. . . . Oh, I used to love to go down to Fourteenth Street and hear Maggie Cline sing 'Thow 'Em Down, McCloskey.' . . .

"I used to soak my hands in brine and my fists were like brick. . . . You could buy a schooner of beer for 3 cents. . . . I voted for Coolidge. . . . In 1888 I fought Johnny Williams for thirty-six rounds . . . got $71. . . . They say that Steve Brodie didn't jump from the Brooklyn Bridge. They're liars. I saw him. I was there. . . .

"All day I could tell you about things. . . . Jersey Jimmy, the national pickpocket, had a saloon in the Bowery. Sometimes you'd find dead people sitting at the bar. After a wake they'd bring dead guys in, set 'em at the bar, and begin to drink. When they finished, the bartender'd say, 'Who's paying?' They point to the dead guy at the bar and walk out."

Billy Ray now lives with his sister and her husband at 130 Ashford Street, Brooklyn. He avoids fights, despises television, loves mostly to talk in saloons. On his ninetieth birthday he showed up at the Neutral Corner saloon, on Eighth Avenue near Stillman's Gymnasium and would not let anybody buy a drink.

TROUPE OF MIDGET WRESTLERS WON'T WORK FOR SMALL CHANGE

New York Times, 1958

TITO INFANTI, WHO from a distance looks no larger than a fifth of Scotch, is one of the nation's fastest, smartest and richest midget wrestlers.

He weighs 93 pounds, stands 4 feet 7 inches, and dresses like the Cisco Kid. He earns $70,000 a year grappling with midgets, dwarfs and assorted gnomes all around the world eleven months a year.

Tomorrow afternoon Tito will arrive in a chauffeur-driven Cadillac from Florida. Tomorrow night he will team with another little man, Farmer McGregor, in a tag-team match at Madison Square Garden. This bout will precede the main event involving king-sized men—the Antonino Rocca-Miguel Perez team vs. the Graham Brothers.

Tito and McGregor will be opposed by Pee Wee James, a 3-foot 7-inch dwarf, and Major Tom Thumb, a 3-foot 10-inch former carnival showman who can tear a deck of cards in half.

Tito Infanti, born 30 years ago in Mexico to a 6-foot father and a 5-foot 6-inch mother, is one of twenty-six midget wrestlers now working on an average of three or four nights a week. He claims to have bashed his way through thousands of matches and to have won them all—except for a few here and there.

To cut traveling expenses, Infanti sometimes rides to work with other midget wrestlers. The Cadillac comfortably seats eight midgets and a driver. The driver usually is a beefy fellow named Lou Klein. Occasionally Klein wrestles as a "villain," but mostly he works as the midgets' combination chauffeur, valet and fixer of flats.

When Tito has a date, and wishes to have the car to himself, he clamps an eight-inch extension onto the brake and accelerator pedals.

Tito, who once courted a 5-foot-7-inch belle, now is infatuated with a 4-foot-11-inch waitress named Daisy and plans to marry in January.

"Women chase us midgets all over," said Tito. "They think we're cute. Whatever money I don't save, I spend on women, suits and shoes." He owns forty suits and seventeen pairs of size 4½ shoes.

Realizing that he would never be a bullfighter, and not wishing to appear in the circus, Tito Infante decided early that, if he was going to amount to anything at all, he must learn to wrestle.

So ten years ago he got in touch with Bert Ruby, the noted Detroit booking agent for midget wrestlers, and, after seven months of gymnastic work and instructions, was ready for the tour.

Television helped to popularize him as it did other midget wrestlers—Fuzzy Cupid, Lord Littlebrook, Cowboy Bradley, Little Beaver, and, among others, the famous Sky Low Low, an eighty-six-pounder who reportedly can lift 460 pounds on his shoulders.

Possessing the agility of a mongoose, and the knack of curling up opponents like French horns, Tito Infante was immediately successful. But after a few more years of this business, Tito wishes to retire opulently to a squire's life in California, where he is known by his real name, Danny Frian.

BARBELL KING:
MUSCLE OVER MIND

New York Times, 1958

BRUTAL MEN WITH muscles used to beat up skinny Bob Hoffman, kick him around and steal his girls. So Bob bought a set of barbells and soon his biceps were popping from his T-shirt. The bigger he got, the more barbells he bought, until finally he bought a whole barbell factory. Then he picked a fight with Charles Atlas.

"Atlas once claimed that weightlifting made you muscle-bound," Hoffman said the other day at his muscle factory in York, Pa. "I threatened to punch him in the nose, but he apologized."

Nobody has challenged Bob Hoffman since his change from the weakling of the "before" advertisement to the body beautiful of the "after" ad. Though he turned 60 a few days ago, he still can lift 250 pounds with one hand, and break chains with his 52-inch chest.

For occasional diversion, he will strap an anvil to his stomach, lie on the floor, and have his herculean buddies bang against his duodenum with sledge hammers.

In fact, a long policy of muscle over mind has helped make

Bob Hoffman a millionaire. With the nation currently on a health kick, Hoffman's York Barbell Company so far this year has sold more than 70,000 barbells—a record for the concern.

Hoffman's fame among muscle men has spread from here to Moscow. He coaches the United States Olympic weight lifters, manufactures various kinds of health foods and has written popular books on assorted subjects—"How to be Strong and Healthy," "Broad Shoulders," "The Big Chest Book" and "Your Sex Life Before Marriage."

Hoffman's life before barbells was, by his own description, miserable and insecure. As an adolescent, he never took his shirt off on public beaches.

"I had typhoid fever, was skinny, and was frequently laughed at," Hoffman recalled. Adding to his woes was his father, a chesty man who frequently took off his shirt, twitched his muscles and squeezed things.

"Since I wasn't strong, I wanted to make a success of business," Hoffman said. "And I did." In Pittsburgh, his home, he began by selling coal burners and made money but was always fatigued. "At 30 I felt like a man of 60," he said. That's when he bought the barbell.

At 40, his 6-foot 3-inch frame had filled out to 240 pounds, and he was lifting 263 pounds with one hand. He began to go places, do things, forget names, but remember physiques. With the money he had, he invested in the barbell business, and his factory now employs 100 workers.

Bob Hoffman gets up at 7:30 A.M., but never goes to sleep before 2 A.M. He sleeps on a hard bed, his feet hanging over the edge to relieve leg tension. He is a ruddy, robust man.

"Exercise is the only thing that matters," he said. "If you exercise you can do anything—smoke, drink, overeat and raise hell."

DENTIST PUTS THE BITE IN THE FIGHT

New York Times, 1958

WHENEVER DR. WALTER H. Jacobs sees a fighter get banged on the mouth, hit in the teeth or butted on the gums, he immediately begins to worry—not about the fighter, but about the fighter's mouthpiece. Dr. Jacobs is a dentist who makes mouthpieces and nothing disturbs him more than to see somebody knock his dental work.

He often attends fights expressly to watch his mouthpieces oppose other dentists' mouthpieces.

"Naturally, I like to see fighters wearing my mouthpieces win," he was saying yesterday at his office at 124 West Ninety-third Street. "But when two of my mouthpieces are fighting against each other, I must remain, of course, neutral."

Dr. Jacobs, a former amateur lightweight, started making mouthpieces in 1936. He takes an interest in his patients' boxing careers. He watched Harold Johnson, a patient, score a tenth-round knockout the other night over Sonny Ray. He hopes to go to Madison Square Garden tonight to watch his mouthpiece worn by Len Matthews in action against Willie Toweel.

*   *   *

Joe Louis and Floyd Patterson, former heavyweight champions, have had their teeth protected by Dr. Jacobs' tailormade mouthpieces. Dr. Jacobs has made 2,030 of them. They are made of soft velum rubber and Dr. Jacobs keeps one on his desk for use as an eraser.

"Some of the toughest fighters in the world become full of fear in a dentist's chair," Dr. Jacobs said, looking abstractedly into the upper molar of his eraser.

"Who, for instance?" he was asked.

"Lew Jenkins," he said, summoning up a vision of the rugged former lightweight champion. "He'd break into a sweat."

"Which fighter had the biggest mouth?"

"Abe Simon, the heavyweight," he said.

"Smallest?"

"Fred Apostoli, the middleweight champ of 1938."

"Which pieces were the most difficult to make?"

"Well, the one I made for Panama Al Brown, I guess," he said. "Panama Al had no upper teeth when he was bantamweight champ in 1929. I make a plastic impression of a fighter's mouth first, you know, and the mouthpiece fits right over the teeth. When Panama Al made a comeback in 1938, he had no teeth at all."

Dr. Jacobs repeatedly has tried to get the New York Rangers to wear mouth guards, even though the hockey team is minus some teeth.

But the club has turned him down. The skaters talk and shout to each other while in action, the management says, and such conversation would be impossible or incomprehensible with mouths full of rubber.

The advantage of a mouthpiece is that it prevents the teeth from cutting the lip, cheeks and tongue. It also helps prevent the teeth from chipping. It does not protect a fighter from a knockout.

Nobody knows who invented the mouthpiece, but Dr. Jacobs said the first fighter to use it was Ted Kid Lewis, the welterweight, in 1921. Before that, he said, fighters often bit on small pieces of match sticks when they fought.

Pugilists at first were reluctant, for reasons for vanity, to use the protective device. Two holdouts against them were Jack Dempsey and Gene Tunney. But the succeeding heavyweight champions—Schmeling, Sharkey, Carnera, Baer, Braddock and Louis—all wore them.

Dr. Jacobs notes with pardonable pride that none of his mouthpieces have been broken, chipped or split. But occasionally, when knocked out of a fighter's mouth, one flies out of the ring and comes close to landing in Dr. Jacobs' lap.

TIMEKEEPER AS QUIET
AS A CLOCK

New York Times, 1959

CLOCKS CAN BE wrong, sundials undependable, hour-glasses faulty, but George Bannon, the official timekeeper at Madison Square Garden, has not been a second off in over a half-century.

Since 1898 he has operated like an imperishable grand-father's clock at ringside, his green eyeshade dusty, his face in the shadows, his bony fingers holding a watch that sparkles under ring lights.

George Bannon, who is 78, has sat through the cigar smoke of 7,000 fights. He has rung the bell more than 100,000 times. He has ticked off the glorious moments for the Jack Demp-seys, Gene Tunneys, Beau Jacks and Tony Zales. And he will be back in the Garden on Friday night for the Charley Scott-Benny Paret welterweight fight.

Though he has been an official part of more fights than any man in the world, George Francis Bannon is rarely noticed. He is quiet. He avoids interviews. People who have known him for thirty years can tell you little about him. What can you say about George Bannon? He is always there.

He was there when Joe Louis beat Max Schmeling, when Benny Leonard dropped dead to the floor, when Floyd Patterson was beaten by Ingemar Johansson. He was there when teeth were knocked out, when fans threw chairs into the ring and when blood from the eye of Alex Miteff trickled all over his dark, shiny suit and silver clock.

"Sometimes," Bannon says, "I turn around and look at the seats and I remember who used to sit in the front row. Nowadays some people ask me, 'What's holding you up?' And I just say, 'I'm overdue.'"

George Bannon, who used to make pianos in the Bronx, always had a good ear for sound. In his spare time he used to keep time for track meets and fights in the Fairmont Athletic Club on East 137th Street and then he drifted into the time-keepers' job at the old Madison Square Garden on Madison Avenue in the Twenties.

If George Bannon had been involved in something such as Chicago's famous "long-count" incident, or if Bannon's clocks would one night suddenly stop, then perhaps there would be more drama in the life of boxing's Father Time.

But no. George is colorless, but correct. He seems to be sleeping at ringside before the fight. Then there is a solid "Bong!" George is awake. The clocks tick. The three-minute rounds go quickly for George and so does the fight.

"Don't you ever get excited at fights?" somebody asked him after a fight at the Garden recently.

"No more," George said. Then he picked up his clock and two watches and, without saying another word, turned and left for the Bronx.

DIAMONDS ARE A BOY'S BEST FRIEND

New York Times, 1961

O NE DAY RECENTLY, when an ad agency photographer was about to take a picture of Roger Maris smoking a Camel, the Yankee slugger held up his hand in protest. "No, no," he said. "Don't shoot from that side. Do it from the other side. My nose is straighter there."

This preoccupation with the niceties of posing for money demonstrates baseball's newest weapon—the sales pitch. Today baseball stars, undoubtedly influenced by the Tetley Tea Taster and Commander Whitehead, have become arbiters of excellence. They endorse food products from *paté de foie gras* to Skippy Peanut Butter. They suggest smoking practically every brand of cigarette except Pot (marijuana).

This week the sales pitching will be stepped up as the stars' whiskered jaws jut forth on television cameras during the world series. They will look sharp, feel sharp, and slice off perhaps $1,000 a commercial. And there will be more to come for many of them in the months ahead.

Maris, Mickey Mantle and the other stars will earn more off-the-field money this year than they ever have in the past.

One reason was the Mantle-Maris home-run splurge, which revived interest in baseball in commercial areas where it had been dormant. The second, and perhaps more important, reason is the activity of a small, imaginative, amiably pushy man who once was waterboy for the University of Pittsburgh football team. His name is Frank Scott and he is the business agent for sixty of the best baseball players (as well as for a few golfers, football and basketball players) in the professional ranks.

Scott, 43 and given to habits of dress no more conservative than those of a rich jockey, is a welcome and familiar figure in the locker rooms of ball parks because—to borrow a phrase from Fitzgerald—he smiles with a face full of money.

"Hey, Scotty," the players shout when they see his hound's-tooth jacket and chartreuse trousers blazing through the room, "where's my loot?"

"It's on the way," Scott will say or, just as often, will pull out a handful of checks and distribute them to the proper players.

Scott is quick to capitalize on an incident involving a player—even if it is not particularly spectacular—in an effort to earn extra money for the athlete as well as a 10 per cent cut for himself. Some years ago, when an Associated Press camera caught Mickey Mantle blowing bubblegum in centerfield, many of Mantle's critics found new evidence that Mickey was just a big, thick muscle man with an immature mind. Mantle was embarrassed by the photo, which appeared in hundreds of newspapers. Scott, however, immediately called up the Bowman Bubble Gum Company and sold Mantle's endorsement of their product for $1,500.

When Joe Adcock of the Milwaukee Braves got hit on the head by a pitch during a game with the Dodgers, but was spared serious injury because he was wearing a helmet, Scott had

Adcock and his helmet on three television shows within the next three days. On another occasion, when Adcock, in a moment of wild optimism, tried to score from second while the catcher held the ball, Scott got him on the Dave Garroway morning show (for $250) to explain his bonehead play.

And when Pittsburgh's Dale Long hit home runs in eight consecutive games, Scott quickly got him $3,108 worth of television and magazine fees before he hit a slump.

Last year, he got Bill Mazeroski, the Pittsburgh star of the world series, $1,000 as a television mystery guest and this year he sold Casey Stengel's book and magazine rights for a fee reported to be well into six figures—more money than Stengel had made in salary during twenty years in baseball.

"There's absolutely no limit to the amount of outside money big-name professional athletes can make." Scott has said, "provided they're hot. When Don Larsen stepped on the mound to pitch that sixth game of the series in 1956, he was worth about $150 for an off-diamond appearance. By the time the sixth inning rolled around, and he still hadn't given a hit or walk, his asking price had doubled. Heading into the ninth, the figure had gone up to $500. At the completion of his perfect game, I was asking no less than $1,500 per appearance for him, and getting it."

Scott might never have created this zany business had he not been fired from his position as road secretary for the Yankees in 1950. (He had progressed from his waterboy job with Pittsburgh to road secretary for the Brooklyn Dodgers football team, then, after four years in the Navy, to the Yanks.)

Scott attributes his dismissal to a "difference of opinion on policy" with George Weiss, then general manager of the club, who felt his road secretary was becoming too "buddy-buddy" with the players. This was almost unavoidable, says Scott, because part of his job was to check on the availability of players being sought as banquet speakers, television guests or product endorsers.

Sometimes when Yankee players received money for a television appearance they would tell Scott what they had been paid and ask, "Was that enough?" Scott did not know. "There were no standards in those days," he says. "Sometimes the players received no money at all for endorsements—only some of the sponsor's products."

Scott learned this one evening while visiting Yogi Berra. Scott's watch had stopped and he asked Mrs. Berra for the correct time. She said wait a minute and she would get him a watch.

"She came back with a whole drawerful of watches," Scott recalls. "I asked Yogi where he got them all. Yogi said, 'I been on a lot of programs and appearances. They pay me in watches.' I said, 'You mean those guys don't give you a check?'" Yogi nodded sheepishly.

Scott soon after founded Frank Scott Associates. He signed up the players he knew best—Phil Rizzuto, Berra, Ed Lopat—and set about trying to earn extra cash for them. He made it a point not to interfere with the player's primary responsibility to the club. He also made it a point not to promise his clients big money.

"I never guarantee them a dime," he says. "I tell them only that I will represent their interest in negotiating off-field deals and that they must well themselves *on* the playing field if we're going to make any money *off* of it. I tell them, 'If you don't win, you get nothing—and I get 10 per cent of nothing.'"

Soon, as he signed up Willie Mays, Jackie Robinson, Johnny Mize and others, the ball-club officials realized the value of having a Frank Scott around. When organizations or firms called the front office requesting the services of a player for an appearance or an endorsement, they merely had to say, "Call Frank Scott." They knew Scott from his Yankee days and trusted him.

Despite all this, however, Scott really did not thrive until Mantle's season of 1956. That year Scott was able to take in around $70,000 for Mantle through endorsements of a pan-cake mix called "Batter-Up," Lifebuoy soap (for which Mantle posed in a shower room wearing only suds), Ainsbrooke Paja-mas, Wheaties and Viceroy Cigarettes, among others. Not to mention a Charles Antell Company contract that Scott almost lost when, just as Mantle was to do the hair-tonic television commercial, he absent-mindedly got a skin-close crew cut. It took six weeks for Mantle to grow back enough hair so that the commercial could be made.

At any rate, after this big year, Scott found that he no longer had to seek clients; they sought him. This season he will prob-ably gross more than $80,000 in commissions.

Except for Mantle and Maris, who command the highest fees from the agencies, Scott has established prices that are fairly rigid. Players no longer ask, "Was that enough?" Before a player even embarks on a commercial proposition, the price is stated and a contract signed.

Should one of Scott's clients win the Most Valuable Player award. Scott will not accept less than $1,500 per endorsement on a one-year deal. Should his client have a good season, Scott expects no less than $1,000. Should the player have a so-so season, Scott asks around $750.

As for Mantle and Maris, Scott thinks that each may earn as much as $500,000 in royalties within the next three years.

The most likely place to find Frank Scott these days is jumping in or out of taxicabs. Whenever Mantle or Maris have a morning or afternoon free, Scott is ushering them, along with other stars, into advertising studios.

The other day, with Mantle, Maris and Whitey Ford, he arrived in a midtown Manhattan studio where the players were to be photographed wearing "Big Yank" trousers. Ford was handed Bermuda shorts by the advertising men and the outfielders were given long pants to put on. As they dressed, a half-dozen photographers' assistants arranged the background.

"Mine are too tight," Maris said.

"We'll fix 'em," an ad man assured him.

"Can we take these pants home with us after?" Mantle asked, pushing his thick legs into them.

"Sure, sure," the agency man said, beaming.

"I sit down in mine, I'll rip 'em," said Maris.

"We'll fix them, don't worry," said another ad man.

After the photographer had finished, the three were escorted to another part of the room to make a tape recording that would be played at a "Big Yank" sales conference. A pleasant, elderly lady handed Mantle a typed sheet, then turned on the machine and watched, awe-inspired, as Mantle slowly started to read:

"I just want to say hello to you Big Yanks from us Yankees," Mantle read. "It's been a great season for us and I hope as great . . . as . . . as great in its own way for you. We'll be talking Yankee and Big Yank talk all the way. . . ."

"Wonderful, Mr. Mantle, just wonderful," the lady exclaimed.

Maris read next. Within an hour the three players had earned $5,000 apiece.

Scott next hustled Maris off to a Camel appointment. After handshakes with the cigarette people, the star was placed before the camera and Scott went to use the phone.

"We've known Maris to be a Camel smoker for some time," an agency man confided. "But we wouldn't sign him up for this job until we were absolutely sure he is still smoking them and is not a switch-smoker.

"Oh, we go to ridiculous extremes before we sign players up. It's like detective work. We have men who go through locker-rooms to see what brands the players have in their lockers. When we see photos of people smoking in newspapers, we have the photos enlarged and see what brand it is. We keep a file.

"Mantle switched from Camel to Viceroy, and now he's endorsing Bantrons. Elston Howard doesn't smoke. Yogi, Whitey and Skowron are Camel smokers. Roy Sievers is a seldom-smoker. Hoyt Wilhelm is a switch-smoker who stopped.

"Yeah," he said, "we gotta be careful in this business. Can't have these players endorsing Camel and be smoking other brands, or cigars, or not smoking at all. The F. T. C. would be after us, and people would talk. For spite, you know. Cab drivers would say, 'Yeah, some Camel smoker, he was in my cab with a pipe, and they gave him ninety-thousand.' "

After Maris had finished posing, he and Frank Scott came over.

"Once I was at a place signing autographs and smoking a Camel," said Maris, "when this lady comes up, sees me smoking and jumps down my throat because of it. I said, 'Look, lady, you mind your business, and I'll mind mine.' You gotta live your *own* life."

*　　*　　*

Scott was about to leave with Maris when, like any other base-ball fan, he suddenly looked at him and stopped.

"Hey, Rog," Scott said, "would you object if they got a shot of me with you?"

"The beauty and the beast," said Maris, slowly getting up to pose.

"It's for my den," Scott explained. Then, sitting next to Maris and looking at the photographer, Scott said, "Hey, Dick, I don't want to look like . . . hey, make me look like . . . an authentic business man, hey, Dick?"

ON THE ROAD,
GOING NOWHERE,
WITH THE YANKEES

New York Times, 1979

GOING NOWHERE IN the American League, but going first-class, the Yankees last week boarded a chartered jet at La Guardia Airport and flew into the chilly Midwest to play with diminished passion a summer game as autumn approached.

The fourth-place Yankees' final road trip of the year, and final fling as the 1978 world champions, began against the sixth-place Indians in Cleveland. It was a four-game series played before a sparse but appreciative audience in a cavernous old stadium where the outfield was pockmarked by football cleats and chalked with yard-line stripes: the fans' cheering during the game was softly polite, the bats resounded more loudly than usual against a speeding ball in the echoed emptiness, and the home runs that were hit into the distant seats went unretrieved by spectators for many moments.

Still, the floodlights bathed the diamond as brightly as ever, and the disco music blaring from the rooftop amplifiers during pregame warm-ups set a lively rhythm that the players responded to, particularly the young prospects from the minor leagues who are now traveling with the Yankees: one is a handsome, Stanford-educated catcher named Bruce Robinson, who resembles Warren Beatty; another is a Travolta-type left-hander from New Jersey named Paul Mirabella, and there is also a lean, dark tango dancer of an infielder from the Dominican Republic named Damaso Garcia.

The older players, too, seemed in touch with the tunes and vibrations on the field. Within its precise boundaries, they are secure. After many years of traveling on the road in a wife-less world of male roommates, managers, coaches and masseurs, most veteran ballplayers feel more at home on the grassy fields and hotel lobbies and locker rooms than they do in the suburban houses that most of them will begin to share next week with their wives and children.

This road trip for the Yankees is more than the season's final road show for last year's champions. It is a conclusion to camaraderie, at least for the present; and within the coming winter months, many players will await, quietly and anxiously, the arrival of a contract that will guarantee their return to the special world within the grandstands.

Meanwhile, as the Yankees traveled last Thursday from Cleveland to Minnesota, and then to Toronto for the weekend series with the Blue Jays that ended late yesterday, the players tried to win ball games, more out of pride than purpose. But as was the case with the Yankees throughout the year, winning was difficult; and the antics and allegations of its principal attractions—its owner, George Steinbrenner; its manager, Billy Martin; and its superstar, Reggie Jackson—tended to dominate the headlines as much as the trio has grown accustomed to expect.

And yet, at least where Martin and Jackson are concerned, the recent stories in the press proclaiming Martin's aversion to

Jackson are not in concert with the behavior exhibited by these two fellow travelers last week. One day Jackson and Martin sat amiably together on a bus headed for an airfield, and in the dugout and on the field they communicated each day without apparent strain or rancor.

The other players tend to ignore these publicized polemics as they concentrate on affairs closer to their own egos and financial interests. On the plane carrying the team from Minneapolis to Toronto, Lou Piniella buried his head within the pages of The Wall Street Journal, surveying the stock statistics. Bobby Murcer, Luis Tiant and others played blackjack, dropping cards and $5 bills in neat piles along the aisle. Jim Kaat, Fred Stanley and Willie Randolph listened to music coming from the AM/FM tape player-radios that the majority of players now bring with them on all road trips.

In fact the easiest way to identify a traveling ball club in airports these days is to look for the sight of groups of black and white men strolling together through the corridors, carrying in their hands a Sony or a Panasonic or a Sanyo portable—objects that many matrons and Fifth Avenue doormen once believed to be the exclusive property of Gristede's delivery boys.

Although some Yankees have eclectic tastes in music, it is generally true that the more introspective black ballplayers (such as Randolph, Roy White and Chris Chambliss) prefer jazz to the country-western music favored by such whites as Rich Gossage, Ken Clay, and Jim Beattie. And more hip and high-heeled Yankees (such as Oscar Gamble, Bucky Dent, and a bull-pen catcher from Brooklyn named Dominic Scala—whose favorite off-the-field exercise seems to be brushing his hair) are drawn to the hard, brash beat of disco. In the opinion of the late Thurman Munson, Neil Diamond was a peerless performer; it was the music of this recording artist that was heard during Munson's funeral.

The players continue to listen to their radios as they undress in the locker room. And as further evidence of how these men on the road bring domesticity to their private retreats beneath the grandstands, it is interesting to note that the shelves within each man's locker are cluttered with the same personal items that might be found in the medicine cabinet or bureau top of a suburban home: there are assorted brands of hair sprays, underarm deodorants, brushes, shampoos, bottles of vitamin pills, skin creams, nasal sprays, dental floss. On Murcer's shelf in his locker in Cleveland there are cans of Skoal and in Luis Tiant's there are several long Venezuelan cigars, Bauza No. 1's, for which he pays $1.50 for each and prefers to the $3 Cuban specials that he might be unable to smuggle past the customs inspectors that he sees on his trip to Toronto. On the shelf of Garcia, there is a statue of St. Martin de Porres, and on the shelves of nearly every player today in the big leagues there are electric hairdryers.

Jackson, like many other black ballplayers in the major leagues, uses an Afro comb, but is particularly distinguished for the amount of jewelry he wears around his neck. He adorns himself with three gold chains on which are attached religious medals, Yankee symbols, and trinkets from his women friends; and whenever he runs hard in the outfield, or spins around mightily after swinging his bat, there emanates from his neck a jangling sound of clinking metal worth more than $3,000.

The reading matter seen in the locker room ranges from Hermann Hesse to Playboy; and the language that is heard there is not only unpublishable in a family newspaper but quite possibly in the periodicals published by Mr. Larry Flynt.

*   *   *

When the game begins, at least during these final days of a losing season, the Yankee starters are often removed in the later innings and replaced by rookies. This is when the manager wishes to see how the rookies perform under major league conditions, and as a consequence the second-stringers are particularly inactive and often frustrated as the season draws to a close. But the other evening, a half hour after the final out in Tommy John's 2-0 victory over the Indians—with the stadium seats completely vacated and only a few groundskeepers scraping the mound with rakes—there appeared under the bright lights a solitary figure of a uniformed Yankee running around the outer edges of the ball park. He was broad shouldered and stocky, a compact black man who ran with speed and energy. He ran once around the entire field, following the warning path from right field to left, and then he circled the outer rim of the infield and continued, faster this time, to encircle the entire field a second time, then a third. It was close to 11 P.M., and in the locker room the newsmen were interviewing John, and the attendants were carrying out canvas bags packed with bats to an awaiting bus.

Breathing heavily, the man on the field stopped running, and trotted to the concrete runway toward the locker room, prespiring but feeling relaxed for the first time that night. He was a Yankee utility infielder named Lenny Randle. Though he had not played in weeks, and did not expect to play again for the Yankees this season, he wanted to remain in condition, just in case, should a miraculous moment occur today or tomorrow, and he was summoned to action . . . he would be ready.

NOTES FROM THE TRIP

Talese calls his reporting style "the art of hanging out." He takes notes in a rather unconventional way, on small pieces of shirt-board recycled from his dry cleaned shirts. At night, he goes back to his hotel room and types up the notes on a typewriter. The notes read like mini-scenes, and in them readers can see Talese working out the direction of a story. The following notes are from the first day of a weeklong trip Talese took with the struggling Yankees in 1979.

MR

Sunday, Sept. 16th, 1979 --

No.1 Day--with the Yankees.

The large crowds in the Stadium are less noisy, the tension is gone, and, while the players still try to win, they have for weeks been resigned to the fact that this would not be another championship season. In fourth place, more than fifteen games behind Baltimore, the Yankees were mathematically eliminated two weeks before the end of the season--on Sunday September 16th; and yet a dozen games (?) were left to be played, requiring nighttime flights to Cleveland, to Minnesota, to Toronto--hardly celebratory traveling for a team that last year had been the toast of the baseball world, the darling of advertising agencies, players making commercials, Nettles and his auto commercials, Bent the poster boy...Jackson...

--no, they would play out the season, perform for themselves, their averages, their place in the statistical record; but it would be a final road trip of the year as the World Champion Yankees--which is what the telephone operators continue to pick up the Stadium phone; and after losing to Detroit on a Sunday (Sept 16th), they lumbered off the field through the players hall...in the rotunda (?) under the stadium. You could still hear the noise of the crowd, it was muffled...the organist upstairs was playing something...the players now walking into the lockerroom. Attendants were carrying bats, gear...reporters were waiting...the players, in no mood to talk, talked anyway....There is such distance between these two groups--
--

The writers, somebody said, are too serious...critical..."they think they're still covering the War in Vietnam"; and while the players want to win, if for no other reason to continue to play, they quietly are repelled by the writers...they are not, with few exceptions, verbal people, not as educated as they write rs. The writers are small, cynical men who, years ago, were athletes...and they became, failing at that, critics of the game and critical of the men who were good enough to play it professionally. The players--the stars -- the men from the Southern regions, the California...the Latins and blacks--they devoted all to their sport, it being their source of prosperity and escape, and identity...and they lost along the way a chance to communicate...they were isolated ("spoiled" say the writers), but really isolated from that which made the writers what they were. So they travel together, they crowd in the lockers--the sullen players, trying to get undressed, pulling off their jocks, their long shorts, numbers on their underwear...socks...big naked men, with spikes , markings...and--surprisingly in athletes--bellies...these men in their twenties...are crowded around by shorter men, urban...most of them Jewish.. (the players are not Jewish-- they are crackers, blacks...Latins...) ..and rural people, the sportwriters are Jewish, college educated, and they question about the game; and ask for explanations...and the players--the Yankees--they do not want to answer. (the Yankees and ass) There is this edge. The writers "have a job to do," to inform the public...but the public doesnot and the public does care. The public is also escaping from life--they are the fans who cheered and crid tday as one hero retired for ever--the fated Catfish Hunter. The fans watched him recdive gifts..all the products of capitalism...merchandising...Toyota..and (get list)...and Hunter, in his drawl, made an acceptance speech...and much was made over this feast day for a Stadium saint....but now everybody had filed out of the park, and the players , in their inaudible way...were dodging...writers. The player want to take a shower...and they slop in the food that the trainers put on the table...they shove food down their throats..and the locker room is open to the select few--d writers..o.trainers..and the coaches--men who are more out of shape...broadshouldered, pot bellies, the faces of drinking men ..years on the road...all the hotel bars and lonely lobbies in cities of America...they are here...and soon, they will pack, and go on the road together--nights in Cleveland, a depressed area of Cleveland, and then to the straight quiet of Minnesota...and then to the livelier..custo...through customs into the brighter lights of Toronto's night...an then home, a few more days in the stadium against these same losing teams--losers playing losers--and then, alas, home...the real home...across homeplate to the real home..where they will rejoin their families, in this uncertain relationship that players have with wives--a union that depends on separation to survive... --the wive s seeking an identity of their own...not feminists...and the burly men of body...who play the game.

insert: the music...

in the stadium, there is a little chain-smoking organist , near
the press box, who plays this music...this Silent Screen
music, ...to press emotion into the crowd...simulating emotion,
--which the players hate...it is an interference..one more inconvenience
in their concentration--as bad as the sun, the wind, the curves
of the opposing pitchers...but they to̶h̶i̶m̶m̶m tolerate it until they
can, after the game, flip the dials to the music they choose..

Neal Diamond...(this was Munson's favorite.. *(they played at his funeral.)*

Note: when we arrive in the Cleveland bar, during dinner, Martin
plays the juke box...gives dollars to the ba̶r̶t̶e̶n̶k̶m̶ waiter to
keep the music coming...they do not want to be alone without
the SOUND...

We are joined, on this trip, too, by young men--it is the time of rookies, thinner
men, unspoiled by the big leagues, more polite to the ~~much~~ writers--for they are yet
~~unbothismatumater~~ not yet felt the sting of their criticism...these are the new men:

-the blondish, handsome, polite young man named Dave Righetti.

Righetti...went a few respectable innings...and was removed; and the writers told
the story...it was his first game...in a game centered around the last of Catfish.

Righetti was polite, smiled like ~~mmm~~ ...every question ("what's the difference
being up here?" He mentioned that the hitters will not go for certain pitches...what
worked in the minors...the high-minors..doesn't work..the hitters are patient..they
wait...they have waited along time to get up here, and at the plate the wait a long
time until they get the pitch with which to kill you...you have to be smart...a
battle of survival all over the chance to remain...and travel first-class)

They players left the park...~~thousand~~...showered and dressed, as is the Yankee
custom, in jackets and ties. The players wear string ties, which meets (barely) Mr.
Steinbrenner's standard...and in them two expandive airconditioned buses.

The veterans--the Jacksons, Nettles, Oscar Gamble...George Scott in a three-piece suit
a vest, a big man ..black man in this suit...and the Tiant, smoking his cigars...(on
bus, they make fun of his Colonial Yankee frank commercials--"~~Immmatafmama~~ "Its good to
be with a weener")...   ⊗
                                            Vem - ol York

and then to the La Guardia airport...and they carry...so many of them..their
radios. Music is what they have...

GT: no, stop: first...out of the stadium, the crowds, kept back by wooden
barricades...jam for a sight of them...and with each player...walking out the door
toward the bus...the young men (a few writes in the crowd)..looking with wonder-
ment, cheering...envy...awe...at the players in suits and ties...and cheering
them. The game is lost, the season is lost, but these people--dressed in shirts,   ⊗
most of them kids and working men, and women--people who tomorrow will be punching
cash registers in supermarkets..delivering ~~punk~~ groceries for Grestedes...selling
subway tokens, drifting through~~life~~ *they* with nothing to cheer about...obscurely through
life in jobs that makes them ~~going~~..supernumeries..they find, particularly the blacks
among them.. in this one chuck of stately real estate in the dark shambles of the
Bronx...they find something to ~~dinaamma~~..in the plays, in the game, something that they
can relate to, as they cannot to their own jobs, *of to* their own adapted city. They
can relate, too, to the radios that the players carry-- ...People who see black and
Latin..men along Lexington Avenue or Broadway...bopping along the street with radios
...lost in the music...oblivious to the slights and limitations of the city that
they endure...they under stand the music; and so do the players ..who carry the same
things on the rod.
         .....there is Randolph...the Latin players,... even ~~than Himmush~~ Chris
Chambliss, who is a quiee, the son of a minister'..An ~~partChmumamat~~ Indian...and it is
the music...his beautiful wife, a writer, and his four-year old son, he embraced them..
and it is the music that is his diversion...in Cleveland, they cannot watch the hote
tg ..the hoaring game shows...the soap operas..the bad reception...they listen to
the music...and --Donna Summer..(who else?

                                the sleep or think...

--they carry it everywhere...the luggages, the bags/...the clothing...is carryined by
the haggard old white men...the aged travele/s..*they look* like washroom
attendants in ~~raimb~~...the sad, tired faces of old men...who could be on the   ⊗
...there is a ~~tmigm~~ bit of the Bowery on their lined, tired faces...and they carry,every-
thing...and the team moves on..womanless, --no wives allowed--no whores allowed in
hotel rooms...no joy...only the game, the so~~mmum~~ and the music.
                        to the ~~lood~~ a 24R Slergia circo
                        nd

This is what blacks have contributed to the game...in addition to the talent...and
the sociological separation...
--the fans are white, working class ...and young boys...young rich kids...the sons of
white executives...the blacks... : the game is played by the poor whites and blacks/latins
..the teams are owned by the old executive class...and the agents and writers are
Jewish... it is the uni~~tedmachineman~~ is a bit of the ~~times~~

--

On the bus...the coaches and mgr sit in the front, as coaches and manages have
always sat--from the yellow high school buses..and the players slip away in
the back...with the writers...those few who still remain on the trip...they
~~remain~~ sit by themselves..

--SECOND STRING writers..the first-team baseball writers have now moved to
Cincinnati, Ca~~lifornia~~ lA Kansas City...to the cities were the pennant ~~games~~
races are still alive; while the other papers...the smaller suburban papers...
they save money on this trip ...and other papers may send their second trip..their
older men who have lost the energy and taste for the game...the less capable...of
the typist...the young ones..or no one.

It is this journey ~~that~~ that we begin ..to Cleveland...home ~~and~~ state of the
owner, Steinbrenner, who remains in New York...and watches the game in his luxury
suite..overlooking the field...sitting with the captains of industry, and tycoons..
politicals..and a bishop...and c~~ongressmen~~ honored ~~as~~ guests..and governs or aspiring
mayors..or real estate tycoons....; ~~which~~...

The pecking orde-

The plane... The seating is the same: up front, in first class section of Delta..
Martin...smoking a thin cigar...across the aisle from him, his coaches..his fellow
from another era--old ball players gone to seed...bodies beginning to spread...ill-
fitting in clothes...the red-faced Art Fowler, who has a sense of humor...diversion
.~~John~~ Fowler, who is only seen on television walking with his belly out to the
mound to ~~bring~~ comfort or caution ~~when~~ a Yankee pitcher in trouble...a position he has
been in long ~~ago~~ ago--in many towns--now he is in his traveling suit, nd Steinbrenner
tie and shirt...with feminist classes...these aviatory classes...and also on the
plane...the other coaches..Mike Ferraro, C~~harlie~~ Lau...Torborg..Hegan...alumni of the
game...still in it...daring not venture out to another world...lucky to reamin a
part of it...
stature-

The players in the rear section, protected from the enforcers...with the high seats.

Martin--he is in a good mood...a ~~victory~~ defeat today, but it has been a season of
defeats...a~~mong~~ fights and deaths... the death of Munson, which brought some sense t
to the team (Dent's marriage revived as a resultof this)) ...a former owner...a job saved for
Martin? ...the fight...Gossage remains...only he; Jackson who prompted the fracas with
his remark...and Cliff Johnson, a strong man not much liked by his teammates...no
remorse over his departure...although a strong right-handed hitting man who ~~coul~~
catch as well as th~~em~~...inadequate young men who were Munson's s~~tumbl~~ backups...
Johnson is long gone.
--Rivers...Chambliss saw him...in Texas...

-These are not men ~~who~~ afflicted with the sensiblit es of the writers, orpoets...
their poetry is in their movements on the field, this is there art, their ballet
.. they are as articulate as ~~a~~ Birishadkov...as moody as ...and the Gunnov t..
and ...they can do what no men can do...catch a fly ball...running..the whole motion
of the body..hitting a ball thrown nearly a 90 miles an hour, curving, moving,
~~headed at his bittr.. they.. the never.. this.. rising injury.. this.. and they~~
are

These men are fulfilling the fantasies and youthful ...failures of everyman who dreamed of being a star athlete. All the real estate men in town, the owners of boxes, the entrepreneurs...the employers..the slumlords and landlords, and corporate vice presidents...and Councilmen who appear for the World Series games with their peroxided wives...they are private failures...in their youth; and since youth is the impressionable time, they are wondering if they ever made it up--andhere are the men that they can measure themselves by...was it worth it...their failure..to be replaced by what these men know...these players...in their final years of youth, are traveling and playing the game...and, in some cases, making extraordinary salaries (but only in some cases--Jackson,Gamble,Gossage...Gullet..without playing--he's gone home)...while others, Pinella...they are earning less than they deserve...and the bitterness is there..

--

What did Roy White...who hit a pinch homerun...a handsome, sensitive man..he dressed, combed his hair while talking...prenning in front of the mirror to be admired ...dressed up to go on a buss.. slipped on his wonderful white Bill Blass shirt, a shirt with the epaulets...and over it his tie and jacket.. he said...he could not play enough games...did not hit left-handed enough...which in the stadium was hisownly chance..he played less this year than ever...

Thirteen years with the Yankees...never a "day" for him...while the Catfish , a big-budget player....paid a fortune, but never the star he was with Oakland... the southerner...the type of ballplayer that prevailed when in the pre-war years.. the rube, the farmer...the last of the farming boys...who came up through farm systems...now this urban game...inter-city game...playedin parks in the depressed areas of cities of Americas...regions of storage ..garages..and factories, and vast tenement housing...and winos and unfed cat s...and junkies...the castles protected by guards...and Burns guards...and , into these areas..the limouses of the captain..sand the new cars of theplay s--the players from other regions--the players from the South, the midwest...dying to get back to the midwest, and out of the big alien city...--

- White...a man of sensitivyt...He must havefelt, as Catfish got more gifts that even Catfish must acknowledge he deserved....must havewndered: "Why not me"?

--

The gifts were sponsors giving away their own products..there is is on the tube, advertisimements for the products..manuscriters exhibiting their own generosity of spirit, for thetelevisio audience...

--

Why not me-- thinketh (?) White.

--

On the road at night: the plane...and walk off the plane in Cleveland...the backrupt city...in the nice hotel: Stouffer's Inn on the Square..in Cleveland,Ohio ..the luggge, with the NY on it...like the blue uniform warmup jackets...the luggag crewds...transport all the accoutrements...and the players, with theirradios..go up...to their rooms...and the writers...it is last, bedtime..

--

--

Martin on the bus from the Cleveland airport...to the hotel... He sits in the front...on the side seats..his coaches...the bumpy ride...the bus rattling windows.. "Need some putty in those windows," shouts Martin, good-humored...and their is the laughter..one of the players,a Latino, in the back has a bottle of wine...and is sipping..it ...and there is much banter...and the affable Fowler is talking about ...teams...they are reminiscing...it is not for the press--but these coaches are talking about the old days...and Martin is talking about peoplewho have traded him...

inse t note on Nettles: Kane said he is like his old idol,
no, Davis..no..name, Maris..there was 180 millions,
know something about the players..Nettles was cool, but
quietly suspicious of these people...his anti-semeti
remark...to the Jewish sportswriters...Hecht)

5=

Flowe Say the Pirate an sche Serial road, - Love -

and Fowler is making funny sexual references...getting a hardon from the
bumping ride...Martin is telling Fowler that this new young pitching star,
Davis, has his wife or somebody along...and Martin doesn't want it:"this
ain't no fucking honeymoon." Martin, a city body...an Italian with an
anglicized name..speaks like a fucking Texan.. he talks like Dean Martin,
the dark-haired, swarthy..common cowboy....some many urban types...Bobby
(Dylan) adopt that Southern comfort..drawl...(Dyl.............

*→ that
Ran Ind,
tho grah st*

It is lonely...around the hotel. The squre, on this Sunday night, is quite...
——

The players are retired to their rooms, their music....no women in the
hotel..s...
——

In the elevator....Jackson sees a new pitcher...asks his name...the guy
tells him (?)..and Jackson nodds, "Oh, yea h, they tell me you throw the
little pellets..."...

No woman..it is a man's world, the barracks world...men at war, though
the armise has been declared...and there will be victims...trades,
releases..and they will go back wence they came...or to jobs...
—-they do not like, joining the fans in this respect...
——

The final drink of the night:

I wander off, bored...to a bar that the cab driver says is the only
lively Sunday night spot in Cleveland...it is : SWINGOS bar... -→

where Martin, Mike Ferraro, Art Fowler, and the traveling secretary
Bill Kane..are at the bar. They passed up the Delta airplane food..and are
ordering...it is nearly empty, the ████..it is the bar in Swingos...where there
usually is a band...but Martin is there ...and he is ███ briefly...they are men
of the night.. *Lead ver* *Billy Hollifler*
--and in walks a lovely black woman...with breasts..large...and an innocence
face--a lovelier version of Diane Ross...and Martin notices here. She might be a
Sunda night hooker...one might assume...and Martin smiles at her...and...she
..buys her a drink...the bartender is told to buy her a drink....she is friendly
..and an innocent..manner about her..."You're very pretty," Martin says, being
quite sincere, and , though the word is casually used, this is accurate: in
the strictest sense of that--she is lovely, she does not hard the hard
wore look of a striving whore...nor the ███ battered features...she couldbe a
bible singer...except she is alone. in this place...and says , when Martin
asks whmh where s she is front, she says Chicago...and she is going to be
driving back there in a few hours. What brings her to Cleveland? Why go back?
He talks..they talk...the coaches on one side of the bar..and the blck
young women, soon to drive her car back to Chicago...on some mysterious turn of
events...the dialoque...The bartener, introducing her, "This is Billy Martin,"
but she smiled, she had never heard of him...she is in another word...the
world of music...that the radios...play. *— But she ercepts his tre with a smb ⊕*

The night ends...I leave...leave Martin and his decons...to the black
lady of the night, soon to depart...directly?...to Chicago...

THE STORY BEHIND THE
SIGNAL TO BRUSH BACK
CLIFF JOHNSON

New York Times, 1979

THE MOST DISASTROUS single event of the Yankees' year of frustration was a postgame locker-room brawl in which the team's star relief pitcher, Rich Gossage, injured his throwing hand fighting with a big, burly second-string catcher named Cliff Johnson. Gossage subsequently missed most of the season, and though five months have now passed since the incident—during which Johnson was traded to the Cleveland Indians—there is latent enmity on the part of some Yankees toward their former teammate. And when Cliff Johnson was batting against the Yankees in Cleveland last week, in a game that the Indians won by 16–3, a fastball was aimed high at his body and hit him on the left arm, which he had suddenly lifted to protect his face.

Appearing to be momentarily confused, Johnson then strode determinedly toward the mound and, rubbing his arm, glared at the Yankee pitcher, a right-hander named Bob Kammeyer, and shouted, "I know you got better control than that!" Johnson repeated the statement several times as he got closer to Kammeyer, but before he could reach the pitcher several players and an umpire interviewed, and Johnson was ordered to first base.

Kammeyer, a prematurely balding Stanford graduate, who is nearly as tall as the 6-foot-4-inch Johnson but who seemed frightfully frail by comparison, remained on the mound saying nothing—and certainly not admitting that he had thrown the pitch intentionally, in accordance with the signaled desires of his catcher, who had received the "brush-back" sign from the manager in the dugout, Billy Martin.

After the next Cleveland hitter slapped a single past the mound and into center field Bob Kammeyer, who had already given up seven hits and had yet to retire a single batter in his calamitous fourth inning, was replaced by another Yankee pitcher. But as Kammeyer walked slowly back to the bench, Martin was not noticeably disturbed by his pitcher's performance. On the contrary, Martin moments later approached the dejected pitcher, uttered words of encouragement and handed him five $20 bills.

This scene was observed, at least in part, by a number of Yankee players. And another person who had deduced what had occurred was the Cleveland Indians' public-address announcer, Ned Welc, whose field box was next to the Yankee dugout and afforded a view of the interior. Having watched hundreds of baseball games attentively and knowledgeably during his five years as the Cleveland field announcer, Ned Welc believed that he could distinguish between a "beanball" and a pitch inadvertently thrown wild.

After the inning was over, Welc joined over the rail and spoke to the visiting club's bat boy, a Cleveland high school student of his acquaintance who was serving in the Yankees' dugout that night. The bat boy told Welc that he had been standing next to Martin when the Yankee manager, in a clear voice, expressed the wish that Cliff Johnson be "knocked down," and that the Yankee pitcher, Bob Kammeyer, later received $100, presumably for fulfilling Martin's desire so efficiently.

Welc telephoned the Cleveland Indians' publicity executive in the press box and said: "The damnedest thing just happened! Billy Martin told his pitcher to hit Johnson, and then he paid him money for doing it!" The Cleveland executive, Joe Bick, listened with interest but said nothing to the reporters seated nearby along the upper-deck press rows.

On the following day, although Cliff Johnson and other Indians had learned of the exchange of cash, they did not openly discuss it. However, ballplayers have a way of making amends; and as the Indians now engage in a three-day series against the Yankees at the Stadium in the final week of the season, it is reasonable to assume that Cliff Johnson in particular will want to demonstrate some semblance of retribution, at least in the form of productive hitting, against an organization that he feels has treated him somewhat shabbily this year.

While nobody on the Yankees would want to become publicly associated with the tactics that guided Kammeyer's eyesight against Johnson last Tuesday night in Cleveland, they will say privately that such behavior is almost as commonly a part of the game today as it was in baseball's more rampant pretelevision era. On the modern Yankees, as on all other teams throughout professional baseball, there are signs that the managers or coaches may impart to their pitchers, via their catchers, to "brush back" a dangerous free-swinging hitter.

Because a pitcher's aim is frequently imperfect, an intended "brush" often becomes a direct hit. Indeed, sitting on the Yankee bench when Johnson was hit in Cleveland was a rookie New York infielder named Dennis Werth, who in 1977 lost a number of teeth and required 25 stitches across the lips after being "brushed" in the mouth while playing in the minors with the Syracuse Chiefs. Werth is still visiting his orthodontist as a result.

It was nevertheless emphasized by some Yankees in Cleveland last week that Cliff Johnson, prior to being nicked by Bob Kammeyer, had earlier in the game knocked two balls out of the park; and thus Kammeyer, the Yankees' third pitcher in four innings, could hardly be expected to view Johnson benignly, particularly inasmuch as there lingered along the Yankee bench the memory of Johnson's role in the locker-room fracas with Gossage that damaged the team's chances of defending the titles it had won in two previous World Series.

The Johnson-Gossage altercation happened on April 19 at Yankee Stadium after an afternoon loss to the Baltimore Orioles, when the season was only two weeks old. Afterward, in the Yankee locker room, there were many sullen men, and none more so than the second-string catcher, Cliff Johnson, who, though Thurman Munson had been given a day's rest, had been denied the catching assignment in favor of a rookie named Jerry Narron.

It was a frustrating time in Johnson's career. Having come to the Yankees from the Houston Astros in the midsummer of 1977, he had significantly contributed to the Yankees' championship season, batting .299 in 51 games, accounting for 12 home runs and 31 runs batted in and competently filling in as the catcher when Munson needed a rest. But after an off year in 1978, during which he played in only 78 games and hit below .200—and an equally unimpressive spring in 1979, which found him mostly on the bench—the shelved slugger was incessantly depressed, and he often pondered the possibility that, at the age of 31, his career was nearly over and that soon he would have to think of another means of supporting his wife and two children back in San Antonio.

As Johnson sat in front of his locker after the Baltimore game, slowly getting undressed and brooding, a ball of tape came flying in his direction, missing him and smacking against the floor. It was Rich Gossage who had thrown it, doing what players do regularly in locker rooms to one another, a form of frolic as old as the game itself. On this particular afternoon, Cliff Johnson was not to be easily humored. Still, he remained seated on the stool, muttering in a soft, growling voice to Gossage, "Man, with your control, I don't have to worry about getting hit."

Reggie Jackson, undressing nearby, then asked aloud, "Hey, Cliff, how'd you hit Gossage when you were both in the National League?" Gossage had pitched for Pittsburgh before joining the Yankees as a $2 million free agent. He is a big, blond country boy with brash confidence to match his talent, and before Cliff Johnson could reply to Jackson, Gossage had interjected, "He couldn't hit what he couldn't see." As Cliff Johnson winced, Gossage added, "He only heard the sound of the ball popping in the catcher's mitt."

Having so cavalierly dispensed with Johnson's prowess as a hitter, Gossage walked toward the shower room. But seconds later, standing near the urinal, he heard Johnson behind him asking, "Do you think you can back that up?"

Gossage paused for a second, studying Johnson's dark frowning face, then answered, "Yeah, I think I can."

Gossage and Johnson, the two largest men on the Yankee

squad—Johnson weighed 217 pounds, and Gossage was only seven pounds lighter—stared at each other. Then, as Johnson later recalled the moment, he slapped Gossage across the back—a gesture implying disgust more than an attempt to inflict bodily harm. But Gossage remembered differently. He claimed that Johnson had slapped him across the side of the head, after which, in a fit of rage, Gossage threw a combination of punches, one of which caught Johnson in the mouth and brought blood from his lips.

Suddenly they both were swinging, struggling, swearing. As Gossage slipped to the floor, they continued to grapple and pummel. The only other player in the room was the 165-pound infielder Brian Doyle. And while he briefly tried to separate the men, their fury and size discouraged his enthusiasm as a peacemaker. Other players, hearing the noise, finally did arrive to separate the combatants, but by this time Gossage had hurt the thumb of his pitching hand, and for him the season was virtually over—as it would subsequently prove to be for the Yankees.

The Baltimore Orioles, leaving Yankee Stadium on that April day after their 6–3 comeback victory, went on to win 51 of their next 67 games. The Yankees, deprived of the presence of the relief pitcher who had been so instrumental in last year's winning season, played little better than .500 ball.

Although Cliff Johnson did play occasionally for the Yankees while Gossage was inactive, and did hustle when he played—he dislocated two fingers while lunging past the catcher to score in Kansas City, and he bowled over and hospitalized an umpire while scoring on another occasion—he would be traded by mid-June to the Cleveland Indians. There he would prove to be very compatible with the team and productive as a player. In 61 games he had hit 13 homers, had batted in 46 runs and was hitting more than .260 as the New Yorkers arrived in Cleveland last week.

As the Yankee players warmed up on the sidelines prior to the first of the four-game series, they saw Cliff Johnson in the batting cage swatting towering drives into the distant left-field seats.

A few of the players—Fred Stanley, Reggie Jackson and Luis Tiant—called out to him in what passes in the league for friendly banter.

"Hey, cheeseburger, cheeseburger," Stanley yelled, imitating the comic John Belushi of the "Saturday Night Live" show. "You staying out of trouble?"

"Hey," Reggie Jackson yelled, "I understand that the man with the boats wants you back."

"Yeah?" said Johnson, sourly. "Well, it'll cost him a boat-load of money."

Noticing that the Yankees' George Scott, acquired recently from the Red Sox, was now wearing Johnson's old Yankee number, 41, Johnson scowled, but then smiled and clapped Scott across the back. Then Johnson turned as he heard, behind the batting cage, the voice of Jerry Narron calling to him. Suddenly, Johnson was angry. "Hey, man, I've been hearing some mean stuff you've been saying." Narron retreated, saying nothing more. Gossage was nowhere in sight.

But 10 minutes later, as the Yankees' second string was taking infield practice, Johnson, in the dugout, spotted Gossage standing behind a protective screen at first base. He trotted out toward Gossage, who turned slowly.

"How you feeling?" Johnson asked.

"Good," Gossage said.

"I see you're back to normal," Johnson added, referring to Gossage's effective relief appearances in recent weeks.

"Yeah," Gossage said. There was silence, and then the two men parted.

The game began. Rick Waits was pitching for Cleveland. And with Cliff Johnson driving in what proved to be the winning run with a double, Cleveland won the first of the four-game series, 5-1. Cleveland also won the second game of the twilight-night doubleheader, 6-5. On the following night, in the first of two times at bat, Cliff Johnson hit home runs. In the fourth inning he faced the Yankees' third relief pitcher, Bob Kammeyer. The count was 2-2 when Kammeyer unleashed the ball toward Johnson's head—the "brushback" pitch that Martin had called for.

The Yankees were already behind by 10-0. Neither team was going anywhere in the American League, and within another inning, Martin would remove most of his regulars from the lineup. Still, Johnson was ordered hit, and later the next day after checking with the few Yankee teammates with whom he remains on good terms, Johnson verified that Kammeyer's pitch had been intentional.

Two days later, the Indians were in Baltimore playing the Orioles, and around the batting cage—which is where the players from the visiting and home teams invariably exchange gossip in items that rarely make the sports pages—there was a discussion about Martin's tactics against Johnson. Nobody was especially surprised by the story. It sounded to them like something Martin was very capable of doing. Except in this instance, the information may not be totally correct. Martin *did* order Johnson brushed; and Martin *did* hand Kammeyer $100 when he returned to the dugout, but the $100 was not presented as a reward for hitting Johnson. What Martin said, in a compassionate tone not generally attributed to his nature, was: "Here, take this, and tonight go out and get drunk with Mirabella and Anderson [the two other battered pitchers] . . . Get drunk and forget about today, and come back strong tomorrow."

RACE, REPORTERS AND
RESPONSIBILITY

New York Times, 1997

TODAY WITHIN A school auditorium in Fairfax, Va., President Clinton's advisory board on race will conduct another in its dialogues that will probably evoke both constructive and contentious comments from speakers representing many aspects of social and business life in America. That is, with one exception—the athletes who make their living in the National Basketball Association.

And yet at the risk of seeming frivolous, I am suggesting that the N.B.A. is one of the nation's least racist industries; while the league's critics may define professional basketball as an enslavement of black energy by white management. I believe there are few places in the country where thousands of black and white fans and hundreds of players are more comfortable with one another than they are on game nights within N.B.A. arenas.

Liberal and conservative pundits are uninvolved here. There are no minority quotas in the N.B.A. During games white fans can, and do, scream out criticisms of a black player without undue concern that their comments will be racially interpreted.

Nowhere in America are people more colorblind. And so I am surprised by suggestions in the media that Latrell Sprewell, a black player, may have been reacting to racism when he tried to choke P. J. Carlesimo, his white coach, at a practice session earlier this month in Oakland. I was also surprised that some commentators thought that racism-played a part in the retaliatory response by the Golden State Warriors when the team canceled his lucrative contract and by the league's predominantly white management in suspending him for a year.

One of the player's legal advisers, Johnnie Cochran, a peerless exponent of racism as a weapon of defense, appeared often on news broadcasts and in the press, condemning the league's ruling as a rush to judgment.

But the rush to judgment, in my opinion—as one who has watched professional basketball for more than 40 years, beginning in the 1950's as a sportswriter—was fomented by the media themselves in hastily surrendering their air time and news space to effective attention seekers who are using the facts for their own purposes and whatever publicity value might accrue to them.

This is how the Rev. Al Sharpton first gained recognition a decade ago—as the flamboyant and race-mongering spokesman on behalf of Tawana Brawley, the young black woman who claimed in 1987, when she was 15, that she had been raped and sodomized by a gang of white men.

A special grand jury ultimately called this accusation a fabrication, but Ms. Brawley is now back in the headlines along with Mr. Sharpton and with more charges of racism. At the State Supreme Court in Poughkeepsis. Mr. Sharpton and two of Ms. Brawley's black supporters, Alton H. Maddox and C. Vernon Mason, are defending themselves in a defamation suit filed by Steven A. Pagones, one of the white men whom they had earlier identified as being among Ms. Brawley's rapists.

The charges have gotten uglier. William E. Stanton, Mr. Pagones's white lawyer, was denounced in court as a racist by Mr. Maddox.

"It's clear that Mr. Stanton is a racist, a bald-faced racist," Mr. Maddox said. "He doesn't believe anything a black woman says."

"I served in Vietnam with black men and saw them die," Mr. Stanton countered.

"You probably shot them," Mr. Maddox replied, eliciting what one journalist described as approving murmurs from his adherents.

Later on the courthouse steps Mr. Stanton was said to be embittered and in pain as he faced the press. "You print everything these people say," he said.

I am a First Amendment absolutist, and I am not advocating any outside restriction upon the press. What I am pleading for instead is a heightened sense of fairness by editors and television news managers, a bit more restraint on their part against the character assassination of people they report on. Why should Alton Maddox be permitted to single out Mr. Stanton in the press as a racist when there is not an iota of evidence to justify this?

And why should a white basketball coach now be forced to defend himself against charges of racism, just as his job seems to be in jeopardy—as the sports pages these days constantly remind us—because he failed to find a winning formula with a team headed by a black star who seemed intent on beheading him?

And again, where is the proof that any racial feelings existed between these two? Athletes and their coaches have often vented their frustrations with physical abuse upon one another. The sports world is populated by many very physical and very aggressive people. But their altercations should not be identified as racist merely because some opportunistic and newsworthy person might suggest that this is true.

If the prizefighter Mike Tyson had bitten off the ear of a white opponent instead of Evander Holyfield's, could this have been projected as an act of racial hatred? If Indiana's basketball star, Reggie Miller, had taunted a white fan at courtside in Madison Square Garden a few years ago instead of Spike Lee, would it have been reported as racially motivated?

During this month and next, as the President's conversations on race continue across the country, might the time be appropriate for the press itself to review the methods by which it evaluates and reports on this troublesome and not always definable subject, one which leads us to so much misunderstanding in America?

THE FIGHTER'S SON

New York Times, 1998

THERE WAS ONCE a tattooed and florid little blue-eyed Sicilian-born prizefighter named Martin Sinatra, who, wishing to enhance his employment opportunities in America at a time when there were no discernible advantages to having an Italian surname (except in the Mafia), presented himself in the ring as "Marty O'Brien."

I mean no disrespect to this man who compromised his identity in the interest of commerce, for it has historically been a very common practice, one followed by many of this nation's foreign-born whenever they have sought to masquerade within the American mainstream—or, in the specific case of Mr. Sinatra and his sobriquet, to appeal more readily to the large number of American boxing promoters of Irish descent and to the many other Irish-Americans who in those distant days were among the nation's most ardent fight fans.

In the case of the fighter's only son, however, compromise of any kind would always be anathema, and thus he was destined to live a life that would be as turbulent as it was triumphant, a headline-making existence that, over the course of half a century, the rest of us (particularly we Americans of Italian heritage) would find inspirational because it gave us the courage, finally, to fully acknowledge and respect who we are.

THE LOSER

G AY TALESE WROTE enough stories about Floyd
Patterson—thirty-seven of them—to fill a small book.
Never before that or since then has he had a relationship with
a subject that compared to the one he had with Patterson. The
fighter and the entourage that surrounded him reminded him
of Jed and Buster, two black men who worked at Talese Town-
ship pressing clothes. "These were battered guys," Talese says.
"They were 4Fs. They were military rejects." Talese often worked
alongside them, putting hangers on a rail.

Like Patterson, many of the people who surrounded him
were busted up, either as fighters or in the boxing match of
life. "They were all beaten at one point, maybe just from neighborhood fights, but they were all battered," Talese says of
Patterson's entourage. "They were a disreputable group of rejects. What I thought was so wonderful is they had great humil-
ity even though they were walking weapons. There's a sadness
about them and when someone would talk to them decently, as
I did, they sort of opened up to me."

The ability to make people comfortable enough to reveal

things they have never told their wives or mistresses is one of the unseen strengths in Talese's career. For starters, he has never dressed any differently just because the people he is writing about don't share his regard for three-piece suits. "That would be disrespecting them," he says. "What you're doing is presuming you know them, you're presuming you know what it is they like to see. I have no social pretentions, but I have mobility. I am socially mobile. I feel I can move into anybody's territory without taking off my vest. What I think is important and what influences people to let me in the door, it's because my manner is courteous. I want to hear about their lives. I want to listen."

The stories in this section concern Patterson's stunning first-round knockout at the hands of Sonny Liston—the build up to the fight, the dialogue from the hazy moments right after ("A right hand wasn't it? I think it was."), the long drive home dressed in a disguise. Ultimately, his remarkable *Esquire* piece "The Loser" opens in an "abandoned country club house with a dusty dance floor." Talese puts into words the interior monologue running through the fighter's head. Patterson *thinks* in Talese's narrative. And Patterson reveals things boxers never put into words, like the euphoria that accompanies being knocked out and the hurt, the feeling of being beaten, that follows.

MR

PORTRAIT OF THE
ASCETIC CHAMP

New York Times, 1961

FLOYD PATTERSON'S DRAMATIC triumph over Ingemar Johansson last June—an international comeback topped
only by Haile Selassie's—made him a big hero again, but it did
not change his ways; he remains a heavyweight ascetic, a man
whose habits have long baffled boxing's epicures, free-loaders
and smart-money scholars.

Patterson thrives on solitude and meditation, and he often
prays. Before the first round of each fight he makes the sign of
the cross, but he never prays to win; he asks only that no serious
injury come to himself or his opponents, and that is what he will
be doing before the first round in Miami Beach on March 13, the
night he risks his title against Johansson.

The two men are vastly different. Johansson likes publicity
and the high life, and possibly knows as much about the
female form as any man since Vesalius. When he knocked
Patterson out two years ago, it was a setback for austerity, a
victory for the Copacabana. Since nearly everybody thought
Johansson would win the second fight, too, Patterson was very
unpopular last winter, and on one occasion was snowbound

for three days within his camp, then in Connecticut, before anybody noticed his predicament and came to dig him out.

But things, of course, have changed. Patterson's repossession of the title restored him to grace, and this winter his training camp—earlier in Spring Valley, N. Y., and now in Miami Beach, where he will remain until the fight—is a busy place. Each day he is visited by civic leaders, sycophants and sports writers who pay homage, ask the usual questions and get from him the usual answers: Yes, I think the third fight with Ingemar will be tough; No, I'm not overconfident; Yes, I'll be right in there swinging from the opening bell; Yessir, good-by, thanks for coming.

Then, as their cars disappear, Patterson either trains some more, watches television or reads. When he finds a word he doesn't understand, he looks it up in the four-pound dictionary that is always kept on his bureau. Recently, while still in Spring Valley, he looked up "enigma," which is what a boxing magazine had called him in an article. Patterson seemed amused to find out that he was "something puzzling or inexplicable." So he phoned his wife in Long Island to ask her if she was aware she was married to a man who was puzzling or inexplicable. She wasn't.

While Patterson is not inexplicable, he is at 26, a highly sensitive and shy individual. "I was always shy," he says. "Lots of times in school I'd know the answer and say to myself, 'Raise your hand, you dope, you know it.' But I couldn't. And finally, if nobody could answer it, the teacher would have to tell the class. And I'd be kicking myself inside. Maybe I would have been the smartest one in school—if I could have only raised my hand."

It is odd—or perhaps not so odd—that the world's best

fighter is a man largely dominated by a sense of inferiority. For the longest time he could not hold his head up, could not look into the eyes of other fighters at the weigh-in, could not speak with confidence.

"My main fight," he admitted not long ago, "was to feel I was as good as other people. Oh, how I used to sit and watch Cus [D'Amato, his manager] talk, and how I admired the way he looked people right in the eye, and could express himself. When I had to talk before a group, I'd break out in a hot sweat.

"I'm a lot better now, but I remember the funny feeling I had in Rome last year as I waited for my audience with the Pope. When he came out, I kneeled and kissed his ring. I touched his hand, and I was sweating. I was scared of messing up. It was like the feeling I had one time in New Jersey as I stood in the back of a church during mass, before the first Johansson fight, and I was asked if I'd like to pass around the basket for the collection. I said okay, but then I saw myself passing the basket, and hitting an elderly lady in the face, and spilling the money all over the floor. I decided not to pass the basket. But," he added, "I didn't mess up with the Pope."

His extreme shyness, until quite recently, even inhibited him from standing up for his rights outside the ring; more than once he has been insulted and provoked by drunks and wise guys, and the only time he hit back was after an attacker had cut him with a knife.

"Back in 1957, the year after I'd won the title," he recalled, "I was driving from my camp to take my wife, Sandra, to the movies. On Lewis Avenue in Brooklyn I noticed a cab racing behind me and blowing his horn like a wild man. I'd stopped for a light, and there was very little room for him to swing around me and make a right turn; but he tried anyway, and smashed my tail light off.

"So I pulled over and was reaching in the glove compartment for my insurance and registration card when I saw him rush out of the cab at me. He was a big guy, much larger than I am, and he reached right through the window and grabbed me by the neck. I tried to explain. But he collared me and pulled out a small knife and cut me on the hand here." Patterson displayed a jagged scar on a knuckle of his right hand.

"So I got out of the car, hit him with a left hook and right hand, and then propped him against a fence. I should have called the police, but I was scared. I was scared because I wasn't supposed to be away from camp—Cus didn't know I was out—and although I was only a few blocks from Sandra, I turned right around and drove back to camp. Later I telephoned to tell her what had happened. I was so nervous . . ."

It is natural, but incorrect, for people to confuse Patterson's diffidence with a lack of confidence. As a fighter, he is supremely sure of his talent. Before the second Johansson fight, with the odds heavily against his winning, he told Sandra, "Somebody is going to be carried out of that ring, and I don't think it'll be me." But he would not make such a remark publicly, and would have been embarrassed to see it in print. He is extremely modest.

If Patterson seems more assertive in public now, it is partly because he has learned that modesty is scorned in his profession; that to be nice is regarded as a sign of weakness by the Eighth Avenue operators and contract-makers. "I used to watch at press conferences the way Ingemar spoke up," Patterson said. "He'd say, 'I will do this,' 'I will do that.' 'I will say when.' And I used to think, doesn't he realize he can't talk to people that way? But he could. Although I would never talk to people that way, I learned quite a bit from him. Quite a bit. I imagine many people learned quite a bit from him."

Floyd Patterson has learned quite a bit about life, too, since his fights with Johansson. Before them he was almost naïve; since them he has become an expert on fair-weather friendships, and now separates his true friends from the phonies by the way they responded to him, spoke of him, or wrote about him after Johansson knocked him out in the first fight.

Nothing gratified him more during those lonely months of defeat than the hundreds of Swedish letters saying that, while they were happy Johansson had won, they were also sorry Floyd had lost, and that they still considered him an excellent fighter. Not nearly so many encouraging letters came from people in this country.

Patterson decided that when he was again the champion, he would visit Sweden and repay the kindness in person. This he did last summer.

"When my sparring partners and I landed in Sweden, the interpreter's daughter kissed me on the cheek," he said, "and an elderly lady kissed my hand. I was so moved that I kissed her hand and said, 'Thank you, thank you.' Everywhere I went in Sweden I saw there was no color line."

At one point during his European tour, however, he received a long-distance call from his wife saying that she was having trouble getting admitted to a beauty salon in Rockville Centre, L. I.

"They'd made appointments with her, and then repeatedly broke them," Patterson said. "So I phoned my attorney's wife, Mrs. Julius November, and she got in the place without appointments. I wanted to make this incident known; I didn't want colored people to go there and receive the embarrassment my wife received. But even worse was when my wife said, 'You know those people who run the place are Swedes.' I said, 'Oh, no, no, they can't be Swedes.' She checked again and found she was right. And I didn't know what to say."

Since then Floyd has endured other racial slurs. A month ago a friend phoned to say it would be unwise for the Pattersons to think further about buying a home in Scarsdale. And recently, when another friend said he'd found a hotel in Florida that would be proud to have the heavyweight champion as its guest, Patterson politely refused, saying, "What happens if I lose the championship?—then can I go back to that hotel and pick up my clothes?"

Patterson is not a rabble-rouser, but he finds hypocrisy hard to stomach. So it was understandable that he would demand a guarantee that segregation be disallowed in the seating arrangements for the coming fight. His demands have been met.

"I used to think Jesus was a white man," he said. "All the pictures I've ever seen of Him showed Him white. But I no longer can accept Him as a white man. He either is a Jesus of no color, or a Jesus with skin that is all colors."

Then he added, "My feelings are rather delicate. You can hit me and I won't think much of it. But you can say something and hurt me very much."

Partly as a result of having been hurt by the digs of sports writers and sometime friends, and partly because of his own nature, Patterson leads a quiet, largely introverted life. He eschews night clubs and usually attends only charity dinners. In addition to his family, his few intimates include his lawyer, Julius November; a Brooklyn priest, Father Archibald McLeese; his trainers, Dan Florio and Buster Watson, and his manager,

D'Amato. There have been pleas by boxing promoters and writers for the break-up of the Patterson-D'Amato alliance, on the ground that D'Amato has ruined Patterson's chances of getting more fights and thus developing into a better champion. But the fighter and manager have a strong relationship.

"Cus never cheated me," Floyd said, a statement which in boxing circles is the highest compliment a manager can receive.

Patterson's association with his manager began when he started working out in D'Amato's gymnasium on the lower East Side. At first, according to D'Amato, Floyd was a "kind of stranger." By the time he was 15 he was working out regularly, and had grand hopes that boxing would provide the means to get himself and his family out of the Brooklyn slum into which they moved after leaving North Carolina.

Floyd, one of eleven children born to a laborer and a domestic, had had a somber childhood in a crowded apartment. Before he had reached 11, he seemed headed for an illustrious career as a juvenile delinquent. A chronic truant from school, he could neither read nor write, rarely spoke and could not face anyone who spoke to him.

He was sent to the Wiltwyck School for incorrigible boys near Esopus, N. Y. There he met a teacher, the late Vivian Costen, who gave him individual tutoring. "She was like a mother to me," Floyd said. "I began to catch on. I was learning to read. I even liked school."

At Wiltwyck Miss Costen and the athletic director, Walter Johnson, encouraged Patterson to take up boxing, and from then on his interest in the sport never subsided; he had finally found something he could do well, and he put all of his heart into it.

*   *   *

He continued to train later, while attending P. S. 614, one of New York's schools for maladjusted children, and Alexander Hamilton Vocational High School, and at 16 he won the Golden Gloves open middleweight title. Next he gained nine amateur titles and then, in 1952, won the Olympic middleweight championship.

With D'Amato as his manager, Patterson turned professional the same year and, getting heavier and better, started his rise toward the heavyweight championship.

Not all of his triumphs were impressive, however. A light heavyweight named Dick Wagner gave him a good jolting at the Eastern Parkway Arena in 1953 before losing a close contest, and Patterson lost a decision there later to Joey Maxim. But D'Amato was picking Patterson's opponents carefully—too carefully, same critics argued—and it remained for Patterson to knock out Archie Moore in 1956, and thus win the heavyweight title at 21, to quiet the boys in the back room.

With the title in his possession, the new champion had very few worthy challengers. Patterson's first title defense, in 1957, was against Tommy (Hurricane) Jackson, an unorthodox fighter who had a big rating on television but was not really a good fighter; the referee stopped the dull fight in the tenth round. Then they dug up a white tiger named Pete Rademacher who had never fought professionally before. Rademacher landed a surprising punch that momentarily floored Patterson in the second round, but Rademacher did nothing else and was knocked out in the sixth.

In 1958, Patterson was matched against a backwoodsman named Roy Harris, scion of a Texas family of armadillo lovers and tobacco chewers. The fight, another dull one, ended with a victory for Patterson in the twelfth, although Harris recorded a debatable knockdown in the second.

Patterson has said that Rademacher's punch definitely knocked him down, but that he was off-balance before the Harris punch. He fights out of a crouched position, with both gloves in front of his face, his eyes peeking over the leather, and often is off-balance. In earlier days he would sometimes jump in the air and swing with both feet off the ground.

While he may be comparatively easy to knock down, he also is astonishingly successful at getting up, as he demonstrated in the first Johansson fight, when he got up seven times and was doing so again when the referee stopped the fight.

Floyd has said that 50 per cent of the punches he sustains do not hurt him. The other 50 per cent, especially those to the ribs and solar plexus, do hurt very much, and often he feels them as long as four days after the fight.

"But regardless of which 50 per cent it happens to be, you must always keep the same look on your face," he says. "Sometimes if a fighter gets hit in the head, he'll smile to let the other guy know it didn't hurt, even if it did. After a fighter gets in a good punch, he'll look at the other fighter's face to study his facial reaction: and if the expression changes, and he looks hurt, then the fighter who landed the punch is swarming all over him.

"A good fighter must learn how to maintain a straight face after he gets hit with a good punch."

When the fighter sits in his corner between rounds, attended to by the cut-men and mouth-washers, the manager usually tries to pep him up, point out what he is doing wrong, and often tells him he is losing if he is winning or winning if he's losing. Sometimes what is said in the corner during or before a fight will have a dramatic effect on the fight itself.

"Before the second fight with Johansson," Floyd remembers, "my trainer, Buster Watson, who is a very funny guy and always makes me laugh, all of a sudden got very serious. He looked at me just before the bell and said. 'This is it, Pat.' I can't explain why it got to me. Maybe it's because Buster never talks that way. I don't know. But it got me in the right mood at the start of the fight."

That encounter lasted until 1 minute 51 seconds of the fifth round; then Johansson was on the floor for good. For Patterson—the first man ever to regain the heavyweight title—the victory was more than revenge upon the Swede: it was a slap against those sports writers who had called him a pancake champion; against the so-called friends who had dropped him; against the people who were not there with shovels when he was snowbound in Connecticut.

But the victory was not his greatest comeback. Floyd Patterson, born in a cabin in Waco, N. C., and the inheritor of more handicaps than he'd care to mention, meanwhile had won a much more important fight against ignorance, delinquency, poverty and insecurity.

With the money he has earned—money other fighters have squandered on frivolity, or had stolen from them by unscrupulous managers—he has guaranteed the college education of his children, the well-being of his wife, and enabled his parents and relatives to move out of the slums.

"My mother looks younger now than she did eight years ago," Patterson says proudly. "This is due to what I could give her from my earnings in boxing."

And this has made up for all the pain and the knocks, all the humiliation and disappointments that boxing has brought him.

PATTERSON, INDIFFERENT AT FIRST, FINALLY TURNS ON BARKING DOG

New York Times, 1962

ELGIN, ILL., SEPT. 19—Each afternoon Floyd Patterson takes a four-mile walk down a narrow road through the corn fields and invariably a noisy white farm dog hears him and comes charging behind him, challenging and snapping.

Patterson had always ignored the dog, but yesterday, having taken all the abuse he could from one animal, he turned quickly and waited for it to attack. It retreated. Patterson laughed; it confirmed for him the cliché about barking dogs and today he was wondering whether Sonny Liston might have something in common with the dog.

"From the way Liston's been acting and boasting at his camp," Patterson said, "it seems he is out to prove something. Maybe he's worried." Then he said, "I'm just as confident as he is. But his is on the surface; mine is within."

Patterson, the champion, was not predicting the winner of their world heavyweight title fight, of course, nor was there anything cocky in his demeanor. In fact, he admitted that he could be knocked out and said that his wife, Sandra, had decided to fly to Chicago to see the fight next Tuesday—rather than watch it on closed-circuit television from her home—so she will be on hand to console him should Liston win.

But there is about the Patterson camp these days a lack of tension and a serenity that is conspicuously absent in Liston's. At the Liston camp, the biggest nuisances are the sports writers; at Patterson's the only nuisances are the mosquitoes.

Whereas Liston's behavior is unpredictable, Patterson appears each afternoon, patiently and quietly, at a news conference to answer the same questions he was asked yesterday and the same questions he will be asked tomorrow: How do you feel? How much do you weigh? How many rounds did you spar?

Today they even got a tape to measure his fist (13¾ inches) and were comparing it unfavorably to Liston's (14 inches) until one sage remembered that Primo Carnera's fist was 14½ inches and recalled that he was lucky to beat Victor Mature in Old Testament movies.

Even after the half-hour news conference was over and after all the cameras and aluminum gadgets were toted on to the trucks and driven down the dusty road forty miles back to Chicago, some men lingered around Patterson. They felt all had not been seen or said. They perhaps felt Patterson would reveal the sagging, sad emotion they expect of one who is supposed to be destroyed by Liston.

But then, after smiling and waving good-by, Patterson walked alone toward his small frame house and disappeared. Then the sparring partners played table tennis in the shade of a tree or slept. And the manager, Cus D'Amato, resumed reading his Civil War book ("Lee reminds me of Joey Maxim," he said). The lawyer, Julius November, got into a huddle with the promoters on the porch and talked money.

*　　*　　*

And then this whole fight camp, nestled in this vast green flat-land of ever-rustling corn stalks, took on a Sleepy-Time Down-South atmosphere. So the men from Chicago left camp.

An hour later, Patterson, wearing khakis, a tee shirt and cap, came out of the house and began his walk down the road past the farms, past the dog.

Usually he is alone for these walks. Today he had two visi-tors, including the novelist James Baldwin, who had just flown in from research in Africa and was trying to learn something about boxing. One hour before, he presented two of his best sellers, "Another Country" and "Nobody Knows My Name," to Patterson, inscribing them "For Floyd Patterson. . . . Because we both know whence we come, and have some idea of where we're going. . . ."

Then the author was given a tour of the grounds by one of Floyd Patterson's articulate press aides, Ted Carroll, who said: "Mr. Baldwin, this is a training camp. And this countryside matches the personality of the champion. While his trade is vio-lent, Mr. Baldwin, his personality is unruffled, bucolic. Is that a good word, Mr. Baldwin?"

Baldwin nodded.

"Any questions?"

"Nothing I can think of," the novelist said.

"Don't be bashful," the aide said.

"Now," Carroll continued, "in a training camp there are sparring partners, a cook, an assistant cook and two trainers, one trainer is Dan Florio. The other, Buster Watson, is an old friend of the champ—an old family benefactor. I don't know if you want to use that word?"

Baldwin could not seem to make up his mind at the moment.

Then the novelist and Floyd Patterson took a walk and, two

hours later, returned. Patterson shook hands with Baldwin and then went back to his house. Baldwin thanked him, and then said about Patterson: "There is a kind of gentleness and a kind of toughness I've seen all my life."

LISTON AIDES EXTOL
HIS GAIETY, BENEVOLENCE
AND RUGGEDNESS

New York Times, 1962

AURORA, ILL., SEPT. 20—Sonny Liston, who has been billed as the toughest man to hit Chicago since Dillinger—it has even been suggested that Liston has no warm spot for Robert Frost—actually is a highly sensitive, gentle soul, his manager said today, and efforts were then made to illustrate this point.

"Liston," said Jack Nilon, "had six or eight groups of kids from Chicago reform schools over here the other day, and he sat them all down and straightened them out."

"He gave 'em autographed photos and a Coca-Cola," said Archibald Pirolli, Liston's public relations executive.

"Pepsi Cola," said Nilon.

"But," Pirolli went on, "the only thing the public hears about is Liston's record. There have been 9,635,721 words written so far about his criminal record."

"If you only knew Liston," he went on, "if you only saw how him and his wife are like two lovebirds—they're never more than five feet apart unless he's training—you'd see what a good guy he is, and how he'd fool around with you, and laugh, and pull your tie, and . . ."

"And," Nilon cut in, "when he becomes heavyweight champion, he'll add some life to this boxing game."

Most visitors to this camp today agreed that Liston would win the title from Floyd Patterson next Tuesday. And some even welcomed the "life" he would add to the game.

"I am frankly a little tired of reading about Patterson's id and all the amateur psychology business," said one boxing observer in the limousine en route from Chicago to Liston's camp 42 miles away. "At least, in Liston, we'll have a brawler who can finish a fight with one punch."

All day long here, and elsewhere, the debate goes on between those who contend that Patterson's triumph would be a victory of good over evil.

Others agree that boxing, after all, is not run for the 4-H Club and that Liston is precisely the type of gladiator needed to pack arenas as they were jammed in the good old days of Roman lion orgy.

Liston is inevitably cast as the "heavy" in these discussions despite arguments to the contrary by Nilon and Perolli.

When Liston appeared today he was wearing a white cap, a blue sports suit and a jovial smile.

"What was your toughest fight, Sonny?" he was asked.

"My toughest fight was getting this fight," Liston said, pleased.

"Will you defend your title once a year?"

"Probably."

There were more interesting questions, but when it was all over Nilon said: "One thing you guys never seemed to mention is how Liston can take a punch."

"Liston," he went on, "you can hit him with an ax."

"Or baseball bat," said Perolli. "And he'll still come after you."

PATTERSON HAS 4 FRIENDS, TOO, BUT HE'LL HAVE TO FIGHT ALONE

New York Times, 1962

ELGIN, ILL., SEPT. 23—In Floyd Patterson's corner Tuesday night will be one trainer who will stretch his elastic trunks between rounds. Another trainer will tend the water bottle, mouthpiece and cuts, a third will keep an eye on everything the challenger is doing.

A fourth individual (the manager), will do most of the talking between rounds. He may possibly tell Patterson he is losing when he is winning, or winning when he is losing.

All four men will be tense and restless at 9 P.M., New York Time, when they escort Patterson into Comiskey Park and begin to tape his hands and help him dress. Then Patterson, the calmest man in his own corner, probably will fall asleep for an hour.

Shortly before 10:30 P.M., the four will follow Patterson into the ring for the duration of the fight, their voices will be shrieking, their eyes intense. When each round ends, their eight busy hands will go into blurry motion for the 60-second intermission.

The manager, Cus D'Amato, carrying the stool, will be the

first to jump into the ring. While Patterson is sitting, Buster Watson, the assistant trainer, will be tugging at the champion's trunks to aid his breathing.

On the left side of Patterson will be the chief trainer, Dan Florio, a top fighter himself forty years ago. He will be swabbing Patterson's face with sterilized pads, holding the mouthpiece, clutching the bottle—and applying smelling salts to Patterson's nose if the fighter is groggy.

Standing on the right side of Patterson and holding an ice bag to the champion's temples will be Dan's brother, Nick Florio. Nick's genius is in perceiving flaws in the opponent's tactics.

"Nick don't miss a trick," said Dan. "Remember the second Johansson fight? Nick noticed Johansson was dropping his left hand, and Floyd was able to hit him with an overhand right and a hook. Johansson was never the same after that."

All four men in Patterson's corner have in common their dedication to the fighter, but, as individuals, they are very different. Dan Florio is a quiet worrier. Nick seems entirely without emotion. D'Amato is all emotion, and does most of the talking in the ring.

Watson, Floyd's closest friend, possesses a schizophrenic quality.

Until the day of the fight, he is a flashy, chatty comic. He swaggers around the camp in flamboyant sportswear or zooms about in his fancy Cadillac. Patterson is greatly amused by him. He is what every champion wants—a combination companion-court jester.

On the day of the fight, however, Watson's big eyes seem to get larger. He begins to sit alone, or next to Ernest Fowler, Patterson's chauffeur. They stare at each other silently, or sometimes they look and just shake their heads, and glance at the ceiling.

Watson, Dan Florio and Fowler live with Floyd Patterson eight months of the year, neglecting their families and private lives. Dan controls the training camp, supervises Patterson's meals, regulates the schedule and hires and dismisses the sparring partners.

D'Amato usually lives away from the training camp until a month before the fight, although he is always breezing in or out, usually unannounced, with news of controversies, schemes and plots, all of which he demonstrates with gestures while pacing back and forth across the floor.

All legal matters, of course, are handled by Patterson's lawyer, Julius November, who also is in contact with Patterson daily by phone, if not in person.

Patterson usually responds, but not always, to the swirling activity around him. However, he makes all his own decisions, in or out of the ring.

While waiting for the fight today, he played cards, watched television, read, took walks and did not seem at all worried about the battle with Sonny Liston.

Tuesday night, he will undoubtedly be a lot better off for having someone tote in the stool, wash off his face, nurse his bruises, etc. But he will probably not be aware of the noise in his corner or the movement. He will be only watching Sonny Liston.

CHAMPION TALKS ABOUT SLEEP
AND RAIN AND WATCHES HIS
ENTOURAGE CLOSE CAMP

New York Times, 1962

ELGIN, ILL., SEPT. 24—Floyd Patterson walked down the winding country road today past the cows and horses clustered behind rustic fences. Every now and then a farmer's voice from the green fields beyond would echo: "Good luck, Floyd. Hope you win, champ."

Patterson would wave back and continue on his two-mile walk in semi-silence. But when it started to drizzle a bit this afternoon, he asked those tagging along with him:

"If it rains as hard before the fight, they won't postpone it, will they?"

"Doubt it," somebody said.

This was what he wanted to hear.

"You ever been rained out before?"

"Yes, in the first Johannson fight," Patterson said. "Rained out and knocked out." Then he said, "Oh, it's a miserable feeling when, on the day of the fight, it rains."

"Get you nervous?"

"I don't show it," he said. "I just get sleepy. The more nervous I am, the sleepier I get. In 1956, in Chicago, I fell asleep in the car on the way to the Archie Moore fight. During my amateur days, before a fight, I used to sleep sitting up in a chair. Now I have a table in the dressing room. Sleeping is more comfortable."

An hour later, when Patterson walked back toward the white farm house that has been his training headquarters for the past month, he saw the sparring partners and trainers carrying suitcases into their cars.

The carpenters were dismantling the boxing ring up on the hill. The cook, having emptied the kitchen and defrosted the icebox, was now placing bread along the grass in the back for the birds. This was moving day.

At night, Patterson and his entourage would be living in a Chicago hotel. There was something pensive in the way everybody moved and packed this afternoon—like circus people when they're taking down the tents.

At 2:30, while Dan Florio, Patterson's chief trainer, was in the village picking up Patterson's laundry, some of the sparring partners went to the Elgin drugstore for a final soda.

Patterson walked around the house for a moment. Then he said:

"It's always like this the day before the fight. Can you feel it?"

It was difficult to miss. Last night it had been a merry camp, with everybody laughing during dinner at the jokes of Patterson's hilarious friend and trainer, Buster Watson. Later, everybody played gin rummy and Patterson won $18.

But today, for the first time in months, they did not hear the rhythm of the punching bag, or the snap of the skip rope against the floor. No carload of newsmen invaded the quietude to ask Floyd how he felt, and whether he could beat Sonny Liston.

So today, everyone just stood around. Patterson has now done hundreds of miles of roadwork, boxed dozens of rounds, jumped thousands of times through a flying rope in preparation for this fight. But today, there was nothing to do but wait.

FLOYD CAUGHT BY
'A GOOD PUNCH'

New York Times, 1962

CHICAGO, SEPT. 25—"What happened, Floyd?" they asked. The former champion shrugged his shoulders and then, sitting upright on a bench before the crowd jammed into his dressing room, said, "I got caught with a good punch."

"A right hand, wasn't it?"

"I think it was."

"Did you hear the referee counting over you?"

"Not clearly at first," Patterson said. "When I did begin to hear, I thought I heard him say '8' and I jumped up."

"How soon will you fight him again?"

"Soon," Patterson said.

"I suggest, gentlemen," said Cus D'Amato, the manager at his side, "that you confine the questions to the fight area itself."

"Were you to press him low at the body?"

"Yes," Patterson said. "That was my plan, yes."

"Were you hurt before that right-hand punch?" (Liston said later he won with left hooks, but nobody in Patterson's dressing room—including the champion and his entourage—was having any. They were talking only of the right-hand punch.)

Patterson was not hurt. His face was marked only by disappointment. He has, in his contract, the right to fight Liston again within 12 months. The promoter, Tom Bolan, said that Patterson's first words when leaving the ring were, "When's the next one going to be?"

Patterson conceded that he never was able to get started. He is notoriously slow at warming up in the ring, and his strategy was to stay away from Liston for a few rounds, fight from a crouch, and protect himself from Liston's barrage until he could get his own combinations going.

But he never got the chance tonight.

After the knockout, Patterson's mother jumped into the ring and embraced her son. Then, after being led into his dressing room, Patterson remained in seclusion for a half hour.

Fifteen minutes later, Patterson's wife, Sandra, came out of the dressing room, her eyes red, her head bowed.

Then some of his other relatives—his brothers, and his cousins—came out along with his trainers. All sorts of questions were asked. They had nothing to say.

MASKED EX-CHAMPION

New York Times, 1962

F LOYD PATTERSON WAS so humiliated after the first-round knockout by Sonny Liston on Tuesday night in Chicago that he drove all the way back to New York disguised as a bearded beatnik. He had a beatnik beard glued to his chin, a thick mustache across his upper lip, dark glasses over his eyes, and a hat tilted forward on his head.

"I just didn't want anyone to see me," he explained yesterday at Highland Mills, N. Y., the camp where he trained for the Liston fight, and to which he returned late Wednesday night after a 22-hour journey from Chicago in a borrowed car.

He was accompanied from Chicago by his long-time friend, the vocalist Mickey Alan, who sang the Star Spangled Banner before the Liston fight. The mustache that Patterson wore was the same one he had in his pocket as he entered the Polo Grounds before his second fight against Ingemar Johansson; had he lost a second time to the Swedish heavyweight, Patterson would have tried to escape unrecognized through the crowd.

*　　*　　*

Defeats in the ring, particularly those in which he performs poorly, leave him with a sense of embarrassment and guilt. He does not want to face people at such times. He wants, instead, to hide—just as he used to hide as a child in a hole above the tracks of the High Street subway station in Brooklyn: a hole he climbed into by a ladder and within which he used to sit for hours in the darkness listening to the trains rumbling by, and imagining himself safe from all that he feared.

Before his first fight with Johansson, Patterson elaborated on his plan of escape; he hired a disguise expert from Newtown, Conn., to make a beard and mustache that, in the event of a defeat, Patterson could wear when leaving the dressing room and getting into his car.

He also planned to have two cars waiting outside for him after each fight. If he won, he would hop in the car that would take him back to his hotel and to people; if he lost, he would get into a second car always pointed toward the quickest route out of town.

The second car would also be packed ahead of time with enough clothing and supplies for the trip ahead, Patterson explained yesterday; he would not have to stop and run the risk of meeting people after a defeat, and having to explain why he lost.

So it was in Chicago last Monday, the day before the Liston fight. Patterson arranged for two cars to be outside Comiskey Park—one pointed toward the parkway bound for New York; the other pointed toward the hotel where, if he won, he would have celebrated.

In his pocket, he had the mustache he did not have to wear after the second and third Johansson fights, both of which he won. The beard that had been made for him for those fights had become shaggy in the meantime, and so, on the day before the fight, he had a Chicago beard salesman bring one to the hotel where Patterson had been staying.

It cost Patterson $65, and he also gave the man a $50 ticket to the fight, the former champion said yesterday.

When the fight ended after 2 minutes 6 seconds of the first round, and after Patterson held a brief news conference in his locker room, he slipped out of Comiskey Park through a pre-planned route and hopped into the car headed for New York. At the wheel was Alan, a former prize fighter who became a singer with large financial backing from Patterson.

The two drove through Illinois and into Ohio before anybody recognized Patterson, the fighter said yesterday. He said that once, when he had stopped the car momentarily to stretch his legs, a policeman stopped and asked Patterson for his driver's license.

He did not have it. Then Patterson removed part of his disguise, arousing the policeman's suspicions even more—until he recognized the fighter. The policeman did not take Patterson into custody; instead he wished him luck in the return match against Liston, and wished him a swift journey home.

Patterson, not wanting to go to his home in Yonkers, drove directly to the training camp at Highland Mills, and he and Alan spent the night there, he said.

"The next day I asked Mickey to leave," Patterson said. "I spent the day watching television—I definitely did not want to listen to the radio, and all the news about Liston—and later I decided to take a walk. I went into the gymnasium. And, suddenly, I got the urge to train—believe it or not, even though it sounds silly. Unfortunately I had none of my gear with me.

"So I walked around, and I thought about all the training,

all the hours I'd spent getting ready for the Liston fight; now it was all out the window."

Later Thursday afternoon, Patterson said that his chauffeur, Ernest Fowler, who had been instructed to bring Patterson's Lincoln to Highland Mills, arrived; later that night, both Patterson and Fowler left the camp for Patterson's home.

Sandra, his wife, said yesterday, "I hardly recognized him with that bushy, black mustache. He'd taken off the beard by this time because he said it was irritating his chin. He played with the kids for a while, and then went to meet Mr. November."

Julius November, Patterson's lawyer, was due at New York International Airport from Chicago after 9 P.M., the fighter said; after picking up the lawyer, Patterson said they discussed business, but did not reveal the content.

Later, Patterson said he returned to Highland Mills, but today plans to return to his home.

He said he would not go into hiding, as he seemed to do after suffering the knockout in his first fight with Johansson. He said he soon plans to resume training for his return match with Liston, and said he does not feel that the world has come to an end.

"In the next fight, I don't say the result will be different," Patterson said, "but I guarantee this: I'll give a much, much better account of myself."

THE LOSER

Esquire, 1964

A T T H E F O O T of a mountain in upstate New York, about sixty miles from Manhattan, there is an abandoned country clubhouse with a dusty dance floor, upturned bar stools, and an untuned piano; and the only sounds heard around the place at night come from the big white house behind it—the clanging sounds of garbage cans being toppled by raccoons, skunks, and stray cats making their nocturnal raids down from the mountain.

The white house seems deserted, too; but occasionally, when the animals become too clamorous, a light will flash on, a window will open, and a Coke bottle will come flying through the darkness and smash against the cans. But mostly the animals are undisturbed until daybreak, when the rear door of the white house swings open and a broad-shouldered Negro appears in gray sweat clothes with a white towel around his neck.

He runs down the steps, quickly passes the garbage cans, and proceeds at a trot down the dirt road beyond the country club toward the highway. Sometimes he stops along the road and throws a flurry of punches at imaginary foes, each jab punctuated by hard gasps of his breathing—*"hegh-hegh-hegh"*—and then, reaching the highway, he turns and soon disappears up the mountain.

At this time of morning farm trucks are on the road, and the drivers wave at the runner. And later in the morning other motorists see him, and a few stop suddenly at the curb and ask, "Say, aren't *you* Floyd Patterson?"

"No," says Floyd Patterson, "I'm his brother, Raymond."

The motorists move on, but recently a man on foot, a disheveled man who seemed to have spent the night outdoors, staggered behind the runner along the road and yelled, "Hey, Floyd Patterson!"

"No, I'm his brother, Raymond."

"Don't tell *me* you're not Floyd Patterson. I know what Floyd Patterson looks like."

"Okay," Patterson said, shrugging, "if you want me to be Floyd Patterson, I'll be Floyd Patterson."

"So let me have your autograph," said the man, handing him a rumpled piece of paper and a pencil.

He signed it—"Raymond Patterson."

One hour later Floyd Patterson was jogging his way back down the dirt path toward the white house, the towel over his head absorbing the sweat from his brow. He lives alone in a two-room apartment in the rear of the house and has remained there in almost complete seclusion since getting knocked out a second time by Sonny Liston.

In the smaller room is a large bed he makes up himself, several record albums he rarely plays, a telephone that seldom rings. The larger room has a kitchen on one side and, on the other, adjacent to a sofa, is a fireplace from which are hung boxing trunks and T-shirts to dry, and a photograph of him when he was the champion, and also a television set. The set is usually on except when Patterson is sleeping, or when he is sparring across the road inside the clubhouse (the ring is rigged over what was once the dance floor), or, when, in a rare moment of painful honesty, he reveals to a visitor what it is like to be the loser.

"Oh, I would give up anything to just be able to work with Liston, to box with him somewhere where nobody would see us, and to see if I could get past three minutes with him," Patterson was saying, wiping his face with the towel, pacing slowly around the room near the sofa. "I *know* I can do better. . . . Oh, I'm not talking about a rematch. Who would pay a nickel for another Patterson-Liston fight? I know *I* wouldn't. . . . But all I want to do is get past the first round."

Then he said, "You have no idea how it is in the first round. You're out there with all those people around you, and those cameras, and the whole world looking in, and all that movement, that excitement, and 'The Star-Spangled Banner,' and the whole nation hoping you'll win, including the president. And do you know what all this does? It blinds you, just blinds you. And then the bell rings, and you go at Liston and he's coming at you, and you're not even aware that there's a referee in the ring with you.

"Then you can't remember much of the rest, because you don't want to. . . . All you recall is, all of a sudden you're getting up, and the referee is saying, 'You all right?' and you say, 'Of *course* I'm all right,' and he says, 'What's your name?' and you say, 'Patterson.'

"And then, suddenly, with all this screaming around you, you're down again, and you know you have to get up, but you're extremely groggy, and the referee is pushing you back, and your trainer is in there with a towel, and people are all

standing up, and your eyes focus directly at no one person—
you're sort of floating.

"It is not a *bad* feeling when you're knocked out," he said.
"It's a *good* feeling, actually. It's not painful, just a sharp grog-
giness. You don't see angels or stars; you're on a pleasant
cloud. After Liston hit me in Nevada, I felt, for about four or
five seconds, that everybody in the arena was actually in the
ring with me, circled around me like a family, and you feel
warmth toward all the people in the arena after you're knocked
out. You feel lovable to all the people. And you want to reach
out and kiss everybody—men and women—and after the Liston fight somebody told me I actually blew a kiss to the crowd
from the ring. I don't remember that. But I guess it's true because that's the way you feel during the four or five seconds
after a knockout.

"But then," Patterson went on, still pacing, "this good feeling leaves you. You realize where you are, and what you're
doing there, and what has just happened to you. And what follows is a hurt, a confused hurt—not a physical hurt—it's a
hurt combined with anger; it's a what-will-people-think hurt;
it's an ashamed-of-my-own-ability hurt . . . and all you want
then is a hatch door in the middle of the ring—a hatch door
that will open and let you fall through and land in your dressing room instead of having to get out of the ring and face those
people. The worst thing about losing is having to walk out of
the ring and face those people."

Then Patterson walked over to the stove and put on the kettle
for tea. He remained silent for a few moments. Through the
walls could be heard the footsteps and voices of the sparring
partners and the trainer who live in the front of the house. Soon
they would be in the clubhouse getting things ready should Patterson wish to spar. In two days he was scheduled to fly to

Stockholm and fight an Italian named Amonti, Patterson's first appearance in the ring since the last Liston fight.

Next he hoped to get a fight in London against Henry Cooper. Then, if his confidence was restored, his reflexes reacting, Patterson hoped to start back up the ladder in this country, fighting all the leading contenders, fighting often, and not waiting so long between each fight as he had done when he was a champion in the 90 percent tax bracket.

His wife, whom he finds little time to see, and most of his friends think he should quit. They point out that he does not need the money. Even he admits that, from investments alone on his $8-million gross earnings, he should have an annual income of about $35,000 for the next twenty-five years. But Patterson, who is only twenty-nine years old and barely scratched, cannot believe that he is finished. He cannot help but think that it was something more than Liston that destroyed him—a strange, psychological force was also involved, and unless he can fully understand what it was, and learn to deal with it in the boxing ring, he may never be able to live peacefully anywhere but under this mountain. Nor will he ever be able to discard the false whiskers and mustache that, ever since Johansson beat him in 1959, he has carried with him in a small attaché case into each fight so he can slip out of the stadium unrecognized should he lose.

"I often wonder what other fighters feel, and what goes through their minds when they lose," Patterson said, placing the cups of tea on the table. "I've wanted so much to talk to another fighter about all this, to compare thoughts, to see if he feels some of the same things I've felt. But who can you talk to? Most fighters don't talk much anyway. And I can't even look another fighter in the eye at a weigh-in, for some reason.

"At the Liston weigh-in, the sportswriters noticed this, and said it showed I was afraid. But that's not it. I can never look *any* fighter in the eye because . . . well, because we're going to fight, which isn't a nice thing, and because . . . well, once I actually did look a fighter in the eye. It was a long, long time ago. I must have been in the amateurs then. And when I looked at this fighter, I saw he had such a nice face . . . and then he looked at *me* . . . and *smiled* at me . . . and *I* smiled back! It was strange, very strange. When a guy can look at another guy and smile like that, I don't think they have any business fighting.

"I don't remember what happened in that fight, and I don't remember what the guy's name was. I only remember that, ever since, I have never looked another fighter in the eye."

The telephone rang in the bedroom. Patterson got up to answer it. It was his wife, Sandra. So he excused himself, shutting the bedroom door behind him.

Sandra Patterson and their four children live in a $100,000 home in an upper-middle-class white neighborhood in Scarsdale, New York. Floyd Patterson feels uncomfortable in this home surrounded by a manicured lawn and stuffed with furniture, and, since losing his title to Liston, he has preferred living full-time at his camp, which his children have come to know as "daddy's house." The children, the eldest of whom is a daughter named Jeannie, now seven years old, do not know exactly what their father does for a living. But Jeannie, who watched the last Liston-Patterson fight on closed-circuit television, accepted the explanation that her father performs in a kind of game where the men take turns pushing one another down; he had his turn pushing them down, and now it is their turn.

The bedroom door opened again, and Floyd Patterson, shaking his head, was very angry and nervous.

"I'm not going to work out today," he said. "I'm going to fly down to Scarsdale. Those boys are picking on Jeannie again. She's the only Negro in this school, and the older kids give her a rough time, and some of the older boys tease her and lift up her dress all the time. Yesterday she went home crying, and so today I'm going down there and plan to wait outside the school for those boys to come out, and . . ."

"How old are they?" he was asked.

"Teenagers," he said. "Old enough for a left hook."

Patterson telephoned his pilot friend Ted Hanson, who stays at the camp and does public-relations work for him, and has helped teach Patterson to fly. Five minutes later Hanson, a lean white man with a crew cut and glasses, was knocking on the door; and ten minutes later both were in the car that Patterson was driving almost recklessly over the narrow, winding country roads toward the airport, about six miles from the camp.

"Sandra is afraid I'll cause trouble; she's worried about what I'll do to those boys; she doesn't want trouble!" Patterson snapped, swerving around a hill and giving his car more gas. "She's just not firm enough! She's afraid . . . and she was afraid to tell me about that groceryman who's been making passes at her. It took her a long time before she told me about that dishwasher repairman who comes over and calls her 'baby.' They all know I'm away so much. And that dishwasher repairman's been to my home about four, five times this month already. That machine breaks down every week. I guess he fixes it so it breaks down every week. Last time, I laid a trap. I waited forty-five minutes for him to come, but then he didn't show up. I was going to grab him and say, 'How would you like it if I called *your* wife *baby?* You'd feel like punching me in the nose, wouldn't you? Well, that's what I'm going to do—if you ever call her *baby* again. You call her Mrs. Patterson; or

Sandra, if you know her. But you don't know her, so call her Mrs. Patterson.' And then I told Sandra that these men, this type of white man, he just wants to have some fun with colored women. He'll never marry a colored woman, just wants to have some fun."

Now he was driving into the airport's parking lot. Directly ahead, roped to the grass airstrip, was the single-engine green Cessna that Patterson bought and learned to fly before the second Liston fight. Flying was a thing Patterson had always feared—a fear shared by, maybe inherited from, his manager, Cus D'Amato, who still will not fly.

D'Amato, who took over training Patterson when the fighter was seventeen or eighteen years old and exerted a tremendous influence over his psyche, is a strange but fascinating man of fifty-six who is addicted to Spartanism and self-denial and is possessed by suspicion and fear: He avoids subways because he fears someone might push him onto the tracks; never has married; never reveals his home address.

"I must keep my enemies confused," D'Amato once explained. "When they are confused, then I can do a job for my fighters. What I do not want in life, however, is a sense of security; the moment a person knows security, his senses are dulled—and he begins to die. I also do not want many pleasures in life; I believe the more pleasures you get out of living, the more fear you have of dying."

Until a few years ago, D'Amato did most of Patterson's talking, and ran things like an Italian *padrone*. But later Patterson, the maturing son, rebelled against the father image. After losing to Sonny Liston the first time—a fight D'Amato had urged Patterson to resist—Patterson took flying lessons. And before the second Liston fight, Patterson had conquered his fear of heights, was master at the controls, was filled with renewed confidence—and knew, too, that even if he lost, he at least possessed a vehicle that could get him out of town, fast.

But it didn't. After the fight, the little Cessna, weighed down by too much luggage, became overheated ninety miles outside of Las Vegas. Patterson and his pilot companion, having no choice but to turn back, radioed the airfield and arranged for the rental of a larger plane. When they landed, the Vegas air terminal was filled with people leaving town after the fight. Patterson hid in the shadows behind a hangar. His beard was packed in the trunk. But nobody saw him.

Later the pilot flew Patterson's Cessna back to New York alone. And Patterson flew in the larger, rented plane. He was accompanied on this flight by Hanson, a friendly, forty-two-year-old, thrice divorced Nevadan who once was a crop duster, a bartender, and a cabaret hoofer; later he became a pilot instructor in Las Vegas, and it was there that he met Patterson. The two became good friends. And when Patterson asked Hanson to help fly the rented plane back to New York, Hanson did not hesitate, even though he had a slight hangover that night—partly due to being depressed by Liston's victory, partly due to being slugged in a bar by a drunk after objecting to some unflattering things the drunk had said about the fight.

Once in the airplane, however, Ted Hanson became very alert. He had to, because, after the plane had cruised awhile at 10,000 feet, Floyd Patterson's mind seemed to wander back to the ring, and the plane would drift off course, and Hanson would say, "Floyd, Floyd, how's about getting back on course?" and then Patterson's head would snap up and his eyes would flash toward the dials. And everything would be all right for a while. But then he was back in the arena, reliving the fight, hardly believing that it had really happened.

*   *   *

And I kept thinking, as I flew out of Vegas that night, of all those months of training before the fight, all the roadwork, all the sparring, all the months away from Sandra . . . thinking of the time in camp when I wanted to stay up until 11:15 P.M. to watch a certain movie on *The Late Show*. But I didn't because I had roadwork the next morning. . . .

And I was thinking about how good I'd felt before the fight, as I lay on the table in the dressing room. I remember thinking, "You're in excellent physical condition, you're in good mental condition—but are you vicious?" But you tell yourself, "Viciousness is not important now, don't think about it now; a championship fight's at stake, and that's important enough and—who knows?—maybe you'll get vicious once the bell rings." . . .

And so you lay there trying to get a little sleep . . . but you're only in a twilight zone, half asleep, and you're interrupted every once in a while by voices out in the hall, some guy's yelling "Hey, Jack," or "Hey, Al," or "Hey, get those four-rounders into the ring." And when you hear that, you think, "They're not ready for you yet." So you lay there . . . and wonder, "Where will I be tomorrow? Where will I be three hours from now?" Oh, you think all kinds of thoughts, some thoughts completely unrelated to the fight . . . you wonder whether you ever paid your mother-in-law back for all those stamps she bought a year ago . . . and you remember that time at 2 A.M. when Sandra tripped on the steps while bringing a bottle up to the baby . . . and then you get mad and ask, "What am I thinking about these things for?" . . . and you try to sleep . . . but then the door opens, and somebody says to somebody else, "Hey, is somebody gonna go to Liston's dressing room to watch 'em bandage up?" . . .

And so then you know it's about time to get ready. . . . You open your eyes. You get off the table. You glove up, you loosen up. Then Liston's trainer walks in. He looks at you; he smiles. He feels the bandages, and later he says, "Good luck, Floyd," and you think, "He didn't have to say that; he must be a nice guy . . ."

And then you go out, and it's the long walk, always a long walk, and you think, "What am I gonna be when I come back this way?" Then you climb into the ring. You notice Billy Eckstine at ringside leaning over to talk to somebody, and you see the reporters—some you like, some you don't like—and then it's *"The Star-Spangled Banner,"* and the cameras are rolling, and the bell rings. . . .

How could the same thing happen twice? How? That's all I kept thinking after the knockout. . . . Was I fooling these people all these years? . . . Was I ever the champion? . . . And then they lead you out of the ring . . . and up the aisle you go, past those people, and all you want is to get to your dressing room, fast . . . but the trouble was in Las Vegas they made a wrong turn along the aisle, and when we got to the end, there was no dressing room there . . . and we had to walk all the way back down the aisle, past the same people, and they must have been thinking, "Patterson's not only knocked out, but he can't even find his dressing room." . . .

In the dressing room I had a headache. Liston didn't hurt me physically—a few days later I only felt a twitching nerve in my teeth—it was nothing like some fights I've had: like that Dick Wagner fight in '53 when he beat my body so bad I was urinating blood for days. After the Liston fight, I just went into the bathroom, shut the door behind me, and looked at myself in the mirror. I just looked at myself, and asked, "What happened?" and then they started pounding on the door, and saying, "Com'on out, Floyd, com'on out; the press is here, Cus is here, com'on out, Floyd." . . .

And so I went out, and they asked questions, but what can you say? What you're thinking about is all those months of training, all the conditioning, all the depriving; and you think, "I didn't have to run that extra mile, didn't have to spar that day; I could have stayed up that night in camp and watched *The Late Show....* I could have fought this fight tonight in no condition." ...

"Floyd, Floyd," Hanson had said, "let's get back on course."

Again Patterson would snap out of his reverie and refocus on the omniscope and get his flying under control. After landing in New Mexico, and then in Ohio, Floyd Patterson and Ted Hanson brought the little plane into the New York airstrip near the fight camp. The green Cessna that had been flown back by the other pilot was already there, roped to the grass at precisely the same spot it was on this day five months later when Floyd Patterson was planning to fly it toward perhaps another fight—this time a fight with some schoolboys in Scarsdale who had been lifting up his little daughter's dress.

Patterson and Ted Hanson untied the plane, and Patterson got a rag and wiped from the windshield the splotches of insects. Then he walked around behind the plane, inspected the tail, checked under the fuselage, then peered down between the wing and the flaps to make sure all the screws were tight. He seemed suspicious of something. D'Amato would have been pleased.

"If a guy wants to get rid of you," Patterson explained, "all he has to do is remove these little screws here. Then, when you try to come in for a landing, the flaps fall off, and you crash."

Then Patterson got into the cockpit and started the engine. A few moments later, with Hanson beside him, Patterson was racing the little plane over the grassy field, then soaring over the weeds, then flying high above the gentle hills and trees. It was a nice takeoff.

Since it was only a forty-minute flight to the Westchester airport, where Sandra Patterson would be waiting with a car, Floyd Patterson did all the flying. The trip was uneventful until, suddenly behind a cloud, he flew into heavy smoke that hovered above a forest fire. His visibility gone, he was forced to the instruments. And at this precise moment, a fly that had been buzzing in the back of the cockpit flew up front and landed on the instrument panel in front of Patterson. He glared at the fly, watched it crawl slowly up the windshield, then shot a quick smash with his palm against the glass. He missed. The fly buzzed safely past Patterson's ear, bounced off the back of the cockpit, circled around.

"This smoke won't keep up," Hanson assured. "You can level off."

Patterson leveled off.

He flew easily for a few moments. Then the fly buzzed to the front again, zigzagging before Patterson's face, landed on the panel, and proceeded to crawl across it. Patterson watched it, squinted. Then he slammed down at it with a quick right hand. Missed.

Ten minutes later, his nerves still on edge, Patterson began the descent. He picked up the radio microphone—"Westchester tower . . . Cessna 2729 uniform . . . three miles northwest . . . land in one-six on final . . ."—and then, after an easy landing, he climbed quickly out of the cockpit and strode toward his wife's station wagon outside the terminal.

But along the way a small man smoking a cigar turned toward Patterson, waved at him, and said, "Say, excuse me, but aren't you . . . aren't you . . . Sonny Liston?"

Patterson stopped. He glared at the man, bewildered. He

wasn't sure whether it was a joke or an insult, and he really did not know what to do.

"Aren't you Sonny Liston?" the man repeated, quite serious.

"No," Patterson said, quickly passing by the man, "I'm his brother."

When he reached Mrs. Patterson's car, he asked, "How much time till school lets out?"

"About fifteen minutes," she said, starting up the engine. Then she said, "Oh, Floyd, I just should have told Sister, I shouldn't have . . ."

"*You* tell Sister; *I'll* tell the boys."

Mrs. Patterson drove as quickly as she could into Scarsdale, with Patterson shaking his head and telling Ted Hanson in the back, "Really can't understand these schoolkids. This is a religious school, and they want $20,000 for a glass window—and yet, some of them carry these racial prejudices, and it's mostly the Jews who are shoulder-to-shoulder with us, and . . ."

"Oh, Floyd," cried his wife, "Floyd, I have to get along here . . . you're not here, you don't live here, I . . ."

She arrived at the school just as the bell began to ring. It was a modern building at the top of a hill, and on the lawn was the statue of a saint, and behind it a large white cross. "There's Jeannie," said Mrs. Patterson.

"Hurry, call her over here," Patterson said.

"Jeannie! Come over here, honey."

The little girl, wearing a blue school uniform and cap, and clasping books in front of her, came running down the path toward the station wagon.

"Jeannie," Floyd Patterson said, rolling down his window, "point out the boys who lifted your dress."

Jeannie turned and watched as several students came down the path; then she pointed to a tall, thin curly-haired boy walking with four other boys, all about twelve to fourteen years of age.

"Hey," Patterson called to him, "can I see you for a minute?"

All five boys came to the side of the car. They looked Patterson directly in the eye. They seemed not at all intimidated by him.

"You the one that's been lifting up my daughter's dress?" Patterson asked the boy who had been singled out.

"Nope," the boy said, casually.

"Nope?" Patterson said, caught off guard by the reply.

"Wasn't him, Mister," said another boy. "Probably was his little brother."

Patterson looked at Jeannie. But she was speechless, uncertain. The five boys remained there, waiting for Patterson to do something.

"Well, er, where's your little brother?" Patterson asked.

"Hey, kid!" one of the boys yelled. "Come over here."

A boy walked toward them. He resembled his older brother; he had freckles on his small, upturned nose, had blue eyes, dark curly hair, and, as he approached the station wagon, he seemed equally unintimidated by Patterson.

"You been lifting up my daughter's dress?"

"Nope," the boy said.

"*Nope!*" Patterson repeated, frustrated.

"Nope, I wasn't lifting it. I was just touching it a little."

The other boys stood around the car looking down at Patterson, and other students crowded behind them, and nearby Patterson saw several white parents standing next to their parked cars; he became self-conscious, began to tap nervously with his fingers against the dashboard. He could not raise his voice without creating an unpleasant scene, yet could not retreat gracefully; so his voice went soft, and he said, finally: "Look, boy, I want you to stop it. I won't tell your mother—that might get you in trouble—but don't do it again, okay?"

"Okay."

The boys calmly turned and walked, in a group, up the street.

Sandra Patterson said nothing. Jeannie opened the door, sat in the front seat next to her father, and took out a small blue piece of paper that a nun had given her and handed it across to Mrs. Patterson. But Floyd Patterson snatched it. He read it. Then he paused, put the paper down, and quietly announced, dragging out the words, *"She didn't do her religion . . ."*

Patterson now wanted to get out of Scarsdale. He wanted to return to camp. After stopping at the Patterson home in Scarsdale and picking up Floyd Patterson, Jr., who is three, Mrs. Patterson drove them all back to the airport. Jeannie and Floyd Jr. were seated in the back of the plane, and then Mrs. Patterson drove the station wagon alone up to camp, planning to return to Scarsdale that evening with the children.

It was 4 P.M. when Floyd Patterson got back to the camp, and the shadows were falling on the clubhouse, and on the tennis court routed by weeds, and on the big white house in front of which not a single automobile was parked. All was deserted and quiet; it was a loser's camp.

The children ran to play inside the clubhouse; Patterson walked slowly toward his apartment to dress for the workout.

"What could I do with those schoolboys?" he asked. "What can you do to kids of that age?"

It still seemed to bother him—the effrontery of the boys, the realization that he had somehow failed, the probability that, had those same boys heckled someone in Liston's family, the school yard would have been littered with limbs.

While Patterson and Liston both are products of the slum, and while both began as thieves, Patterson had been tamed in a special school with help from a gentle Negro spinster; later he became a Catholic convert and learned not to hate. Still later he bought a dictionary, adding to his vocabulary such words as *vicissitude* and *enigma*. And when he regained his championship from Johansson, he became the Great Black Hope of the Urban League.

He proved that it is possible not only to rise out of a Negro slum and succeed as a sportsman but also to develop into an intelligent, sensitive, law-abiding citizen. In proving this, however, and in taking pride in it, Patterson seemed to lose part of himself. He lost part of his hunger, his anger—and as he walked up the steps into his apartment, he was saying, "I became the good guy. . . . After Liston won the title, I kept hoping that he would change into a good guy too. That would have relieved me of the responsibility, and maybe I could have been more of the bad guy. But he didn't. . . . It's okay to be the good guy when you're winning. But when you're losing, it is no good being the good guy."

Patterson took off his shirt and trousers and, moving some books on the bureau to one side, put down his watch, his cuff links, and a clip of bills.

"Do you do much reading?" he was asked

"No," he said. "In fact, you know I've never finished reading a book in my whole life? I don't know why. I just feel that no writer today has anything for me; I mean, none of them has felt any more deeply than I have, and I have nothing to learn from them. Although Baldwin to me seems different from the rest. What's Baldwin doing these days?"

"He's writing a play. Anthony Quinn is supposed to have a part in it."

"Quinn?" Patterson asked.

"Yes."

"Quinn doesn't like me."

"Why?"

"I read or heard it somewhere; Quinn had been quoted as saying that my fight was disgraceful against Liston, and Quinn said something to the effect that he could have done better. People often say that—*they* could have done better! Well I think that if *they* had to fight, *they* couldn't even go through the experience of waiting for the fight to begin. They'd be up the whole night before, and would be drinking, or taking drugs. They'd probably get a heart attack. I'm sure that, if I was in the ring with Anthony Quinn, I could wear him out without even touching him. I would do nothing but pressure him; I'd stalk him; I'd stand close to him. I wouldn't touch him, but I'd wear him out and he'd collapse. But Anthony Quinn's an old man, isn't he?"

"In his forties."

"Well, anyway," Patterson said, "getting back to Baldwin, he seems like a wonderful guy. I've seen him on television, and, before the Liston fight in Chicago, he came by my camp. You meet Baldwin on the street and you say, 'Who's this poor slob?'—he seems just like another guy; and this is the same impression *I* give people when they don't know me. But I think Baldwin and me, we have much in common, and someday I'd just like to sit somewhere for a long time and talk to him."

Patterson, his trunks and sweatpants on, bent over to tie his shoelaces, and then, from a bureau drawer, took out a T-shirt across which was printed *Deauville*. He has several T-shirts bearing the same name. He takes good care of them. They are souvenirs from the high point of his life. They are from the Deauville

Hotel in Miami Beach, which is where he trained for the third Ingemar Johansson match in March of 1961.

Never was Floyd Patterson more popular, more admired than during that winter. He had visited President Kennedy; he had been given a $35,000 jeweled crown by his manager; his greatness was conceded by sportswriters—and nobody had any idea that Patterson, secretly, was in possession of a false mustache and dark glasses that he intended to wear out of Miami Beach should he lose the third fight to Johansson.

It was after being knocked out by Johansson in their first fight that Patterson, deep in depression, hiding in humiliation for months in a remote Connecticut lodge, decided he could not face the public again if he lost. So he bought false whiskers and a mustache and planned to wear them out of his dressing room after a defeat. He had also planned, in leaving his dressing room, to linger momentarily within the crowd and perhaps complain out loud about the fight. Then he would slip undiscovered through the night and into a waiting automobile.

Although there proved to be no need for bringing disguise into the second or third Johansson fights, or into a subsequent bout in Toronto against an obscure heavyweight named Tom McNeeley, Patterson brought it anyway; and, after the first Liston fight, he not only wore it during his thirty-hour automobile ride from Chicago to New York, but also wore it while in an airliner bound for Spain.

"As I got onto this plane, you'd never have recognized me," he said. "I had on this beard, mustache, glasses, and hat—and I also limped, to make myself look older. I was alone. I didn't care what plane I boarded; I just looked up and saw this sign at the terminal reading 'Madrid,' and so I got on that flight after buying a ticket.

"When I got to Madrid, I registered at a hotel under the

name 'Aaron Watson.' I stayed in Madrid about four or five days. In the day time I wandered around to the poorer sections of the city, limping, looking at the people, and the people stared back at me and must have thought I was crazy because I was moving so slow and looked the way I did. I ate food in my hotel room. Although once I went to a restaurant and ordered soup. I hate soup. But I thought it was what old people would order. So I ate it. And after a week of this, I began to actually think I was somebody else. I began to believe it. And it is nice, every once in a while, being somebody else."

Patterson would not elaborate on how he managed to register under a name that did not correspond to his passport; he merely explained, "With money, you can do anything."

Now, walking slowly around the room, his black silk robe over his sweat clothes, Patterson said, "You must wonder what makes a man do things like this. Well, I wonder too. And the answer is, I don't know . . . but I think that within me, within every human being, there is a certain weakness. It is a weakness that exposes itself more when you're alone. And I have figured out that part of the reason I do the things I do, and cannot seem to conquer that one word—*myself*—is because . . . is because . . . I am a coward."

He stopped. He stood very still in the middle of the room, thinking about what he had just said, probably wondering whether he should have said it.

"I am a coward," he then repeated, softly. "My fighting has little to do with that fact, though. I mean you can be a fighter—and a *winning* fighter—and still be a coward. I was probably a coward on the night I won the championship back from Ingemar. And I remember another night, long ago, back when I was in the amateurs, fighting this big, tremendous man named Julius Griffin. I was only 153 pounds. I was petrified. It was all

I could do to cross the ring. And then he came at me and moved close to me . . . and from then on I don't know anything. I have no idea what happened. Only thing I know is, I saw him on the floor. And later somebody said, 'Man, I never saw anything like it. You just jumped up in the air and threw thirty different punches.'"

"When did you first think you were a coward?" he was asked.

"It was after the first Ingemar fight."

"How does one see this cowardice you speak of?"

"You see it when a fighter loses. Ingemar, for instance, is not a coward. When he lost the third fight in Miami, he was at a party later at the Fountainebleau. Had I lost, I couldn't have gone to that party. And I don't see how he did."

"Could Liston be a coward?"

"That remains to be seen," Patterson said. "We'll find out what he's like after somebody beats him, how he takes it. It's easy to do anything in victory. It's in defeat that a man reveals himself. In defeat I can't face people. I haven't the strength to say to people, 'I did my best, I'm sorry, and whatnot.'"

"Have you no hate left?"

"I have hated only one fighter," Patterson said. "And that was Ingemar in the second fight. I had been hating him for a whole year before that—not because he beat me in the first fight, but because of what he did after. It was all that boasting in public, and his showing off his right-hand punch on television, his thundering right, his 'toonder and lightning.' And I'd be home watching him on television and *hating* him. It is a miserable feeling, hate. When a man hates, he can't have any peace of mind. And for one solid year I hated him because, after he took everything away from me, deprived me of everything I was, he *rubbed it in*. On the night of the second fight, in the dressing room, I couldn't wait until I got into the ring. When he was a little late getting into the ring, I thought, 'He's holding me up; he's trying to unsettle me—well, I'll get him!' "

"Why couldn't you hate Liston in the second match?"

Patterson thought for a moment, then said, "Look, if Sonny Liston walked into this room now and slapped me in the face, then you'd see a fight. You'd see the fight of your life because, then, a principle would be involved. I'd forget he was a human being. I'd forget I was a human being. And I'd fight accordingly."

"Could it be, Floyd, that you made a mistake in becoming a prize-fighter?"

"What do you mean?"

"Well, you say you're a coward; you say you have little capacity for hate; and you seemed to lose your nerve against those schoolboys in Scarsdale this afternoon. Don't you think you might have been better suited for some other kind of work? Perhaps a social worker or . . ."

"Are you asking why I continue to fight?"

"Yes."

"Well," he said, not irritated by the question, "first of all, I love boxing. Boxing has been good to me. And I might just as well ask you the question, 'Why do you write?' Or, 'Do you retire from writing everytime you write a bad story?' And as to whether I should have become a fighter in the first place, well, let's see how I can explain it. . . . Look, let's say you're a man who has been in an empty room for days and days without food . . . and then they take you out of that room and put you into another room where there's food hanging all over the place . . . and the first thing you reach for, you eat. When you're hungry, you're not choosy, and so I chose the thing that was closest to me. That was boxing. One day I just wandered into a gymnasium and boxed a boy. And I beat him. Then I boxed another boy. I beat him too. Then I kept boxing. And winning. And I said, 'Here, finally, is something I can do!'

"Now I wasn't a sadist," he quickly added. "But I liked beating people because it was the only thing I could do. And whether boxing was a sport or not, I wanted to make it a sport because it was a thing I could succeed at. And what were the requirements? Sacrifice. That's all. To anybody who comes from the Bedford-Stuyvesant section of Brooklyn, sacrifice comes easy. And so I kept fighting, and one day I became heavyweight champion, and I got to know people like you. And you wonder how I can sacrifice, how I can deprive myself so much. You just don't realize where I've come from. You don't understand where I was when it began for me.

"In those days, when I was about eight years old, everything I got—I stole. I stole to survive, and I did survive, but I seemed to hate myself. My mother told me I used to point to a photograph of myself hanging in the bedroom and say, 'I don't like that boy!' One day my mother found three large Xs scratched with a nail or something over that photograph of me. I don't remember doing it. But I do remember feeling like a parasite at home. I remember how awful I used to feel at night when my father, a longshoreman, would come home so tired that, as my mother fixed food before him, he would fall asleep at the table because he was that tired. I would always take his shoes off and clean his feet. That was my job. And I felt so bad because here I was, not going to school, doing nothing, just watching my father come home; and on Friday nights it was even worse. He would come home with his pay, and he'd put every nickel of it on the table so my mother could buy food for all the children. I never wanted to be around to see that. I'd run and hide. And then I decided to leave home and start stealing—and I did. And

I would never come home unless I brought something that I had stolen. Once I remember I broke into a dress store and stole a whole mound of dresses, at 2 A.M., and here I was, this little kid, carrying all those dresses over the wall, thinking they were all the same size, my mother's size, and thinking the cops would never notice me walking down the street with all those dresses piled over my head. They did, of course. . . I went to the Youth House."

Floyd Patterson's children, who had been playing outside all this time around the country club, now became restless and began to call him, and Jeannie started to pound on his door. So Patterson picked up his leather bag, which contained his gloves, his mouthpiece, and adhesive tape, and walked with the children across the path toward the clubhouse.

He flicked on the light switches behind the stage near the piano. Beams of amber streaked through the dimly lit room and flashed onto the ring. Then he walked to one side of the room, outside the ring. He took off his robe, shuffled his feet in the rosin, skipped rope, and then began to shadowbox in front of the spit-stained mirror, throwing out quick combinations of lefts, rights, lefts, rights, each jab followed by a *"hegh-hegh-hegh-hegh"*. Then, his gloves on, he moved to the punching bag in the far corner, and soon the room reverberated to his rhythmic beat against the hobbling bag—rat-tat-tat-*tetteta*, rat-tat-tat-*tetteta*, rat-tat-tat-*tetteta*, rat-tat-tat-*tetteta!*

The children, sitting on pink leather chairs moved from the bar to the fringe of the ring, watched him in awe, sometimes flinching at the force of his pounding against the leather bag.

And this is how they would probably remember him years from now: a dark, solitary, glistening figure punching in the corner of a forlorn spot at the bottom of a mountain where people once came to have fun—until the clubhouse became unfashionable, the paint began to peel, and Negroes were allowed in.

As Floyd Patterson continued to bang away with lefts and rights, his gloves a brown blur against the bag, his daughter slipped quietly off her chair and wandered past the ring into the other room. There, on the other side of the bar and beyond a dozen round tables, was the stage. She climbed onto the stage and stood behind a microphone, long dead, and cried out, imitating a ring announcer, "Ladieeees and gentlemen . . . tonight we present . . ."

She looked around, puzzled. Then, seeing that her little brother had followed her, she waved him up to the stage and began again: "Ladieeees and gentlemen . . . tonight we present . . . *Floydie Patterson.*"

Suddenly, the pounding against the bag in the other room stopped. There was silence for a moment. Then Jeannie, still behind the microphone and looking down at her brother, said, "Floydie, come up here!"

"No," he said.

"Oh, come up here!"

"*No,*" he cried.

Then Floyd Patterson's voice, from the other room, called: "Cut it out. . . . I'll take you both for a walk in a minute."

He resumed punching—rat-tat-tat-*tetteta*—and they returned to his side. But Jeannie interrupted, asking, "Daddy, how come you sweating?"

"Water fell on me," he said, still pounding.

"Daddy," asked Floyd Jr., "how come you spit water on the floor before?"

"To get it out of my mouth."

He was about to move over to the heavier punching bag

when the sound of Mrs. Patterson's station wagon could be heard moving up the road.

Soon she was in Patterson's apartment cleaning up a bit, patting the pillows, washing the teacups that had been left in the sink. One hour later the family was having dinner together. They were together for two more hours; then, at 10 P.M., Mrs. Patterson washed and dried all of the dishes and put the garbage out in the can—where it would remain until the raccoons and skunks got to it.

And then, after helping the children with their coats and walking out to the station wagon and kissing her husband good-bye, Mrs. Patterson began the drive down the dirt road toward the highway. Patterson waved once and stood for a moment watching the taillights go, and then he turned and walked slowly back toward the house.

STORIES WITH REAL NAMES

I N H I S 1973 book *The New Journalism*, Tom Wolfe credited Gay Talese, and specifically his 1962 *Esquire* piece about Joe Louis, "The King as a Middle-Aged Man," with creating a new kind of journalism that borrowed the tools of fiction writers to tell true stories. "It wasn't like a magazine article at all," Wolfe wrote. "It was like a short story. It began with a scene." Though this is precisely what Talese had always intended—writing stories with real names in the style of Fitzgerald and Shaw—he has resisted "The New Journalism" inventor label. "I have always thought of myself as rather traditional in my approach," Talese has said, "and not so 'new.' I never wanted to do something new. I wanted to do something that would hold up over time, something that could get old and still have the same resonance."

Harold Hayes, the editor of *Esquire*, offered Talese the chance to stretch his writing legs. "I could not contain myself within the twelve-hundred-word limit of daily journalism," Talese said in a *Paris Review* interview. "Wherever I was, I thought that there were stories that other people weren't telling."

Talese did some of his most masterful sports writing at
Esquire—"The Loser," "Joe Louis: The King as a Middle-Aged
man," "Ali in Havana," and the title piece of this collection,
"The Silent Season of a Hero," about Joe DiMaggio's life after
the cheering stopped. Many sports writers argue that it is the
single most memorable sports story ever written. The late
David Halberstam, Talese's friend and an often fine sportswriter himself, declared the story as such in *The Best Sports
Writing of the Century*.

The first time I began reading the DiMaggio piece I was a
graduate student studying new journalism at the University
of Pittsburgh. About halfway through I noticed that my right
hand, holding the next page to be turned, was shaking, as if it
was trying to jump ahead to see what happened next. There is
one paragraph that tightens my throat every time I read it. Talese is with DiMaggio at a special day at Yankee Stadium honor-
ing Mickey Mantle, the legend who came after Joltin' Joe.
"Don't Quit Mick" and "We Love the Mick" banners hung high
in the stadium. Talese wrote:

> The banners had been held by hundreds of young boys whose
> dreams had been fulfilled so often by Mantle, but also seated in
> the grandstands were older men, paunchy and balding, in whose
> middle-aged minds DiMaggio was still vivid and invincible, and
> some of them remembered how one month before, during a pre-
> game exhibition at Old-timers' Day in Yankee Stadium, DiMag-
> gio had hit a pitch into the left-field seats, and suddenly thousands
> of people had jumped wildly to their feet, joyously screaming—
> the great DiMaggio had returned; they were young again; it was
> yesterday.

MR

THE CADDIE—
A NON-ALGER STORY

New York Times, 1960

"...he found himself glancing at the four caddies who trailed them, trying to catch a gleam or gesture that would remind him of himself, that would lessen the gap which lay between his present and his past."

—F. Scott Fitzgerald.

THE HERO OF Fitzgerald's short story, "Winter Dreams," is a former caddie who, at a very early age, dreamed of beating the pro, becoming rich and having someone else carry the bag. He eventually did become rich, and someone else did carry the bag, but he never forgot his caddie days. For him, and for thousands of other young dreamers, the caddie job was the point where the dream began. But it isn't any more.

Caddies have changed. The caddie today is more likely to be an older man, unmarried, perhaps a drifter; or, if he *is* a boy, he certainly is not the Fitzgeraldian hero who treks through "the fairways of his imagination" with lofty thoughts. No longer do most great professional golfers come from caddie yards. No longer is caddying often the first job for a self-made tycoon of the future.

Although a record number of 5,000,000 Americans are now playing golf, the number of caddies has dropped from 400,000 a generation ago to about 200,000 today. In large part they have been replaced on the nation's 5,000 courses by 50,000 electric cars and 250,000 two-wheeled hand carts. But it isn't only automation that has produced the twilight of the caddy. Many boys, in these days of affluence, are reluctant to tote a bag and chase some duffer's hook shots into the woods for a paltry $3 or $4 a round.

To be sure, it is not really important that many boys no longer wish to caddie, or that the carts nowadays make some country clubs look like supermarkets. What is important, so far as professional golf goes, is that ex-caddies usually make the most exciting golfers. As caddie-turned-champion Willie Turnesa says, "If we don't keep young caddies interested in golf, where will we get our future Walter Hagens, Gene Sarazens, Sam Sneads, Ben Hogans, Byron Nelsons?" (All are former caddies.)

Caddies in the old days, in addition to being just plain interested in the game, were often (by their own admission) the brains of the golfer. The first mental giant on record to carry clubs was a man named Andrew Dickson, hired in Scotland in 1681. He rarely lost a ball, conceded all five-foot putts and became immensely popular with his patron, the Duke of York. In those days the caddie—the word is the Scottish spelling of the French *cadet*, meaning "little chief"—held a position similar to that of a squire to the knight. He is still the only person to whom, under the rules, a player can go for advice on choice of clubs or strategy.

*　　*　　*

In America, some of the early great caddies were Joe Horgan, who caddied for a half century; Jack Allen, a confidant of Bobby Jones; and Leggy Ahearn, who knew which clubs Walter Hagen hit best when he was hung-over and which when he was not.

"Back in the Open in 1919, Haig had been drinking the night before, and had a couple of cocktails at noon," recalls Ahearn, who is now 55 and still caddies occasionally at the Winged Foot Country Club in Mamaroneck. "On the fourteenth hole, Haig wanted to use a mashie. He was even at the time with Mike Brady. He pulled the mashie out, but I said, 'No, no, Haig, go to a midiron.' He did. And he hit it up stiff, inches from the pin. He holed out for a birdie 3. And that one-shot edge beat Brady. Haig gave me $160. We got along well. But when I used to see him come to the clubhouse in the morning wearing a tuxedo, I knew we were in for a bad day."

Gene Sarazen gave his caddie much credit for his triumph in the British Open in 1932. Lawson Little was so grateful to his caddie for helping him win the National Open in 1940 that he sent him to college. And when Ed Furgol won the Open in 1954, he gave his caddie $1,000. Snead also has always leaned heavily on a caddie's advice.

But there are times (as one out of ten caddies will admit) when a golfer would be a lot better off without a caddie. In 1946, Byron Nelson lost the National Open by a single penalty stroke because his caddie accidentally kicked his ball.

Those were the days—during the war and immediately after it—when the quality of caddying reached its nadir. Older teenagers were in the Army, drifting men were making more money in factories, and so caddie masters were left with incompetents who often knew nothing about the game at all. Once Jack

Burke, undecided on what club he should use to reach the green, asked his caddie, "What do you think I need to get home?" "Get home?" repeated the caddie. "Man, I don't even know where you live."

The caddie characteristic of the present days falls (or trips) into various categories, although all caddies are united in their contempt for bad tippers ("stiffs"), slow, bad players ("choppers"), and players who own heavy bags filled with extra clubs, shoes, practice balls, umbrellas and jugs (a "house and lot").

One category of caddie is the "Matinee Caddie." He refuses to get up before noon and fastidiously avoids ladies' tournaments because, he says, ladies tip poorly, play slowly, expect extra service and will not concede each other a one-foot putt.

A second type is the "Mad Looper." He loves to walk, will carry anybody's bag, and will make two or three loops (rounds) a day. But he is not very smart. He is of little help to conscientious golfers who depend on a caddie's judgment regarding distances. He is a "bag-toter," as distinguished from a caddie.

Then there are "Vagabond Caddies." These are the best caddies, and they wander about the country, following the sun and money. In the winter they're working for a golf course in Florida, or perhaps in Arizona. They'll work during the summer in the plush clubs of Westchester County, or perhaps spend week-ends at clubs at East Hampton or Montauk Point. They're anywhere from 21 to 60, and can average over $100 a week (much more when they caddie in tournaments).

The fourth type is the "Rabbit." Rabbits are beginners with enthusiasm. Golf was once overrun with these youngsters, and they were the boys who often became famous pros. Caddies who learn golf early in life develop what is called a "caddie-house swing," a natural, rhythmic swing easily distinguished from the jerky motions of business men whose golf began with an expense account.

Though scarce, some Rabbits are still around, and caddie masters always try to give them lots of experience. The usual procedure when a foursome is going out is to send along one older, seasoned caddie (who will carry two bags) and two Rabbits.

"In this way, the older caddie can keep the Rabbits from messing up the game," explains Gene Hayden, a caddie master for three decades in Westchester County. "Rabbits alone would mess around out there, lag behind, whistle. There's an old saying among caddie masters—if you send one boy, you have a boy; if you send out two boys, you have half a boy; if you send out three boys, you have no boys at all."

The absence of great numbers of Rabbits in recent years has meant that golf's tournament professionals have come mainly from college campuses.

According to Charles Price, editor of *Golf* magazine, only one of the top twenty-four money-winners in 1959 was a former caddie: Doug Ford. The twenty-three others were college boys.

While the college boys are fine golfers, none of them has electrified the nation in the way ex-caddies like Snead & Co. did in their prime. The college boys, say some former caddies, are a pack of conformists. None of them would be caught dead in such polkadot shirts and fancy hats as Jimmy Demaret (an ex-caddie) used to wear. They do not fling clubs like Tommy Bolt (an ex-caddie) used to do. They do not show up in the morning wearing tuxedos.

All this may be fine with some people. But is the game itself as exciting, other golf devotees wonder, as it was when the fairways were crawling with Rabbits who had secretly vowed one day to surpass the masters they served?

SUSPICIOUS MAN
IN THE CHAMP'S CORNER

New York Times, 1962

FLOYD PATTERSON'S MANAGER, Cus D'Amato, never rides subways because he fears being pushed onto the tracks, never reveals his home address because he suspects snipers, and has never married because he believes a wife might be duped by his enemies or might try to alter his image as the most mysterious, confusing and emotionally bullet-proof man in boxing. Tuesday night, at Comiskey Park in Chicago, he will be in the heavyweight champion's corner, glaring across the ring at the referee, the sportswriters, the crowd and the challenger, Sonny Liston, whom D'Amato suspects of being backed by hoods from Philadelphia.

For most of his 54 years, Constantine D'Amato has gone through life like a shadow boxer, sometimes jabbing away at ghosts and ghouls visible only to himself, sometimes indulging in public battles with fleshly boxing commissioners, matchmakers and promoters, charging them with trying to eliminate him, underpay or overmatch his fighters and monopolize the sport.

Prior to the last title fight in Chicago—the one in which Patterson knocked out Archie Moore—the champion recalls that D'Amato would nightly push his cot across the entrance to the bedroom in which the fighter and his trainer slept and would be there, often fully clothed, because he feared someone might sneak in and attack Patterson.

"Cus doesn't trust *anybody*," Patterson observed recently. Then, after contemplating the frustration that befalls the prizefighter perpetually in search of peace and solitude among noisy friends, Patterson said, "You know, people think the *prizefighter* is the crazy one. But sometimes I think I'm the only sane one around here."

While there is no doubt that D'Amato's behavior may strike some people as rare, it must not be overlooked that he is the most successful boxing manager in the nation today. Like any first-rate manager, he tries never to overmatch his fighters; he never condones laxity in training, and gets the most money possible from promoters for his men's bouts. But these qualities do not in themselves explain his special success. D'Amato has excelled because his endless suspicion, his seeming paranoia, is precisely the attitude needed to thrive among boxing's barbarians.

"I must keep my enemies confused," D'Amato says. "When they are confused, then I can do a job for my fighters. What I do not want in life, however, is security. The moment a person knows security, his senses are dulled—and he begins to die. I also do not want any pleasures in life. I believe the more pleasures you get out of living, the more fear you have of dying."

Such asceticism seems to have left its mark on Floyd Patterson and helped him become champion. While Patterson has permitted himself such extravagances as a wife, three children and two Lincolns, he mostly secludes himself in the hills, perfecting his craft. He avoids the celebrity's life and making new friends because, he says, both will vanish when he loses his title and he does not want to miss them.

D'Amato became addicted to self-denial at a much earlier age than Patterson. As a boy in the Bronx, he would fast for days so that nobody could intimidate him with threats of starvation. Though the vision in his left eye became impaired after he was struck by a stick in a street fight, D'Amato insisted then (and still insists) on closing his *right* eye while reading and squinting through his bad left eye—a mannerism that seems to symbolize his desire to do everything the hard way.

It would take years of psychiatry to determine the source of his eccentricities. All he remembers about his boyhood thoughts was his preoccupation with death. He used to watch funeral processions passing through the Bronx and he would think, "The sooner death, the better." He said he was sure, as a youth that he was going to Heaven.

Tired of Morris High School after less than two years, but unable to become a fighter because of his bad eye, D'Amato hung around gymnasiums doing odd jobs for a while, and then—despite his eye—was inducted into the Army. He *loved* Army life, confirming friends' views that something was definitely wrong. "I went into the Army prepared to die," he says. So that death would not be something to fear, but rather something to welcome, D'Amato made life as miserable as possible. He shaved only with cold water. He slept on the barracks floor. He stood at attention for hours.

"One day we were on bivouac and everybody was trying to keep the flies out of their food," D'Amato has related. "But I made up my mind that when the next insect landed on my plate I wasn't going to swat it away.

"Well," he continued, "the next insect was a spider. How I hate spiders! Nevertheless, I put a piece of bread over the spider, closed my eyes, and ate it."

D'Amato's military bearing and the way his toothbrush and socks were always precisely arranged during footlocker inspection, greatly impressed the company commander, who one day said, "D'Amato, report to headquarters. You're going to be tested as a non-com."

"Sorry, sir, but I do not know my General Orders," D'Amato said. D'Amato felt he never could learn them and never did.

"Don't worry," the captain assured him. "I took care of that. They won't ask you. Just go down there, give 'em that big salute, and you're in."

An hour later D'Amato returned to the company, dejected.

"What's the matter?" the C. O. asked.

"They asked me to recite the General Orders," D'Amato said.

The C. O., doublecrossed by a fellow officer, flew into a rage. A day later, he arranged for D'Amato to get another chance; this time he thought he had an agreement that no questions about the eleven General Orders pertaining to sentry duty would be asked. But as soon as D'Amato appeared before the officers, gave his big salute and snapped to attention, one officer again shot him a question about the General Orders. And, again, D'Amato was turned down. His C. O. was astonished. D'Amato wasn't. It merely confirmed his mistrust of people.

After his discharge, D'Amato, with money saved and borrowed, bought into a gymnasium on the second floor of an old building at 116 East Fourteenth Street. There, up two creaky flights of steps, in a small room left of the boxing ring, D'Amato slept at night, his only companion a ferocious police dog. During the day, youths wishing to learn boxing could climb the stairs and watch professionals work out and could also receive— free—boxing instruction on the condition that, if they ever turned professional, D'Amato would be their manager. Thus it was that a skinny 14-year-old boy named Floyd Patterson climbed into D'Amato's life one day.

D'Amato would watch closely as boys first entered the gym. He would observe whether they had come alone or with parents or friends. He would note if they hesitated at the door, disturbed by the howling dog tied near the entrance. The manner of their entrance quickly gave D'Amato some insight into them. Some were more afraid than others. They were all a little afraid. But this did not bother D'Amato. "Fear," he would lecture them, "is natural. It is normal. Fear is your friend. When a deer walks through the forest, it has fear; this is nature's way of keeping the deer alert because there may be a tiger in the trees. Without fear, we would not survive."

On the night before their first fight, he would tell them, they would get no sleep—but neither would their opponent. At the weigh-in, he would predict, their opponent would look unbeatable—but this would only be the imagination at work. "Nothing is as bad as your imagination will have you believe," Cus might say. "Not even death."

Fear would go with them, Cus continued, but after the bell rang, fear would disappear; what happened at that point depended on how faithfully the fighters had trained and how much courage they had. They need not worry about facing an opponent who was more experienced or skilled than they, Cus

promised. He would always try to match them against someone they could beat—and he has a rare skill for doing just that.

This is D'Amato's method of building up his fighter's confidence. An early defeat may destroy a young boxer's image of
himself, D'Amato feels. So D'Amato travels from gym to gym
watching other managers' fighters, looking for flesh his tigers
may feast on in future matches. If D'Amato is faced with the
decision of putting his boy in against an opponent who *might*
be better, or having no fight at all, D'Amato will have no fight.
"I'm not in this business to get my guys massacred," he says.

One problem in boxing today, he feels, is that fighters with
insufficient experience are rushed into main events by money-
hungry managers, blood-thirsty promoters and television producers; the fighter gets chewed up by someone he had no business
being in the ring with and his career is quickly over—*years* before it should be, by D'Amato's standards.

D'Amato once co-managed a talented middleweight named
Gene (Ace) Armstrong, who, while Cus was away on a trip to
California, agreed to accept a bout at Madison Square Garden
against Rory Calhoun, with whose promoters Cus has long
shared a mutual contempt. Even though Armstrong knocked
out Calhoun, and followed with other impressive victories,
D'Amato was so displeased by the fighter's moving ahead of the
schedule D'Amato had set that he refused to co-manage him
any longer. In 1959, Armstrong lost to Dick Tiger of Nigeria. He
lost again in 1960 to Tiger, and was knocked out in 1961 by
him, suffering a rib injury as well. Armstrong tried to make a
comeback this summer, after a sixteen-month layoff, against
Luis Rodriguez, but was again knocked out and his career seems
close to being finished.

*　　*　　*

"Each time Tiger beat Armstrong, it had a demoralizing effect," says D'Amato, who would never have agreed to a second match unless he felt a reversal probable. "If I had been manager of Armstrong, he would now be on his way to a championship. If I had managed Benny Paret, I would never have taken on Emile Griffith in that last fight. I saw the way Paret got knocked out the first time, and saw the rough rematch they had [Paret won], and saw how Paret then was beaten by Gene Fullmer before the third Griffith fight that killed Paret. The boxing commissioners could have yelled all they wanted. I *still* wouldn't have agreed to the Griffith fight. The manager has no right to gamble with his fighter's life."

But picking opponents his boys can probably beat is not always easy for D'Amato. He makes some mistakes. And sometimes, despite his suspicions, he is tricked. A few years ago D'Amato, wishing to get a fight for one of his rising young sluggers, agreed to a bout in Sunnyside Gardens against a fighter from Long Island. D'Amato had never heard of him. If the boy from Long Island had any ability, D'Amato reasoned, D'Amato certainly *would* have heard of him because this boy was white and up-and-coming talented white fighters in the New York area are becoming increasingly rare—and easy to spot—these days. So D'Amato blithely concluded that the white boy had no talent.

"But almost as soon as the bell rang I realized my guy wasn't fighting no preliminary fighter," D'Amato recounted, bitterly. "My guy got hit with everything and was knocked down ten times, and I kept yelling to the referee, 'Stop it, stop it!' not wanting to get my guy ruined. After the fight I went into the locker room and my guy looks up and says, 'Cus, I'm sorry I let you down.' 'You didn't let *me* down,' I told him, 'I let *you* down. I overmatched you.'

"Then," D'Amato said, "I went over to collect the money and I heard the phone ring and somebody says it's a long-distance call asking for the result of the match. I knew then that this white boy wasn't no amateur from Long Island; he'd been brought in from another part of the country." He smashed his right fist into his left palm. "I don't make many mistakes like that!"

D'Amato thought Patterson would have no trouble with Ingemar Johansson in the first fight or he would not have agreed to it. "I was, of course, aware of Johansson's right-hand punch," D'Amato said. "But I did not think he had the means of delivering it against Patterson. If you have a big punch, but cannot deliver it, what good is it? It's like having an A-bomb—but if you can't deliver it, it's worthless, it's like having a big rock. Anyway, I did not think Johansson could trick Patterson in the first fight. But he did."

He explained that Johansson did it by repeatedly flicking a lazy, harmless left jab at Patterson—a jab not meant to hurt, but to hypnotize Patterson and get him into the habit of blocking it with a glove, or moving away from the jab in a manner that set Patterson up for a right-hand smash to follow. And so it was that, when Patterson moved away from the left and raised a glove to block the meaningless punch, Johansson came through with a right hand that caught Patterson leaning into it. Patterson was so severely jolted that he never recovered, and the combinations that followed floored him seven times.

Patterson's mistake, D'Amato said, was easily corrected in their rematch. Instead of blocking the lazy left with his gloves, Patterson "slipped" the harmless punch—dodged it without leaning into it, and did not leave his guard open—and soon his superior punching overpowered the Swede.

In their third fight, however, Johansson developed a new punch—a lazy left hook which was to do what the jab had done in the first fight; twice he faked Patterson out of position in the first round and floored him, but Johansson could not finish him off, and soon he began taking more punishment than he was giving. When last seen, he was being helped into his dressing room where the tax men were waiting to peck at him.

Patterson's triumph provided for D'Amato a sense of vindication, it being convincing evidence that he could still pick a loser when he saw one. Then the sportswriters began clamoring for the Liston fight. D'Amato was hesitant. Liston had beaten nearly every heavyweight contender so unmercifully that nobody was eager to take him on. The gamblers in Las Vegas established Liston as the favorite in any fight against Patterson.

One day, irritated at D'Amato's hesitance, Liston decided to visit D'Amato to see if perhaps a heart-to-heart chat (or perhaps the sight of a big, clenched fist) might not speed up D'Amato's decision. Not knowing how to reach D'Amato in New York, Liston spoke with José Torres, another fighter, and boasted that D'Amato was afraid of him. Torres said this was not true, that Cus fears no man, and, to prove it, Torres said he would take Liston to D'Amato's office. This is precisely what Liston wanted Torres to do.

"Cus, look what I have brought you," Torres said as be entered D'Amato's hideaway office. D'Amato looked at the big, dark, hulking figure moving toward him through the doorway. With a scowl, Liston asked, "Cus, why ain't you gonna gimme a fight with Patterson?"

"You clean up those people around you first, and then . . ."

"Cus," Liston cut in. "*You* pick my manager!"

* * *

D'Amato said he was not in the business of picking other fighters' managers. He was not going to discuss the matter further when, however, he saw something in Liston's eyes. "I thought he might slug me," D'Amato admitted, but added that Liston later calmed down and left. "If he *had* taken a swing," D'Amato quickly went on, "*he would not have left that room without marks!* I would have put *marks* on him, MARKS, you can be sure, with my fists, and anything I could throw at him!"

There is a little doubt that, if D'Amato had had his way, there would not have been a Patterson-Liston fight at this time. But D'Amato no longer has the persuasive power he once did with Patterson; the fighter still *listens* to D'Amato, but often rejects the manager's advice, being very much his own man in and out of the ring. The independence that Patterson acquired with his growing maturity has often prompted sportswriters' reports of a Patterson-D'Amato split; such reports always were, and are, exaggerated.

But Patterson simply could not resist the Liston fight. His pride had been hurt when sportswriters began to hint in the papers that Patterson was afraid of Liston. Patterson insisted on the fight even though the New York State Athletic Commission, which considered Liston's background somewhat short of Racquet Club standards, refused to allow the championship to be fought for in New York. There was simply no way D'Amato could dissuade Patterson; and so, for the first time in the fighter's relationship with D'Amato, he has publicly defied the will of the Father Image in the choice of an opponent.

D'Amato will not say exactly why he opposed the Liston fight. He likes to give the impression that he did so because of Liston's police record and because the challenger's Philadelphia backers are allegedly not Main Line. But maybe, in his heart,

D'Amato fears something he will never openly admit. And that is, for the first time in his career as a manager, he has gone ahead and helped make the arrangements for a battle that he thinks his own fighter will lose.

DR. BIRDWHISTELL
AND THE ATHLETES

In 1958, Talese collaborated on a piece with Ray Birdwhistell, an anthropologist who studied young male athletes. Birdwhistell had a controversial view of sports: "that the athlete in America is often a padded pawn who exists to fulfill other person's dreams," Talese wrote. The story was rejected by several publications, including Life *and* Sports Illustrated. *Talese thinks the piece shows "an early glimpse of my leaning toward what would later be called literary nonfiction, or New Journalism, or whatever."*

MR

THE STAR ATHLETE in America performs in a world of whim.

In the course of one week he may be both cheered and booed, bought and sold, beatified and bribed. Song writers idolized him, alumni fawn on him, college professors flunked him. Learned men disagree over whether he is a genius or a lunkhead. "There has never been a good player who was dumb," once wrote Jacques Barzun. But James Thurber, after analyzing a star Ohio State tackle named Bolenciecwcz, wrote, "While he was not dumber than an ox he was not any smarter."

Since scientists have tended to ignore him, the nation has come to know him mostly through television, or through those high priests of games—the sportswriters. For decades now, sportswriters have festooned him with catchy nicknames, pined over his pulled muscles, written about the homeruns he's hit, the punts he's blocked, the trains he's missed.

But at Temple University nowadays there is a forty-two-year-old social anthropologist named Ray Birdwhistell who is attempting to delve much deeper than the sports experts into the world of the American athlete. On and off for twenty years Dr. Birdwhistell has traveled around the country watching athletes on the field, in the locker room, at home, in school, driving cars, chasing or being chased by women.

He has made the playing field his laboratory. And he has found that the athlete in America is often a padded pawn who exists to fulfill other people's dreams; a tool who gets a second-rate high school and college education, has little time for auxiliary reading, and dwells in a society that regards his brain as somehow inferior. Dr. Birdwhistell has found athletes to be generally shy around young girls and especially close to their mothers—much closer, in fact, than the so-called Mama's Boy.

"The athletes of high school age that my associates and I studied in Midwestern schools tended to form an 'All-Male World'," Dr. Birdwhistell was saying at his office in Philadelphia the other day. "The athletes tended to date girls later, and not as often, as non-athletes. High school coaches would gather the boys around and tell them that women wreck a player's physique, ruin his conditioning, burn him out. I noticed that the coaches' jeremiads on women, often eloquent and sometimes convincing, usually followed games in which players were hurt, struck out, passed out—or, as the coaches put it: 'dogged it.' While observing students in Illinois, Ohio, Kentucky, and Indiana, I found that young athletes, if they dated at all, tended to date in groups, or in 'teams'—to double-date, triple-date, or gang-date.

"In other words," Dr. Birdwhistell said, "a normal development pattern for boys was often impossible in this All-Male Society where girls were regarded as somehow threatening and destructive."

"How long does this smear campaign against girls go on?" he was asked.

"Sometimes right through college," he said. "Some colleges deny athletic scholarships to athletes who marry. So, when these young high school athletes reach college, many of them continue this spasmodic relationship with girls. And it was not surprising to find, in 1952, following a study through Kentucky and Indiana, that a high percentage of college athletes were becoming involved with, and *marrying*, the first girl they dated several times. The normal courtship experience, which teaches the youngster how to delay as well as speed up marriage, was denied these athletes, and they just never seemed to learn how to defend themselves against a marrying woman."

Since most coaches considered girls only slightly less desirable than a separated shoulder, many high school athletes were forced to depend almost exclusively upon their mothers for female attention. It was Mom who watched their games, encouraged them, begged them to be careful, and comforted them after they'd been hurt, Birdwhistell said. The powerful trace of Mom-ism that Birdwhistell encountered wherever he went caused him to believe that the relationship between the athlete and Mom is stronger than even the relationship between Mom and the non-athletic "Mama's Boy."

"What about Fathers, where do they fit in here?"

"Out of some two thousand freshmen college athletes who were interviewed, less than one hundred of them could ever remember having a heart-to-heart conversation with their fathers of more than ten minutes," Birdwhistell said. "But this does not mean that fathers are not concerned with their sons' athletic prowess. Far from it. Most fathers push their sons too much. This is a father's way of living out his own adolescence (although a father may secretly resent it if his son succeeds in becoming powerful.) Symbolically, the athletic son might even be described as fulfilling his father's masculine role in the family. The pushing father, the doting mother and the arrested adolescent often make up the structure of the family which produces the athlete. If a boy had an understanding, non-pushing father, the Mom-ism probably would not be so prevalent in sports."

"Does this family relationship to the athlete affect him in any other way?" he was asked.

"Well, possibly as a result of this relationship," Birdwhistell said, "we get some insight into athletic injuries—or what was found to be an abnormally high amount of 'accident prone-ness' among schoolboy athletes. That is, the boys were getting hurt to gain attention or affection."

The more active lives led by athletes was not the only reason they got hurt more than other kids, said Dr. Birdwhistell. "During one study it was found that athletes were getting hurt in and out of season. Athletes seemed to put themselves into situations in which they'd get hurt. After a study of Buffalo high school boys two years ago, a whole series of them admitted that they usually got hurt when they're afraid they're *going* to get hurt. Obviously, they're planning on getting hurt; that is, unconsciously, they're setting up a situation in which they *will* get hurt. It's a situation rather similar to the fact that in the average factory about ten percent of the men will have about 80 per cent of the accidents. Or a small proportion of automobile drivers will have a major portion of the accidents. No one has ever done a conclusive study that I know of on auto accidents among athletes, but I'll bet the incidence is very high."

Dr. Birdwhistell, who now lives in the Philadelphia suburbs with his wife and two daughters, actually got started on this sports kick back in 1940 while traveling about the Southwest with a group of Chicago anthropologists studying the Sioux, the Navajo, the Zuni, the Papago, and Hopi Indian tribes. Birdwhistell immediately became attracted to the Hopis, especially to the way they played their games. They did not emphasize playing to win; being "outstanding" was shameful and cooperation was stressed over individual achievement. The Hopis did not like body contact in sports, hated football, but loved track meets, particularly as associated with the running events. "Running to them was symbolically a way of making the wind come, and bringing good weather," Dr. Birdwhistell said. "This justified the competition. Otherwise competitiveness indicated pushiness, a 'bad spirit,' even elicited suspicion of being in league with witches. The more I learned about Hopi games, the more I came to realize that sports are as expressive of the life of the people as are, say, religious ceremonies. A game to be played by a group must be expressive of implicit values in that culture. Games which do not express such values are dull. For example, the national game in America—baseball—puts top emphasis on the same thing that is considered uppermost in American culture—'home.' In baseball you have a man who begins at home, attempts to leave,

and who can only return when he is successful. Before returning home he must avoid threatening defenders in the areas of
insecurity that lay between the bases. Even the bases are only
havens of temporary security—to be really safe, he has to get
home and start over. Nearly all popular games in America,"
Birdwhistell said, "have this structure: They deal with areas of
danger, and areas of safety; with threateners and defenders;
with getting to a home, where you can stay, and then going
through the whole routine again."

With this knowledge, he returned in 1942 to Chicago, and
he was rather surprised to discover that midwestern school
athletes traveled like a tribe, had fewer social contacts than
other students, and made relatively poor adjustments to girls.
These boys ranged in age from thirteen to seventeen. Wearing
their bright varsity sweaters, or other symbolic emblems, they
walked together, ate together, and dwelled almost exclusively
together in this All-Male Society that included The Coach,
The Field, The Locker Room, Other Athletes, and The Team
Manager—the latter more often than not a highly-efficient but
physically handicapped youth who always sat next to the coach
on the team bus, and who, like the sportswriter, was part of the
necessary claque. "The manager has the inside information for
the campus," said Dr. Birdwhistell, "the sportswriter for the
general public."

Dr. Birdwhistell, himself a former high school athlete in Cincinnati, though an "insufficiently devoted" one, became intrigued
with the behavior and symbolism within the Athlete's World—
and he thus began his safari, a safari that led him through
miles of locker rooms and dirty towels and brought him in
contact with hundreds of coaches and athletes, all of whose
names and schools he insists on keeping secret. Throughout his
initial venture into the All-Male World he wondered what

made athletes different, what were their problems, what *really* mattered in their society of pads and dirty socks? He began to seek answers by watching athletes at their youngest, most disorganized level—on the sandlots playing pick-up games of baseball. He saw them, noisy and beardless, running wildly around the bases—bases represented by rocks, pieces of wood, or garbage can covers. They all were between the ages of eight and fifteen. Some of them were big and were able to hold their bat way down at the end, and murder the ball. The power hitters arrived casually at the playing field, their hands in pockets, their manner exuding the quiet confidence of one who is sure he will be chosen.

The boys who were not so sure of themselves tried to buy their way in by providing the equipment the teams needed— bats, new baseballs and extra gloves. They would place the equipment on the ground, under a tree, and wait hopefully while two of the better players flipped a coin, and then began choosing-up sides.

"I'll take Jake," said one boy, obviously a leader.

"I'll take Hank," said the other leader.

"Then *I'll* take Pugs."

And on they went, until all but one had been selected. The last boy was often a lean, bespectacled no-hit no-field specialist who stood alone under the tree trying to seem unconcerned. He was used to being picked last.

"Okay, I'll take Lester," the other leader would say, as if finally resigning himself to a minor disease. "Lester, you play right field." And the boy nobody wanted would usually pick up his glove (an expensive one perhaps signed by Mickey Mantle!) and sprint out to right field. Very few balls are hit to right field, and that is precisely why the boy was sent out there.

"Before long I noticed that the most agile young boys—often

the *leaders* of the gang—preferred the shortstop position, which was apparently the top-status position among adolescent base-ball players," said Dr. Birdwhistell. "Next in status came second base, then left field. Third base was taken by the youth with an arm strong enough to throw to first base. First base went to a tall boy who could catch. The catcher, if there were enough players to have one, was usually a slow, sturdy kid who did not mind getting hit with the ball, or who had enough patience to chase the young pitcher's wild pitches, a hardly prestigeful position. Catchers often were kids who would drive a motorcycle."

"What about the pitcher?" he was asked.

"The pitcher," Dr. Birdwhistell said, "had little prestige in these sand-lot pick-up games. In pick-up games the emphasis was merely on getting the ball over and letting the batter hit. It was only in the neighborhood games, or in organized Little League–type of competition, that the pitcher became the most important defensive player on the field."

Twenty runs an inning were common in these games, and teams sometimes won by scores of 93–54, or 121–86.

"The shortstop position was naturally the most sought-after by the leaders because it was the spot with many 'opportunities,'" said Dr. Birdwhistell. "Since many balls were hit around second base and out in left field by the predominantly right-handed hitters, these fielders also had many 'opportunities' to look good.

"I also noticed," said Dr. Birdwhittell, "that many of these shortstops and second basemen tended to be shorter kids— early-matured kids with quickness as their attribute. These shortstops stood in contrast to the later physical maturers, the long-boned, awkward sandlot players. In fact, many of these shorter shortstops tended to stick to these positions through high school, and some even went up to Major League baseball that way—where they make great 'little men' like Rizzuto, Reese, and the like, and are idolized by the public who identify with these Little Davids."

"What about the rightfielder—what happens to him?"

"Many of these sandlot rightfielders, disappointed with their status, eventually give up team sports," said Dr. Birdwhistell. "Perhaps they concentrate on girls and bookish things, or study the piano. A number of them shift to individual sports as they mature. Tennis, track, squash and golf probably owe a great deal to these early disappointments. These disappointed right-fielders go off by themselves to mature in private. You find a lot of them among your pole vaulters, discus throwers, wrestlers—guys in events where they never talk to anyone. They stand out there all day throwing that damn javelin. What they need is some privacy in their development. On the other hand, being a frustrated rightfielder is excellent training for future managers and sportswriters."

When Dr. Birdwhistell moved from the sandlots to study the high school athlete, he was not surprised that the "little men" quarterbacks occupied many of the brainy, top-status spots on football teams. Since the Pleistocene period, sportswriters have been calling nearly every quarterback a "field general," "signal caller," or "the leader." But Birdwhisttell *was* surprised to learn that many coaches considered the quarterback ethnically supe-rior to the fullback, and the tackle only socially superior to an orangutan.

"Or, to be more specific," Birdwhistell says, "up to ten years or so ago many school coaches believed that the toughest line-men and hardest-hitting fullbacks necessarily come from slums or coal mines; are products of the hyphenated groups—i.e., the poorer classes of Polish-Americans, Italian-Americans, Irish-

Americans, Swedish-Americans, depending on the part of the country. The theory was that the hungry hyphenated groups, frustrated in a social system set against them, would produce angry anthropoids with a penchant for body contact and head-banging.

"I also found, during a pre-War tour of the Midwest and South, that most fullbacks and linemen—except the ends—generally came from working class families. On the other hand, the ends and other backs were, at least in high school, more often the sons of professional men, teachers, successful merchants, or, to be more exact—the Anglo-Saxons, whom coaches regarded as being brighter as backfield men than the ethnic groups."

"What about Negros, where did they fit in?"

"There were some coaches who had a brilliant theory on how to handle a Negro back," Birdwhistell said. "For some strange reason, coaches, like many of their fellow Americans, were prone to believe that Negros had especially tender shin bones; and coaches recommended, 'Kick'im in the shins.' This is part of the same theory that immigrants had hard heads and were 'too dumb to be hurt.' "

"Do these theories still prevail?" he was asked.

"They've faded," Dr. Birdwhistell said, lighting a cigarette. "Mostly due to the post-War emphasis on the T-formation, in which many hyphenated groups (and Negros) have become brilliant quarterbacks, these theories, and similar ones, no longer hold up. Sports, in fact, have become a central arena of democracy—whether because there is a greater supply of athletes among Negros, so they get a chance; whether because coaches themselves are often ethnic, ex-linemen; whether because the war and G.I. Bill provided new opportunities—for a whole series of reasons, the democracy of the bleachers has been extended to the playing field and discrimination is greatly reduced nowadays."

"What theories or special problems do basketball coaches have?"

"Basketball coaches in college have often a very interesting problem," he said. "When I was at the University of Louisville I attended at least half of the basketball practices for five years, and I was most interested in how coaches took these extraordinarily big boys, particularly the centers, and taught them to be aggressive. Big boys, you understand, are taught as children in our society to be gentle. They are taught not to use their strength on smaller boys. 'Pick on your own size,' is what irate mothers say to big bullies. Anyway, these coaches have the problem of making these big boys, these 6-feet 5-inchers, aggressive enough to play center. They have to make them *mean*. And one thing I've noticed is that coaches develop a device of systematically frustrating the boy—like, say he comes into college with only one shot, say a right-handed hook shot. Then the coach makes him shoot only with his *left* hand. And generally it didn't take long before the big boy became pretty frustrated, and pretty mean. It's a very cute thing to see happen, this taking a big person who has been taught *not* to be aggressive, and making him aggressive. Sheer size won't work unless the boy is made to be mean. Making him frustrated is one way coaches accomplish this; the other way I've already mentioned—getting the poverty-stricken boys from ethnic groups, the boys who are frustrated in their social system anyway, and making *them* the body-contact specialists."

"What sport do you most enjoy?"

"I probably get the biggest kick out of basketball because of its patterns, and the swiftness with which it moves. Many of the players are better than the best dancers in a ballet."

"What about baseball?"

"My feelings on baseball are relatively simple: I am a fan of fans. I enjoy watching the crowd at the game. America does not do very well in supporting the underdog; we are much better with winners at the box office. Also, we are one of the few societies in the world that can take three games between two teams and turn it into something called 'tradition.' It's most amazing. When Americans came across the ocean they left the past behind them. Americans are an exceedingly NOW people, and yet our sportswriters are ever making these 'traditions.' Some sportswriters will even write of a game, "this is the *beginning* of a traditional series.' Sportswriters have become the high priests of this religion; if one doesn't look to the sportswriters, one can't possibly understand America's sports patterns. The sportswriter is, in addition to the theologian, also the historian and writer of bibles. He is tremendously important; people will hasten out after a ball game to read what opinion they should have about the game, or they'll carry a little radio to the park with them to find out what is going on down on the field."

"What feelings do school teachers and professors hold toward the athlete?" he was asked.

"There is the supposition among some school teachers that most athletes are flunking material," Dr. Birdwhistell said. "Throughout my pre-war and post-war study, I have observed that on every school faculty—from grade school on up to college—there exist at least three factions: 1) teachers who over-indulge athletes; 2) teachers who fear or despise them; and 3) teachers who don't indulge in stereotypes."

The first category, says Birdwhistell, consists mostly of teachers who themselves are former athletes, or are themselves rather immature. "Every good coach makes it his business to know the teachers who are 'friends' of the Athletic Department," Dr. Birdwhistell said. It is the desire of every ambitious coach to place his minions in only those classes taught by "friends." Friends never flunk the athlete during season. Friendly teachers, of course, are always greeted with enthusiasm around the Athletic Department, are invited to team banquets, and are regarded as gentlemen, possibly scholars, by the coaches.

Teachers who despise athletes are, Birdwhistell suggested, individuals who as children possibly felt themselves snubbed by athletes, or maybe lost status battles to athletes, or perhaps they just resent the fact that athletes are treated ofttimes like sacred cows by an ambitious administration. Irwin Shaw, in his novel "The Troubled Air," was remarkably accurate in this description of a typical first meeting in a college class between the anti-athlete teacher (Clement Archer) and the football hero (Victor Herres):

> "...Archer called the roll. Herres answered with a clipped 'Here' and Archer remembered the name. Quarterback on the football team, another mark against him. Probably there'd be a hearty, embarrassed visit from Samson, the coach, in a month or two, with a plea to keep the boy eligible until Thanksgiving, even though he cut half his classes. Not this time, Samson, old boy, Archer resolved in advance, not for this particular young hero in a bow tie. He can come in with both eyes closed and swinging on crutches after scoring twenty touchdowns on Saturday afternoon, but I won't give an inch..."

In all truth, however, it does not take a bitter, athlete-hating teacher to prove that athletes are sometimes ill-equipped to pass any standard college course except Gym I. It has long been Dr. Birdwhistell's contention that most athletes *themselves* secretly think they can not (or should not) show eptitude in the class room. Athletes have been reared in a society where sports experts and broadcasters have lavishly publicized any star athlete who is an A-student, as if to suggest that he is a kind of freak who accomplished a great, scholarly feat despite a tremendous medical handicap—no brain.

"It is very hard for most of us to believe that a good brain can come in a good body," Birdwhistell said. "We've had a double assumption in our American society: we assumed that the athlete, like the beautiful blonde, tends to be dumb. And we also play it the other way around: the brilliant man tends to be emaciated, tends to wear eye-glasses, and so on.

"Because of the assumption in our society that athletes usually are not very smart," Birdwhistell continued, "the students and teachers join in this myth. Thus, the athletes tend to give-up sooner in their classes. And teachers often confuse the weariness that comes from long hours of athletics, or a lack of practice with words, with stupidity. The most serious charge that I can make against athletics in America is that it takes some of our best brains and convinces them that they're dumb; convinces them somehow that if they're good in sports they'll not be good in education.

"But the fact of the matter is," Birdwhistell said, "if you give the average athlete the right kind of I.Q. test—not one based on cleverness with words, but in an area in which he's working— then you will see some really fantastic intellectual maneuvers from athletes. I've seen two big linemen who could scarcely stay in school because of their lack of interest . . . play a football game in their head in which each maneuvered twenty-two men offensively and defensively. And they played it like two chess players. Only faster. It was a really remarkable intellectual achievement."

But what is most pathetic, says Birdwhistell, is that a major proportion of athletes, despite all the glory and gold they get, really go under-rewarded in the end. In a sense they function merely to provide Roman circuses for the customers. But when they no longer can run swiftly, or hit the curve, most of them are shipped back to mediocrity. And that athletic mind, which Birdwhistell believes has great potentiality, is most often lost to the nation in crucial times such as these.

"Besides the choice of becoming coaches, and scouts, and sporting goods salesmen," Birdwhistell said, "more athletes should be prepared in college for a future career in, say, mathematics or science. I believe that the college athletic scholarship should be for six years—not four—and that the athlete should have the last two years for only serious study, and no sports activity whatsoever."

This additional schooling would help develop the athlete for future leadership off the field, Birdwhistell contends, and will perhaps also provide the athlete with the scholastic background he will need for that big contest in the future when he must battle for a good job against those many studious, ambitious, embittered ex-right fielders who, when all the tumult and shouting ends, usually finish first.

JOE LOUIS: THE KING
AS A MIDDLE-AGED MAN

Esquire, 1962

H I, SWEETHEART!" JOE Louis called to his wife, spotting her waiting for him at the Los Angeles airport.

She smiled, walked toward him, and was about to stretch up
on her toes and kiss him—but suddenly stopped.

"Joe," she said, "where's your tie?"

"Aw, sweetie," he said, shrugging, "I stayed out all night in
New York and didn't have time—"

"All *night!*" she cut in. "When you're out here all you do is
sleep, sleep, sleep."

"Sweetie," Joe Louis said, with a tired grin, "I'm an ole man."

"Yes," she agreed, "but when you go to New York, you try
to be young again."

They walked slowly through the airport lobby toward their
car, being followed by a redcap with Joe's luggage. Mrs. Louis,
the third wife of the forty-eight-year-old former fighter, always
meets him at the airport when he is returning from a business
trip to New York, where he is vice president of a Negro public-
relations firm. She is an alert, pleasingly plump woman in her

forties who is a very successful trial lawyer in California. She had never known a prizefighter before she met Joe. Previously, she had been married to a fellow lawyer, a Phi Beta Kappa—a man she once described as being "exposed to books, not to life." After her divorce, she vowed she wanted a man "exposed to life, not to books."

She met Joe in 1957 through an introduction from a West Coast lady friend, and, two years later, to the surprise of her courtroom associates in Los Angeles, she married him. "How in the hell did *you* meet Joe Louis?" they kept asking, and she usually replied, "How in the hell did Joe Louis meet me?"

Arriving at the car, Joe Louis tipped the redcap and opened the door for his wife. Then he drove past palm trees and quiet neighborhoods for a few miles, and finally turned into a long driveway that flanks an impressive, ten-room, Spanish-style house that is worth $75,000. Mrs. Louis bought it a few years ago and filled it with Louis XV furniture—and eight television sets. Joe Louis was a television addict, she explained to her friends, adding that he even has a set in his bathroom above the tub; the set is placed at such an angle that Joe, when taking a shower across the room, can peek over the shower curtain and see a reflection of the TV screen through a strategically placed mirror.

"Television and golf," Mrs. Louis said, helping to carry her husband's things into the house, "that's Joe Louis today." She said this unruefully, and, later kissing her husband on the cheek, she suddenly seemed a lot less formal than she had at the airport. After hanging his coat in the closet, she quickly put on a kettle for tea.

"Cookies, honey?" she asked.

"Nah," he said, sitting slope-shouldered at the breakfast table, his eyelids drooping from lack of sleep. Soon she was upstairs, turning down the covers of their gigantic bed, and five minutes later Joe Louis had plunged upon it and was fast asleep. When Mrs. Louis returned to the kitchen, she was smiling.

"In court, I'm a lawyer," she said, "but when I'm home, I'm *all* woman." Her voice was husky, suggestive. "I treat a man *right*, I treat a man like a *king*—if he treats *me* right," she added, pouring herself a glass of milk.

"Each morning I bring Joe breakfast in bed," she said. "Then I turn on Channel 4 so he can watch the *Today* show. Then I go down and get him the *Los Angeles Times*. Then I leave the house for court.

"By 11 A.M.," she continued, "it's time for him to tee off at the Hillcrest Country Club, and, if he plays eighteen holes, he should be finished by three o'clock, and will probably drive over to the Fox Hills Country Club for eighteen more. But if he isn't hitting the ball right, he'll stop after eighteen and go buy a bucket of balls and hit 'em for hours. He don't buy *regular* balls—no, not Joe Louis!—he buys the Select balls, the best, which cost $1.25 a bucket. And he'll hit—if he's real mad—two, three, or four buckets full, $5 worth.

"Some nights he comes home, all excited, and says, 'Well, sweetheart, I *finally* got it today! After all these years playing golf, I just realized what I been doing wrong.'

"But," she said, "a day later he may come home, all mad from throwing clubs, and say, 'I'm never gonna play again!' I'll say, 'But, honey, you told me yesterday you *had* it!' He'll say, 'I *had* it, but I didn't *keep* it!'

"The next morning it might be raining, and I'll say, 'Sweetheart, you gonna play golf today? It's raining.' And he'll say, 'It rains on the course, but it don't rain on the players.' And off to the golf course he goes."

Joe Louis's present wife, Martha, is as different from his first two wives as he is from Martha's Phi Beta Kappa husband.

Joe's first wife, Marva, a sleek Chicago steonographer whom he married in 1935 and remarried in 1946, belonged to his lush years, to the years when he blew most of his $5-million boxing fortune on trinkets, jewels, furs, trips abroad, gambling on the golf course, poor investments, lavish tips, and clothes. In 1939, a year in which he had already purchased twenty suits, thirty-six shirts, and two tuxedos, he also hired tailors to create clothing styles of his own invention, such as two-tone floppy green trousers, suit coats without lapels, and camel's-hair jackets with leather piping. When he was not training or fighting—he won the title by knocking out James J. Braddock in 1937—Joe Louis was doing the town with Marva ("I could make her laugh") or was gambling as much as $1,000 a hole at golf, a game that two sportswriters, Hype Igoe and Walter Stewart, introduced to him in 1936. "One guy built a house in California with the money he took Joe for," an old friend of Louis's said.

Joe's second wife, Rose Morgan, the cosmetics and beauty expert to whom he was married from 1955 to 1958, is a stunning, curvesome woman dedicated to her prosperous business, and she refused to stay up all night with Joe. "I tried to make him settle down," she said. "I told him he couldn't sleep all day and stay out all night anymore. Once he asked me why not, and I told him I'd worry and wouldn't be able to sleep. So he said he'd wait till I fell asleep before going out. Well, I stayed up till 4 A.M.—and then *he* fell asleep." Rose was also disenchanted with him in 1956 when, in an effort to make some money toward the $1 million he owed the government in back taxes, he began touring as a wrestler. "To me, Joe Louis was like the president of the United States," Rose said. "How would you like to see the president of the United States washing dishes? That's how I felt about Joe wrestling."

Joe's third wife, while having none of the obvious sex appeal of his first two, has succeeded where they had failed because she is wiser than they, and because Joe was ripe for taming when he fell in love with Martha. She seems to be many things to him: a combination lawyer, cook, mistress, press agent, tax consultant, valet de chambre, and everything but caddie. And she was obviously pleased recently when her friend, the singer Mahalia Jackson, noticed the closets bulging with Joe's belongings and remarked, "Well, Martha, I guess he's finally ready to settle down; this is the first time in his life he's got all his clothes under one roof."

It does not seem to matter to Martha that she got Joe Louis in his declining years—at a time when he weighs 240 pounds, is going bald, is somewhat less than prosperous, and no longer possesses the quick reflexes either to hit or pick up checks. "There's a soul about this man, and a quietness that I love," she said, adding that her love has been returned. Joe even goes to church with her on Sundays, she said, and often appears in court to watch her handle cases. Though he neither smokes nor drinks, Joe still goes to nightclubs occasionally to hear some of the many musicians and singers he lists among his friends, she says, and she is aware of the number of women who still find Joe Louis sexually appealing and would consider a night with him time well spent. "If those sort of women like living on the side streets of a man's life," Martha said, "I wish them well. But I am his wife, and when I come on the scene they got to get the hell out."

Martha is aware, too, that Joe Louis still is friendly with his former wives—who, after getting divorced from him, went to polar extremes in choosing their future husbands. Marva, after leaving Joe, married a doctor in Chicago. Rose followed her divorce from Joe with a marriage to a lawyer. When Joe is in Chicago, he often calls Marva (the mother of his two children) and sometimes goes over for dinner. When in New York, he does the same thing with Rose. "Joe Louis never really cuts off a woman," Martha observed, more amused than piqued. "He just adds another to his list." Actually, Joe has been responsible for his three wives getting acquainted with each other, and he is delighted that they get along. He introduced his first wife to his present wife at the Patterson-Johansson title fight in New York, and on another occasion he arranged to have his present wife's hair done by his second wife—free.

Joe Louis had told me all about this earlier in the day on the plane during our flight to Los Angeles from New York (where I had spent some time following him around Manhattan and watching him function as a public-relations executive). "I called Rose on the phone," Joe had said, "and told her, 'Now Rose Morgan, don't you charge my wife,' She said, 'No, Joe, I won't.' That Rose Morgan is a wonderful woman," Joe mused, shaking his head.

"You know, I been married to three of the finest women in the world. My only mistake in life was getting divorced."

"Why did you then?" I asked.

"Oh," he said, "in those days I wanted to be free, and sometimes I just wanted to be alone. I was crazy. I'd go out of the house and stay weeks without coming home. Or maybe I'd stay home in bed for days watching television."

Just as he blames himself for the failure of his first two marriages, so does he accept the blame for all of his other difficulties, such as his inability to hold on to his money, and his negligence in paying taxes. During his last visit to New York, some old boxing friends were saying, "Joe, if only you were fighting today, you'd be making twice what you did in the old days, with the money fighters now get from closed-circuit TV and all." But Joe Louis shook his head and said, "I ain't sorry I fought when I did. In my time, I made $5 million, wound up broke, and owe the government $1 million in taxes. If I was fighting today, I'd earn $10 million, would still wind up broke, and would owe the government $2 million in taxes."

Such remarks, simple yet mixed with an almost absurd sense of humor, were delivered often by Joe Louis during the hours I followed him in New York—much to my surprise.

Rightly or wrongly, I had imagined that this middle-aged hero would merely be a flabby version of the rather dim-witted champion that Don Dunphy used to interview over the radio after the knockout of another Great White Hope—and I had assumed that Joe Louis, at forty-eight, would still hold his title as perhaps the most quiet athlete since Dummy Taylor, the Giant pitcher, who was a mute.

Of course, I was aware of those few, famous Joe Louis remarks—like the one about Billy Conn: "Maybe he kin run, but he can't hide"; and Pvt. Joe Louis's answer in World War II when somebody asked how he felt about fighting for nothing: "I ain't fighting for nothing, I'm fighting for my country." But I had read, too, that Joe Louis was incredibly naïve—so naïve that in 1960 he agreed to do public-relations work for Fidel Castro. I had also seen recent news photos of Joe posing outside courtrooms with Hulan E. Jack, the ex–Manhattan borough president who tried to conceal gratuities concerning the remodeling of his apartment. And once Senator John L. McClellan hinted that Louis had received $2,500 for sitting for two hours at the bribery trial of James R. Hoffa; although there were denials all around, the undeniable image of Joe Louis then was that while he was a "credit to his race—the human race," he was now probably a debt to everybody else.

And so it was with some unexpected elation that I found Joe Louis to be an astute businessman in New York, a shrewd bargainer, and a man with a sense of humor often quite subtle. For instance, as we were boarding the plane at Idlewild Airport for Los Angeles and I had to exchange my tourist-class ticket for first class so I could sit next to Joe, I casually asked him how the airlines could justify the forty-five dollar difference in price. "First-class seats are up in front of the plane," Louis said, "and they get you to L.A. faster."

The day before, I had seen Joe Louis argue some extra money out of New York television executives who are doing a television show on his life.

"Hey," Joe said, carefully reading every word of the contract before signing it, "this says you'll pay my plane ticket from L.A. to New York and back, and my hotel bill, but what about my living expenses when I'm here?"

"But, Mr. Louis," one executive said, nervously, "we never discussed that."

"Who's gonna pay? How ma gonna eat?" Louis asked, his voice rising with irritation.

"But, but . . ."

Louis stood up, put the pen down, and would not have signed at all had not the president of the television company finally said, "Okay, Joe, I'm sure something can be worked out."

Assured that it would, Louis then signed, shook hands with everyone, and left the office.

"Well," he said, on the sidewalk, "I won that round."

Then he added, "I know what I'm worth, and I don't want less." He said the movie producers of *Requiem for a Heavyweight* wanted him to appear as a referee but only offered him a fee of $500 plus $50-a-day living expenses. Though the whole part would have kept Louis on the screen only forty-five seconds, Louis said it was worth a fee of $1,000. The producers said that was too much. But a few days later, Louis said, they called him back. He got his $1,000.

Though his tax difficulties have eradicated all his assets—including two trust funds he had set up for his children—Joe Louis is still a man of great pride. He refused the money that hundreds of citizens sent him to help with his government debt, although he still owes the government thousands and could have used the cash. Last year Joe Louis earned less than $10,000, most of it from refereeing wrestling matches (he earns between $750 and $1,000 a night), and from endorsements or appearances. The last big money he made was the $100,000-a-year guarantee he got in 1956 for wrestling. He won all his matches—except those in which he was disqualified for using his fists—but his career ended not long afterward when the 300-pound cowboy Rocky Lee accidentally stepped on Louis's chest one night, cracked one of his ribs, and damaged some of his heart muscles.

Today Joe Louis is a matchmaker with a group of California boxing promoters he formed (United World Boxing Enterprises), and still has his name used by a Chicago milk company; but the only financial interests he has are with the Manhattan public-relations firm of Louis-Rowe Enterprises, Inc., a swinging outfit on West Fifty-seventh Street that handles Louis Armstrong and the new singer Dean Barlow, among other Negro entertainers, and would have had a profitable thing going in Cuba had there not been such an uproar over Joe Louis representing Castro and saying, as he did in 1960, "There is no place in the world except Cuba where the Negro can go in the wintertime with absolutely no discrimination."

Without being a racist, Joe Louis today is very much concerned with the Negro's fight for equality and, possibly for the first time in his life, is quite outspoken on the subject. Frankly, Joe Louis saw nothing wrong in endorsing Cuba in 1960 as a vacationland for American Negroes and is also quick to point out that he canceled his firm's $287,000-a-year contract with Cuba's National Institute of Tourism *before* the United States severed diplomatic relations with the Castro regime. Even now, Louis feels Castro is far, far better for the Cuban people than the United Fruit Company.

When Joe Louis reads newspapers, I noticed that it was not the sports page that got his first attention but rather such stories as the announcement that Lieut. Commander Samuel Gravely, Jr., had become the first Negro in U.S. naval history to command a warship. "Things are getting better," Louis said. I noticed, too, that one afternoon, as he was switching the television dial in search of a golf match, he happened upon a panel show on which a delegate from Ghana was speaking; Louis listened until the African finished before switching to the golf tournament.

While the second Max Schmeling fight was billed by American newspapers as a grudge match in which Louis sought revenge against the "Super Race" that regarded Negroes as an inferior breed, Joe Louis said this was strictly a publicity stunt to build up the gate. Louis said he never really felt hostility toward Schmeling, although he did not like one of Schmeling's friends who strode about the fight camp wearing a Nazi armband. Louis said that he is far more bitter toward Eastern Air Lines than he ever was at the Schmeling camp, having never forgiven Eastern for refusing him limousine service in 1946 from a New Orleans hotel to the airport after Louis had fought an exhibition. Louis, who would have missed his plane had he not gotten there on his own, wrote a letter of protest to Eastern's Eddie Rickenbacker. "He never answered," Louis said.

As a result, Louis said he has never flown Eastern since, even when it would have been much more convenient; he also said he has told many of his friends to avoid the airline and believes this has cost Eastern considerable revenue in the past sixteen years.

It is one of the aims of Joe Louis, and his public-relations partner, Billy Rowe, to convince big business executives that the Negro market, if discouraged or ignored, can be hazardous to sales figures; but if properly encouraged, it can be very profitable. The Louis-Rowe agency claims that each year American Negroes pour $22 billion into big business, spend more than 18 percent of America's travel dollar, and that Negroes in Harlem alone spend $200,000 a day gambling on sports events and the numbers game.

Negroes would spend much more, Louis and Rowe argue, if big business would increase its advertising budget for the Negro market and would make its advertising campaigns more specialized—i.e., would show more Negro models in Negro newspapers selling certain brands of soap, beer, and so forth. This is the message that Rowe delivers when he, accompanied by Louis, visits Madison Avenue ad agencies, insurance companies, stockbrokerages, and racetracks; Rowe, a fast-talking, endlessly articulate man who dresses like a Broadway dude and resembles Nat King Cole (but is handsomer), dominates most conversations, although Louis gets in a good line now and then.

Billy Rowe, who is forty-seven and was once a deputy police commissioner in New York—he still carries a pistol everywhere he goes—occupies a larger, fancier office than Joe at their agency. While Joe has only one of his plaques hanging on the wall—the

"State of Michigan Hall of Fame" plaque—Billy Rowe has covered a wall with eighteen of *his* plaques and scrolls, including commendations for youth work from the Minisink Men's Guidance Council, letters from the governor, and two gold trophies that do not even belong to him. Modesty is not his primary virtue.

Mr. Rowe, who lives in a fourteen-room house (with four television sets) in the suburbs of New Rochelle, arrives at the office a full hour ahead of Louis and has the day's—and some of the week's—appointments all lined up by the time Louis strolls in, usually around 11 A.M., with a big wink for the girl at the switchboard.

"Hey, Dad," Rowe greets Louis, "we got an appointment with the mayor on the thirteenth. We'd had it before, but he's fighting with the governor."

Louis nodded, then yawned, then suddenly became wide-eyed when he noticed walking toward him a voluptuous Harlem nightclub singer named Ann Weldon. Without saying a word, Miss Weldon swished right up to Louis and wiggled close to him.

"You get any closer," Louis said, "I gonna have to marry you."

She swooned and slithered away.

"Hey, Dad," Rowe said, "you gonna eat lunch at Lindy's?"

"Yeah."

"Who's picking up the check?"

"Yonkers Raceway."

"In that case," Rowe said, "I'll join you."

An hour later, headed for Lindy's, Rowe and Louis left the office and jammed into the crowded elevator, where nearly everyone grinned or winced as they recognized Joe Louis.

"Hi, champ," they said. "Hello, Joe."

"Sure wouldn't want to start a fight in this car," the elevator man said.

"No," Joe said, "not enough room for me to run."

"Joe," a man said, shaking Louis's hand, "you sure look in good shape."

"Only in shape for a steak," Louis said.

"Joe," another man said, "seems like only yesterday I seen you fight Billy Conn. Time sure flies."

"Yeah," said Louis. "It do, don't it?"

And on and on it went, as Louis walked down Broadway: cabdrivers waved at him, bus drivers honked at him, and dozens of men stopped him and recalled how they had once traveled 130 miles to get to one of his fights, and how they'd put their heads down to light a cigarette in the first round, then before they could look up, Louis had flattened his opponent and they had missed everything: or how they'd had guests at the house that night to hear the fight, and while they were struggling in the kitchen to get the ice out, somebody came in from the living room and said, "It's all over! Louis knocked 'im out with the first punch."

It was astonishing, most of all to Louis, that they had remembered him so—especially since he has not had a fight since his unwise comeback in 1951, when Rocky Marciano knocked him out. Two years before that Louis had retired undefeated, having defended his title twenty-five times, more than any other champion.

In Lindy's, the waiters, fussing over Louis, led him and Rowe to a table occupied by an official from Yonkers Raceway. Before the lunch was half over, Louis was making a pitch for the track's account, saying that a good public-relations campaign by Louis-Rowe would get more Negroes to the track than ever before. The official said he would present their proposal to the board of directors and would let Louis and Rowe know the result.

"Joe, we better get moving," Rowe said, looking at his watch. "We gotta see Joe Glaser. That Glaser's got so much money that the bank charges him storage." Rowe laughed at his joke and said, "Joe, tell that to Glaser when you see him."

Five minutes later, Louis and Rowe were escorted by Glaser's assistants into the new, plush quarters of Mr. Glaser, the talent-booking man, who pounded Joe on the back and said, loud enough for his assistants in the other offices to hear, "Joe Louis is one of the finest men in the world!"

And Billy Rowe said, because he could not resist, "Joe Glaser's got so much money that the bank charges him storage."

Everybody laughed, except Joe Louis, who glanced sideways at Rowe.

After leaving Glaser's, Louis and Rowe had appointments at the Investors Planning Corporation of America, where they submitted proposals for selling more mutual funds to Negroes; then visited the Cobleigh and Gordon, Inc. agency, where they discussed a Negro newsletter that Rowe and Louis wish to produce; then dropped into Toots Shor's; and finally went to dinner at La Fonda del Sol, where Rowe had arranged for a couple of Harlem nightclub starlets to join them.

"Oh, Joe," one of the girls said, as a Spanish guitar strummed behind her, "when you used to fight, I was a young girl, and in our house we all gathered around the radio—and I wasn't allowed to talk."

Joe winked.

"Joe," another said, "while I'm sitting so close, how's about autographing this menu—for my son."

Louis grinned and playfully pulled from a pocket his hotel key, dangled it, then slid it across the table at her.

"You don't want to let your son down, do you?" he asked.

Everybody laughed, but she did not know whether or not Joe was kidding.

"If I do," she said primly, "I'm sure he'll understand—when he gets older." She slid the key back. Joe howled and signed the menu.

After dinner, Louis and the rest planned to go nightclubbing in Harlem, but I had an appointment to see Louis's second wife, Rose Morgan. Rose now lives in the large, magnificent uptown apartment that overlooks the Polo Grounds and once was occupied by Joe and his first wife, Marva.

Opening the door, Rose Morgan was chic, impeccably groomed, almost exotic in a Japanese loll suit. She led the way across a sprawling, thick rug to a boomerang-shaped white sofa; there, sitting cross-legged and arms akimbo, she said, "Oh, I don't know what it was about Joe. He just got under your skin."

But being married to Joe was not as exciting as being courted by Joe, Rose observed, shaking her head. "When I'd come home from work, 6:30 or 7 P.M., Joe'd be there watching television and eating apples. But," she continued, after a pause, "we're now very good friends. In fact, I just wrote him a letter the other day telling him I found some things of his around and want to know if he wants them."

"Like what?"

"I have the robe he wore when he started boxing," she said, "and his road shoes, and also a film of the first Billy Conn fight. Would you like to watch it?"

Just then, Rose's husband, the lawyer, walked in, followed by some friends from Philadelphia. Rose's husband is a short, portly, manicured man who, after introducing everyone, suggested a round of drinks.

"I'm just showing Joe's fight film," Rose said.

"Hate to put you through all the trouble," I told her.

"Oh, it's *no* trouble," Rose said. "I haven't seen it in years, and I'd love to see it again."

"Is it all right with you if we watch it?" I asked Rose's husband.

"Yes, yes, it's all right with me," he said, quietly. It was obvious that he was just being polite and would rather not have to sit through it; yet there was no way of stopping Rose, for she quickly had the projector out of the closet and soon the lights were off and the fight was on.

"Joe Louis was definitely the greatest of all time," one of the men from Philadelphia said, clinking the ice in his glass. "There was a time when nothing was more important to colored people than God and Joe Louis."

The menacing, solemn image of Joe Louis, then twenty years younger than he is today, moved across the screen toward Conn; when he clouted Conn, Billy's bones seemed to shake.

"Joe didn't waste no punches," somebody said from the sofa.

Rose seemed excited at seeing Joe at his top form, and every time a Louis punch would jolt Conn, she'd go, "Mummmm" (sock). "Mummmm" (sock). "Mummmm."

Billy Conn was impressive through the middle rounds, but as the screen flashed Round 13, somebody said, "Here's where Conn's gonna make his mistake; he's gonna try to slug it out with Joe Louis." Rose's husband remained silent, sipping his Scotch.

When the Louis combinations began to land, Rose went, "Mummmm, mummmm," and then the pale body of Conn began to collapse against the canvas.

Billy Conn slowly began to rise. The referee counted over

him. Conn had one leg up, then two, then was standing—but the referee forced him back. It was too late.

But Rose's husband in the back of the room disagreed.

"I thought Conn got up in time," he said, "but that referee wouldn't let him go on."

Rose Morgan said nothing—just swallowed the rest of her drink.

THE SILENT SEASON OF A HERO

Esquire, 1966

"I would like to take the great DiMaggio fishing," the old man said. "They say his father was a fisherman. Maybe he was as poor as we are and would understand."

—Ernest Hemingway, *The Old Man and the Sea*

I T WAS N O T quite spring, the silent season before the search for salmon, and the old fishermen of San Francisco were either painting their boats or repairing their nets along the pier or sitting in the sun talking quietly among themselves, watching the tourists come and go, and smiling, now, as a pretty girl paused to take their picture. She was about twenty-five, healthy and blue-eyed, and wearing a red turtleneck sweater, and she had long, flowing blonde hair that she brushed back a few times before clicking her camera. The fishermen, looking at her, made admiring comments, but she did not understand because they spoke a Sicilian dialect; nor did she notice the tall gray-haired man in a dark suit who stood watching her from behind a big bay window on the second floor of DiMaggio's Restaurant, which overlooks the pier.

He watched until she left, lost in the crowd of newly arrived tourists that had just come down the hill by cable car. Then he sat down again at the table in the restaurant, finishing his tea and lighting another cigarette, his fifth in the last half hour. It was 11:30 A.M. None of the other tables was occupied, and the only sounds came from the bar where a liquor salesman was laughing at something the headwaiter had said. But then the salesman, his briefcase under his arm, headed for the door, stopping briefly to peek into the dining room and call out, "See you later, Joe." Joe DiMaggio turned and waved at the salesman. Then the room was quiet again.

At fifty-one, DiMaggio was a most distinguished-looking man, aging as gracefully as he had played on the ball field, impeccable in his tailoring, his nails manicured, his six-foot two-inch body seeming as lean and capable as when he posed for the portrait that hangs in the restaurant and shows him in Yankee Stadium swinging from the heels at a pitch thrown twenty years ago. His gray hair was thinning at the crown, but just barely, and his face was lined in the right places, and his expression, once as sad and haunted as a matador's, was more in repose these days, though, as now, tension had returned and he chain-smoked and occasionally paced the floor and looked out the window at the people below. In the crowd was a man he did not wish to see.

The man had met DiMaggio in New York. This week he had come to San Francisco and had telephoned several times, but none of the calls had been returned because DiMaggio suspected that the man, who had said he was doing research on some vague sociological project, really wanted to delve into DiMaggio's private life and that of DiMaggio's former wife,

Marilyn Monroe. DiMaggio would never tolerate this. The memory of her death is still very painful to him, and yet, because he keeps it to himself, some people are not sensitive to it. One night in a supper club a woman who had been drinking approached his table, and when he did not ask her to join him, she snapped, "All right, I guess I'm *not* Marilyn Monroe."

He ignored her remark, but when she repeated it, he replied, barely controlling his anger, "No—I wish you were, but you're not."

The tone of his voice softened her, and she asked, "Am I saying something wrong?"

"You already have," he said. "Now will you please leave me alone?"

His friends on the wharf, understanding him as they do, are very careful when discussing him with strangers, knowing that should they inadvertently betray a confidence he will not denounce them but rather will never speak to them again; this comes from a sense of propriety not inconsistent in the man who also, after Marilyn Monroe's death, directed that fresh flowers be placed on her grave "forever."

Some of the older fishermen who have known DiMaggio all his life remember him as a small boy who helped clean his father's boat, and as a young man who sneaked away and used a broken oar as a bat on the sandlots nearby. His father, a small mustachioed man known as Zio Pepe, would become infuriated and call him *lagnuso*, lazy, *meschino*, good-for-nothing, but in 1936 Zio Pepe was among those who cheered when Joe DiMaggio returned to San Francisco after his first season with the New York Yankees and was carried along the wharf on the shoulders of the fishermen.

The fishermen also remember how, after his retirement in 1951, DiMaggio brought his second wife, Marilyn, to live near the wharf, and sometimes they would be seen early in the morning fishing off DiMaggio's boat, the *Yankee Clipper*, now docked quietly in the marina, and in the evening they would be sitting and talking on the pier. They had arguments, too, the fishermen knew, and one night Marilyn was seen running hysterically, crying as she ran, along the road away from the pier, with Joe following. But the fishermen pretended they did not see this; it was none of their affair. They knew that Joe wanted her to stay in San Francisco and avoid the sharks in Hollywood, but she was confused and torn then—"She was a child," they said—and even today DiMaggio loathes Los Angeles and many of the people in it. He no longer speaks to his onetime friend Frank Sinatra, who had befriended Marilyn in her final years, and he also is cool to Dean Martin and Peter Lawford and Lawford's former wife, Pat, who once gave a party at which she introduced Marilyn Monroe to Robert Kennedy, and the two of them danced often that night, Joe heard, and he did not take it well. He was very possessive of her that year, his close friends say, because Marilyn and he had planned to remarry; but before they could she was dead, and DiMaggio banned the Lawfords and Sinatra and many Hollywood people from her funeral. When Marilyn Monroe's attorney complained that DiMaggio was keeping her friends away, DiMaggio answered coldly, "If it weren't for those friends persuading her to stay in Hollywood, she would still be alive."

Joe DiMaggio now spends most of the year in San Francisco, and each day tourists, noticing the name on the restaurant, ask the men on the wharf if they ever see him. Oh yes, the men say, they see him nearly every day; they have not seen him yet this morning, they add, but he should be arriving shortly. So the tourists continue to walk along the piers; past the crab vendors, under the circling seagulls, past the fish 'n' chip stands, sometimes stopping to watch a large vessel steaming toward the Golden Gate Bridge, which, to their dismay, is painted red. Then they visit the Wax Museum, where there is a life-size figure of DiMaggio in uniform, and walk across the street and spend a quarter to peer through the silver telescopes focused on the island of Alcatraz, which is no longer a federal prison. Then they return to ask the men if DiMaggio has been seen. Not yet, the men say, although they notice his blue Impala parked in the lot next to the restaurant. Sometimes tourists will walk into the restaurant and have lunch and will see him sitting calmly in a corner signing autographs and being extremely gracious with everyone. At other times, as on this particular morning when the man from New York chose to visit, DiMaggio was tense and suspicious.

When the man entered the restaurant from the side steps leading to the dining room, he saw DiMaggio standing near the window talking with an elderly maître d' named Charles Friscia. Not wanting to walk in and risk intrusion, the man asked one of DiMaggio's nephews to inform Joe of his presence. When DiMaggio got the message, he quickly turned and left Friscia and disappeared through an exit leading down to the kitchen.

Astonished and confused, the visitor stood in the hall. A moment later Friscia appeared, and the man asked, "Did Joe leave?"

"Joe who?" Friscia replied.

"Joe DiMaggio!"

"Haven't seen him," Friscia said.

"You haven't *seen* him! He was standing right next to you a second ago!"

"It wasn't me," Friscia said.

"You were standing next to him. I saw you. In the dining room."

"You must be mistaken," Friscia said, softly, seriously. "It wasn't me."

"You *must* be kidding," the man said, angrily, turning and leaving the restaurant. Before he could get to his car, however, DiMaggio's nephew came running after him and said, "Joe wants to see you."

He returned, expecting to see DiMaggio waiting for him. Instead he was handed a telephone. The voice was powerful and deep and so tense that the quick sentences ran together: *"You are invading my rights; I did not ask you to come; I assume you have a lawyer; you must have a lawyer; get your lawyer!"*

"I came as a friend," the man interrupted.

"That's beside the point," DiMaggio said. "I have my privacy; I do not want it violated; you'd better get a lawyer." Then, pausing, DiMaggio asked, "Is my nephew there?"

He was not.

"Then wait where you are."

A moment later DiMaggio appeared, tall and red-faced, erect and beautifully dressed in his dark suit and white shirt with the gray silk tie and the gleaming silver cuff links. He moved with big steps toward the man and handed him an airmail envelope, unopened, that the man had written from New York.

"Here," DiMaggio said. "This is yours."

Then DiMaggio sat down at a small table. He said nothing, just lit a cigarette and waited, legs crossed, his head held high and back so as to reveal the intricate construction of his nose, a fine sharp tip above the big nostrils and tiny bones built out from the bridge, a great nose.

"Look," DiMaggio said, more calmly. "I do not interfere with other people's lives. And I do not expect them to interfere with mine. There are things about my life, personal things, that

I refuse to talk about. And even if you asked my brothers, they would be unable to tell you about them because they do not know. There are things about me, so many things, that they simply do not know."

"I don't want to cause trouble," the man said. "I think you're a great man, and—"

"I'm not great," DiMaggio cut in. "I'm not great," he repeated, softly. "I'm just a man trying to get along."

Then DiMaggio, as if realizing that he was intruding upon his own privacy, abruptly stood up. He looked at his watch.

"I'm late," he said, very formal again. "I'm ten minutes late. *You're* making me late."

The man left the restaurant. He crossed the street and wandered over to the pier, briefly watching the fishermen hauling their nets and talking in the sun, seeming very calm and contented. Then, after he had turned and was headed back toward the parking lot, a blue Impala stopped in front of him, and Joe DiMaggio leaned out the window and asked, "Do you have a car?" His voice was very gentle.

"Yes," the man said.

"Oh," DiMaggio said. "I would have given you a ride."

Joe DiMaggio was not born in San Francisco but in Martinez, a small fishing village twenty-five miles northeast of the Golden Gate. Zio Pepe had settled there after leaving Isola delle Femmine, an islet off Palermo where the DiMaggios had been fishermen for generations. But in 1915, hearing of the luckier waters off San Francisco's wharf, Zio Pepe left Martinez, packing his boat with furniture and family, including Joe, who was one year old.

San Francisco was placid and picturesque when the DiMaggios arrived, but there was a competitive undercurrent and struggle for power along the pier. At dawn the boats would sail out to where the bay meets the ocean and the sea is rough, and later the men would race back with their hauls, hoping to beat their fellow fishermen to shore and sell it while they could. Twenty or thirty boats would sometimes be trying to gain the channel shoreward at the same time, and a fisher-man had to know every rock in the water, and later know ev-ery bargaining trick along the shore, because the dealers and restaurateurs would play one fisherman off against the other, keeping the prices down. Later the fishermen became wiser and organized, predetermining the maximum amount each fisherman would catch, but there were always some men who, like the fish, never learned, and so heads would sometimes be broken, nets slashed, gasoline poured onto their fish, flowers of warning placed outside their doors.

But these days were ending when Zio Pepe arrived, and he expected his five sons to succeed him as fishermen, and the first two, Tom and Michael, did; but a third, Vincent, wanted to sing. He sang with such magnificent power as a young man that he came to the attention of the great banker A. P. Giannini, and there were plans to send him to Italy for tutoring and the opera. But there was hesitation around the DiMaggio household, and Vince never went; instead he played ball with the San Francisco Seals, and sportswriters misspelled his name.

It was DeMaggio until Joe, at Vince's recommendation, joined the team and became a sensation, being followed later by the youngest brother, Dominic, who was also outstanding. All three later played in the big leagues, and some writers like to say that Joe was the best hitter, Dom the best fielder, Vince the best singer, and Casey Stengel once said: "Vince is the only player I ever saw who could strike out three times in one game and not be embarrassed. He'd walk into the clubhouse whistling.

Everybody would be feeling sorry for him, but Vince always thought he was doing good."

After he retired from baseball, Vince became a bartender, then a milkman, now a carpenter. He lives forty miles north of San Francisco in a house he partly built, has been happily married for thirty-four years, has four grandchildren, has in the closet one of Joe's tailor-made suits that he has never had altered to fit, and when people ask if he envies Joe, he always says, "No, maybe Joe would like to have what I have. He won't admit it, but he just might like to have what I have." The brother Vince most admired was Michael, "a big earthy man, a dreamer, a fisherman who wanted things but didn't want to take from Joe, or to work in the restaurant. He wanted a bigger boat but wanted to earn it on his own. He never got it." In 1953, at the age of forty-four, Michael fell from his boat and drowned.

Since Zio Pepe's death at seventy-seven in 1949, Tom, at sixty-two the oldest brother—two of his four sisters are older—has become nominal head of the family and manages the restaurant that was opened in 1937 as Joe DiMaggio's Grotto. Later Joe sold out his share, and now Tom is the co-owner of it with Dominic. Of all the brothers, Dominic, who was known as the "Little Professor" when he played with the Boston Red Sox, is the most successful in business. He lives in a fashionable Boston suburb with his wife and three children and is president of a firm that manufactures fiber-cushion materials and grossed more than $3.5 million last year.

Joe DiMaggio lives with his widowed sister, Marie, in a tan stone house on a quiet residential street not far from Fisherman's Wharf. He bought the house almost thirty years ago for his parents, and after their death he lived there with Marilyn Monroe; now it is cared for by Marie, a slim and handsome dark-eyed woman who has an apartment on the second floor, Joe on the third. There are some baseball trophies and plaques in the small room off DiMaggio's bedroom, and on his dresser are photographs of Marilyn Monroe, and in the living room downstairs is a small painting of her that DiMaggio likes very much: It reveals only her face and shoulders, and she is wearing a very wide-brimmed sun hat, and there is a soft sweet smile on her lips, an innocent curiosity about her that is the way he saw her and the way he wanted her to be seen by others—a simple girl, "a warm bighearted girl," he once described her, "that everybody took advantage of."

The publicity photographs emphasizing her sex appeal often offended him, and a memorable moment for Billy Wilder, who directed her in *The Seven Year Itch*, occurred when he spotted DiMaggio in a large crowd of people gathered on Lexington Avenue in New York to watch a scene in which Marilyn, standing over a subway grating to cool herself, had her skirt blown high by a sudden wind below. "What the hell is going on here?" DiMaggio was overheard to have said in the crowd, and Wilder recalled, "I shall never forget the look of death on Joe's face."

He was then thirty-nine; she was twenty-seven. They had been married in January of that year, 1954, despite disharmony in temperament and time: He was tired of publicity; she was thriving on it. He was intolerant of tardiness; she was always late. During their honeymoon in Tokyo an American general had introduced himself and asked if, as a patriotic gesture, she would visit the troops in Korea. She looked at Joe. "It's your honeymoon," he said, shrugging, "go ahead if you want to."

She appeared on ten occasions before 100,000 servicemen, and when she returned she said, "It was so wonderful, Joe. You never heard such cheering."

"Yes I have," he said.

Across from her portrait in the living room, on a coffee table in front of a sofa, is a sterling-silver humidor that was presented to him, by his Yankee teammates at a time when he was the most talked-about man in America, and when Les Brown's band had recorded a hit that was heard day and night on the radio:

> From Coast to Coast, that's all you hear
> Of Joe the One-Man Show
> He's glorified the horsehide sphere,
> Jolting Joe DiMaggio . . .
> Joe . . . Joe . . . DiMaggio . . . we
> want you on our side.

The year was 1941, and it began for DiMaggio in the middle of May after the Yankees had lost four games in a row, seven of their last nine, and were in fourth place, five-and-a-half games behind the leading Cleveland Indians. On May 15, DiMaggio hit only a first-inning single in a game that New York lost to Chicago, 13–1; he was barely hitting .300 and had greatly disappointed the crowds that had seen him finish with a .352 average the year before and .381 in 1939.

He got a hit in the next game, and the next, and the next. On May 24, with the Yankees losing 6–5 to Boston, DiMaggio came up with runners on second and third and singled them home, winning the game, extending his streak to ten games. But it went largely unnoticed. Even DiMaggio was not conscious of it until it had reached twenty-nine games in mid-June. Then the newspapers began to dramatize it, the public became aroused, they sent him good-luck charms of every description, and DiMaggio kept hitting, and radio announcers would interrupt programs to announce the news, and then the song again: *"Joe ... Joe ... DiMaggio ... we want you on our side."*

Sometimes DiMaggio would be hitless his first three times up, the tension would build, it would appear that the game would end without his getting another chance—but he always would, and then he would hit the ball against the left-field wall, or through the pitcher's legs, or between two leaping infielders. In the forty-first game, the first of a doubleheader in Washington, DiMaggio tied an American League record that George Sisler had set in 1922. But before the second game began, a spectator sneaked onto the field and into the Yankees' dugout and stole DiMaggio's favorite bat. In the second game, using another of his bats, DiMaggio lined out twice and flied out. But in the seventh inning, borrowing one of his old bats that a teammate was using, he singled and broke Sisler's record, and he was only three games away from surpassing the major-league record of forty-four set in 1897 by Willie Keeler while playing for Baltimore when it was a National League franchise.

An appeal for the missing bat was made through the newspapers. A man from Newark admitted the crime and returned it with regrets. And on July 2, at Yankee Stadium, DiMaggio hit a home run into the left-field stands. The record was broken.

He also got hits in the next eleven games, but on July 17 ... in Cleveland, at a night game attended by 67,468, he failed against two pitchers, Al Smith and Jim Bagby, Jr., although Cleveland's hero was really its third baseman, Ken Keltner, who in the first inning lunged to his right to make a spectacular backhanded stop of a drive and, from the foul line behind third base, he threw DiMaggio out. DiMaggio received a walk in the fourth inning. But in the seventh he again hit a hard shot at Keltner, who again stopped it and threw him out. DiMaggio hit sharply toward the shortstop in the eighth inning, the ball taking a bad hop, but Lou Boudreau speared it off his shoulder and threw to the second baseman to start a double play and DiMaggio's streak was stopped at fifty-six games. But the New York Yankees were on their way to winning the pennant by seventeen games, and the World Series too, and so in August, in a hotel suite in Washington, the players threw a surprise party for DiMaggio and toasted him with champagne and presented him with this Tiffany silver humidor that is now in San Francisco in his living room.

Marie was in the kitchen making toast and tea when DiMaggio came down for breakfast; his gray hair was uncombed, but, since he wears it short, it was not untidy. He said good morning to Marie, sat down, and yawned. He lit a cigarette. He wore a blue wool bathrobe over his pajamas. It was 8 A.M. He had many things to do today, and he seemed cheerful. He had a conference with the president of Continental Television, Inc., a large retail chain in California of which he is a partner and vice president; later he had a golf date, and then a big banquet to attend, and, if that did not go on too long and he were not too tired afterward, he might have a date.

Picking up the morning paper, not rushing to the sports page, DiMaggio read the front-page news, the people-problems of '66: Kwame Nkrumah was overthrown in Ghana; students were burning their draft cards (DiMaggio shook his head); the flu epidemic was spreading through the whole state of California. Then he flipped inside through the gossip columns, thankful they did not have him in there today—they had printed an item about his dating "an electrifying airline hostess" not long ago, and they also spotted him at dinner with Dori Lane, "the frantic frugger" in Whiskey à Go Go's glass cage—and then he turned to the sports page and read a story about how the injured Mickey Mantle might never regain his form.

It had all happened so quickly, the passing of Mantle, or so it seemed; he had succeeded DiMaggio as DiMaggio had succeeded Ruth, but now there was no great young power hitter coming up and the Yankee management, almost desperate, had talked Mantle out of retirement; and on September 18, 1965, they gave him a "day" in New York during which he received several thousand dollars' worth of gifts—an automobile, two quarter horses, free vacation trips to Rome, Nassau, Puerto Rico—and DiMaggio had flown to New York to make the introduction before 50,000. It had been a dramatic day, an almost holy day for the believers who had jammed the grandstands early to witness the canonization of a new stadium saint. Cardinal Spellman was on the committee, President Johnson sent a telegram, the day was officially proclaimed by the mayor of New York, an orchestra assembled in center field in front of the trinity of monuments to Ruth, Gehrig, Huggins; and high in the grandstands, billowing in the breeze of early autumn, were white banners that read: "Don't Quit Mick," "We Love the Mick."

The banners had been held by hundreds of young boys whose dreams had been fulfilled so often by Mantle, but also seated in the grandstands were older men, paunchy and balding, in whose middle-aged minds DiMaggio was still vivid and invincible, and some of them remembered how one month before, during a pregame exhibition at Old-timers' Day in Yankee Stadium, DiMaggio had hit a pitch into the left-field seats, and suddenly thousands of people had jumped wildly to their feet, joyously screaming—the great DiMaggio had returned; they were young again; it was yesterday.

But on this sunny September day at the stadium, the feast day of Mickey Mantle, DiMaggio was not wearing No. 5 on his back nor a black cap to cover his graying hair; he was wearing a black suit and white shirt and blue tie, and he stood in one corner of the Yankees' dugout waiting to be introduced by Red Barber, who was standing near home plate behind a silver microphone. In the outfield Guy Lombardo's Royal Canadians were playing soothing soft music; and moving slowly back and forth over the sprawling green grass between the left-field bullpen and the infield were two carts driven by grounds-keepers and containing dozens and dozens of large gifts for Mantle: a six-foot, 100-pound Hebrew National salami, a Winchester rifle, a mink coat for Mrs. Mantle, a set of Wilson golf clubs, a Mercury 95-horsepower outboard motor, a Necchi portable, a year's supply of Chunky Candy. DiMaggio smoked a cigarette but cupped it in his hands as if not wanting to be caught in the act by teenage boys near enough to peek down into the dugout. Then, edging forward a step, DiMaggio poked his head out and looked up. He could see nothing above except the packed towering green grandstands that seemed a mile high and moving, and he could see no clouds or blue sky, only sky of faces. Then the announcer called out his name—*"Joe DiMaggio!"*—and suddenly there was a blast of cheering that grew louder and louder, echoing and reechoing within the big steel canyon, and DiMaggio stomped out his cigarette and climbed up the dugout steps and onto the soft green grass, the noise resounding in his ears; he could almost feel the breeze, the breath of 50,000 lungs upon him, 100,000 eyes watching his every move, and for the briefest instant as he walked he closed his eyes.

Then in his path he saw Mickey Mantle's mother, a smiling elderly woman wearing an orchid, and he gently reached out for her elbow, holding it as he led her toward the microphone next to the other dignitaries lined up on the infield. Then he stood, very erect and without expression, as the cheers softened and the stadium settled down.

Mantle was still in the dugout, in uniform, standing with one leg on the top step, and lined on both sides of him were the other Yankees, who, when the ceremony was over, would play the Detroit Tigers. Then into the dugout, smiling, came Senator Robert Kennedy, accompanied by two tall curly-haired young assistants with blue eyes, Fordham freckles. Jim Farley was the first on the field to notice the senator, and Farley muttered, loud enough for others to hear, "Who the hell invited *him*?"

Toots Shor and some of the other committeemen standing near Farley looked into the dugout, and so did DiMaggio, his glance seeming cold, but he remained silent. Kennedy walked up and down within the dugout shaking hands with the Yankees, but he did not walk onto the field.

"Senator," said the Yankees' manager, Johnny Keane, "why don't you sit down?" Kennedy quickly shook his head, smiled. He remained standing, and then one Yankee came over and asked about getting relatives out of Cuba, and Kennedy called over one of his aides to take down the details in a notebook.

On the infield the ceremony went on, Mantle's gifts continued to pile up—a Mobilette motorbike, a Sooner Schooner wagon barbecue, a year's supply of Chock Full O'Nuts coffee, a year's supply of Topps Chewing Gum—and the Yankee players watched, and Maris seemed glum.

"Hey, Rog," yelled a man with a tape recorder, Murray Olderman, "I want to do a thirty-second tape with you."

Maris swore angrily, shook his head.

"It'll only take a second," Olderman said.

"Why don't you ask Richardson? He's a better talker than me."

"Yes, but the fact that it comes from you . . ."

Maris swore again. But finally he went over and said in an interview that Mantle was the finest player of his era, a great competitor, a great hitter.

Fifteen minutes later, standing behind the microphone at home plate, DiMaggio was telling the crowd, "I'm proud to introduce the man who succeeded me in center field in 1951," and from every corner of the stadium the cheering, whistling, clapping came down. Mantle stepped forward. He stood with his wife and children, posed for the photographers kneeling in front. Then he thanked the crowd in a short speech and, turning, shook hands with the dignitaries standing nearby. Among them now was Senator Kennedy, who had been spotted in the dugout five minutes before by Red Barber and been called out and introduced. Kennedy posed with Mantle for a photographer, then shook hands with the Mantle children, and with Toots Shor and James Farley and others. DiMaggio saw him coming down the line, and at the last second he backed away, casually, hardly anybody noticing it, and Kennedy seemed not to notice it either, just swept past shaking more hands.

Finishing his tea, putting aside the newspaper, DiMaggio went upstairs to dress, and soon he was waving good-bye to Marie and driving toward his business appointment in downtown San Francisco with his partners in the retail television business. DiMaggio, while not a millionaire, has invested wisely and has always had, since his retirement from baseball, executive positions with big companies that have paid him well. He also was among the organizers of the Fisherman's National Bank of San Francisco last year, and, though it never came about, he demonstrated an acuteness that impressed those businessmen who had thought of him only in terms of baseball. He has had offers to manage big-league baseball teams but always has rejected them, saying, "I have enough trouble taking care of my own problems without taking on the responsibilities of twenty-five ballplayers."

So his only contact with baseball these days, excluding public appearances, is his unsalaried job as a batting coach each spring in Florida with the New York Yankees, a trip he would make once again on the following Sunday, three days away, if he could accomplish what for him is always the dreaded responsibility of packing, a task made no easier by the fact that he lately has fallen into the habit of keeping his clothes in two places—some hang in his closet at home, some hang in the back room of a saloon called Reno's.

Reno's is a dimly lit bar in the center of San Francisco. A portrait of DiMaggio swinging a bat hangs on the wall, in addition to portraits of other star athletes, and the clientele consists mainly of the sporting crowd and newspapermen, people who know DiMaggio quite well and around whom he speaks freely on a number of subjects and relaxes as he can in few other places. The owner of the bar is Reno Barsocchini, a broad-shouldered and handsome man of fifty-one with graying wavy hair who began as a fiddler in Dago Mary's tavern thirty-five years ago. He later became a bartender there and elsewhere, including DiMaggio's Restaurant, and now he is probably DiMaggio's closest friend. He was the best man at the DiMaggio-Monroe wedding in 1954, and when they separated nine months later in Los Angeles, Reno rushed down to help DiMaggio with the packing and drive him back to San Francisco. Reno will never forget the day.

Hundreds of people were gathered around the Beverly Hills

home that DiMaggio and Marilyn had rented, and photographers were perched in the trees watching the windows, and others stood on the lawn and behind the rosebushes waiting to snap pictures of anybody who walked out of the house. The newspapers that day played all the puns—"Joe Fanned on Jealousy"; "Marilyn and Joe—Out at Home"—and the Hollywood columnists, to whom DiMaggio was never an idol, never a gracious host, recounted instances of incompatibility, and Oscar Levant said it all proved that no man could be a success in two national pastimes. When Reno Barsocchini arrived, he had to push his way through the mob, then bang on the door for several minutes before being admitted. Marilyn Monroe was upstairs in bed; Joe DiMaggio was downstairs with his suitcases, tense and pale, his eyes bloodshot.

Reno took the suitcases and golf clubs out to DiMaggio's car, and then DiMaggio came out of the house, the reporters moving toward him, the lights flashing.

"Where are you going?" they yelled.

"I'm driving to San Francisco," he said, walking quickly.

"Is that going to be your home?"

"That *is* my home and always has been."

"Are you coming back?"

DiMaggio turned for a moment, looking up at the house.

"No," he said, "I'll never be back."

Reno Barsocchini, except for a brief falling out over something he will not discuss, has been DiMaggio's trusted companion ever since, joining him whenever he can on the golf course or on the town, otherwise waiting for him in the bar with other middle-aged men. They may wait for hours sometimes, waiting and knowing that when he arrives he may wish to be alone. But it does not seem to matter, they are endlessly awed by him, moved by the mystique; he is a kind of male

Garbo. They know that he can be warm and loyal if they are sensitive to his wishes, but they must never be late for an appointment to meet him. One man, unable to find a parking place, arrived a half hour late once, and DiMaggio did not talk to him again for three months. They know, too, when dining at night with DiMaggio, that he generally prefers male companions and occasionally one or two young women, but never wives; wives gossip, wives complain, wives are trouble, and men wishing to remain close to DiMaggio must keep their wives at home.

When DiMaggio strolls into Reno's bar, the men wave and call out his name, and Reno Barsocchini smiles and announces, "Here's the Clipper!"—the "Yankee Clipper" being a nickname from his baseball days.

"Hey, Clipper, Clipper," Reno had said two nights before, "where you been, Clipper? . . . Clipper, how 'bout a belt?"

DiMaggio refused the offer of a drink, ordering instead a pot of tea, which he prefers to all other beverages except before a date, when he will switch to vodka.

"Hey, Joe," a sportswriter asked, a man researching a magazine piece on golf, "why is it that a golfer, when he starts getting older, loses his putting touch first? Like Snead and Hogan, they can still hit a ball well off the tee, but on the greens they lose the strokes."

"It's the pressure of age," DiMaggio said, turning around on his bar stool. "With age you get jittery. It's true of golfers; it's true of any man when he gets into his fifties. He doesn't take chances like he used to. The younger golfer, on the greens, he'll stroke his putts better. The older man, he becomes hesitant. A little uncertain. Shaky. When it comes to taking chances, the younger man, even when driving a car, will take chances that the older man won't."

"Speaking of chances," another man said, one of the group that had gathered around DiMaggio, "did you see that guy on crutches in here last night?"

"Yeah, had his leg in a cast," a third said. "Skiing."

"I would never ski," DiMaggio said. "Men who ski must be doing it to impress a broad. You see these men, some of them forty, fifty, getting onto skis. And later you see them all bandaged up, broken legs . . ."

"But skiing's a very sexy sport, Joe, all the clothes, the tight pants, the fireplace in the ski lodge, the bear rug—Christ, nobody goes to ski. They just go out there to get it cold so they can warm it up."

"Maybe you're right," DiMaggio said. "I might be persuaded."

"Want a belt, Clipper?" Reno asked.

DiMaggio thought for a second, then said, "All right—first belt tonight."

Now it was noon, a warm sunny day. DiMaggio's business meeting with the television retailers had gone well; he had made a strong appeal to George Shahood, president of Continental Television, Inc., which has eight retail outlets in northern California, to cut prices on color television sets and increase the sales volume, and Shahood had conceded it was worth a try. Then DiMaggio called Reno's bar to see if there were any messages, and now he was in Lefty O'Doul's car being driven along Fisherman's Wharf toward the Golden Gate Bridge en route to a golf course thirty miles upstate. Lefty O'Doul was one of the great hitters in the National League in the early thirties, and later he managed the San Francisco Seals when DiMaggio was the shining star. Though O'Doul is now sixty-nine, eighteen years older than DiMaggio, he neverthe-

less possesses great energy and spirit, is a hard-drinking, bois-
terous man with a big belly and roving eye; and when DiMaggio,
as they drove along the highway toward the golf club, noticed
a lovely blonde at the wheel of a car nearby and exclaimed,
"Look at *that* tomato!" O'Doul's head suddenly spun around,
he took his eyes off the road, and yelled, "Where, *where?*"
O'Doul's golf game is less than what it was—he used to have
a two-handicap—but he still shoots in the 80s, as does Di-
Maggio.

DiMaggio's drives range between 250 and 280 yards when
he doesn't sky them, and his putting is good, but he is distracted by a bad back that both pains him and hinders the full-
ness of his swing. On the first hole, waiting to tee off, DiMaggio
sat back watching a foursome of college boys ahead swinging
with such freedom. "Oh," he said with a sigh, "to have *their*
backs."

DiMaggio and O'Doul were accompanied around the golf
course by Ernie Nevers, the former football star, and two brothers who are in the hotel and movie-distribution business. They
moved quickly up and down the green hills in electric golf carts,
and DiMaggio's game was exceptionally good for the first nine
holes. But then he seemed distracted, perhaps tired, perhaps
even reacting to a conversation of a few minutes before. One of
the movie men was praising the film *Boeing, Boeing*, starring
Tony Curtis and Jerry Lewis, and the man asked DiMaggio if he
had seen it.

"No," DiMaggio said. Then he added, swiftly, "I haven't
seen a film in eight years."

DiMaggio hooked a few shots, was in the woods. He took
a No. 9 iron and tried to chip out. But O'Doul interrupted
DiMaggio's concentration to remind him to keep the face of
the club closed. DiMaggio hit the ball. It caromed off the side

of his club, went skipping like a rabbit through the high grass down toward a pond. DiMaggio rarely displays any emotion on a golf course, but now, without saying a word, he took his No. 9 iron and flung it into the air. The club landed in a tree and stayed up there.

"Well," O'Doul said, casually, "there goes *that* set of clubs."

DiMaggio walked to the tree. Fortunately, the club had slipped to the lower branch, and DiMaggio could stretch up on the cart and get it back.

"Every time I get advice," DiMaggio muttered to himself, shaking his head slowly and walking toward the pond, "I shank it."

Later, showered and dressed, DiMaggio and the others drove to a banquet about ten miles from the golf course. Somebody had said it was going to be an elegant dinner, but when they arrived they could see it was more like a county fair; farmers were gathered outside a big barnlike building, a candidate for sheriff was distributing leaflets at the front door, and a chorus of homely ladies was inside singing "You Are My Sunshine."

"How did we get sucked into this?" DiMaggio asked, talking out of the side of his mouth, as they approached the building.

"O'Doul," one of the men said. "It's his fault. Damned O'Doul can't turn *anything* down."

"Go to hell," O'Doul said.

Soon DiMaggio and O'Doul and Ernie Nevers were surrounded by the crowd, and the woman who had been leading the chorus came rushing over and said, "Oh, Mr. DiMaggio, it certainly is a pleasure having you."

"It's a pleasure being here, ma'am," he said, forcing a smile.

"It's too bad you didn't arrive a moment sooner; you'd have heard our singing."

"Oh, I heard it," he said, "and I enjoyed it very much."

"Good, good," she said. "And how are your brothers Dom and Vic?"

"Fine. Dom lives near Boston. Vince is in Pittsburgh."

"Why, *hello* there, Joe," interrupted a man with wine on his breath, patting DiMaggio on the back, feeling his arm. "Who's gonna take it this year, Joe?"

"Well, I have no idea," DiMaggio said.

"What about the Giants?"

"Your guess is as good as mine."

"Well, you can't count the Dodgers out," the man said.

"You sure can't," DiMaggio said.

"Not with all that pitching."

"Pitching is certainly important," DiMaggio said.

Everywhere he goes the questions seem the same, as if he has some special vision into the future of new heroes, and everywhere he goes, too, older men grab his hand and feel his arm and predict that he could still go out there and hit one, and the smile on DiMaggio's face is genuine. He tries hard to remain as he was—he diets, he takes steam baths, he is careful; and flabby men in the locker rooms of golf clubs sometimes steal peeks at him when he steps out of the shower, observing the tight muscles across his chest, the flat stomach, the long sinewy legs. He has a young man's body, very pale and little hair; his face is dark and lined, however, parched by the sun of several seasons. Still he is always an impressive figure at banquets such as this—an *immortal*, sportswriters called him, and that is how they have written about him and others like him, rarely suggesting that such heroes might ever be prone to the ills of mortal men, carousing, drinking, scheming; to suggest this would destroy the myth, would disillusion small boys, would infuriate rich men who own ball clubs and to whom baseball is a business dedicated to profit and in pursuit of which they trade mediocre players' flesh as casually as boys trade players' pictures on bubble-gum cards. And so the baseball hero must always act the part, must preserve the myth, and none does it better than DiMaggio; none is more patient when drunken old men grab an arm and ask, "Who's gonna take it this year, Joe?"

Two hours later, dinner and the speeches over, DiMaggio is slumped in O'Doul's car headed back to San Francisco. He edged himself up, however, when O'Doul pulled into a gas station in which a pretty red-haired girl sat on a stool, legs crossed, filing her fingernails. She was about twenty-two, wore a tight black skirt and tighter white blouse.

"Look at *that*," DiMaggio said.

"Yeah," O'Doul said.

O'Doul turned away when a young man approached, opened the gas tank, began wiping the windshield. The young man wore a greasy white uniform on the front of which was printed the name "Burt." DiMaggio kept looking at the girl, but she was not distracted from her fingernails. Then he looked at Burt, who did not recognize him. When the tank was full, O'Doul paid and drove off. Burt returned to his girl; DiMaggio slumped down in the front seat and did not open his eyes again until they had arrived in San Francisco.

"Let's go see Reno," DiMaggio said.

"No, I gotta go see my old lady," O'Doul said. So he dropped DiMaggio off in front of the bar, and a moment later Reno's voice was announcing in the smoky room, "Hey, here's the Clipper!" The men waved and offered to buy him a drink. DiMaggio ordered a vodka and sat for an hour at the bar talking to a half dozen men around him. Then a blonde girl who had been with friends at the other end of the bar came over, and somebody introduced her to DiMaggio. He bought her a drink, offered her a cigarette. Then he struck a match and held it. His hand was unsteady.

"Is that me that's shaking?" he asked.

"It must be," said the blonde. "I'm calm."

Two nights later, having collected his clothes out of Reno's back room, DiMaggio boarded a jet; he slept crossways on three seats, then came down the steps as the sun began to rise in Miami. He claimed his luggage and golf clubs, put them into the trunk of a waiting automobile, and less than an hour later he was being driven into Fort Lauderdale, past palm-lined streets, toward the Yankee Clipper Hotel.

"All my life it seems I've been on the road traveling," he said, squinting through the windshield into the sun. "I never get a sense of being in any one place."

Arriving at the Yankee Clipper Hotel, DiMaggio checked into the largest suite. People rushed through the lobby to shake hands with him, to ask for his autograph, to say, "Joe, you look great." And early the next morning, and for the next thirty mornings, DiMaggio arrived punctually at the baseball park and wore his uniform with the famous No. 5, and the tourists seated in the sunny grandstands clapped when he first appeared on the field each time, and then they watched with nostalgia as he picked up a bat and played "pepper" with the younger Yankees, some of whom were not even born when, twenty-five years ago this summer, he hit in fifty-six straight games and became the most cherished man in America.

But the younger spectators in the Fort Lauderdale park, and the sportswriters, too, were more interested in Mantle and Maris, and nearly every day there were news dispatches reporting how Mantle and Maris felt, what they did, what they said, even though they said and did very little except walk around the field frowning when photographers asked for another picture and when sportswriters asked how they felt.

After seven days of this, the big day arrived—Mantle and Maris would swing a bat—and a dozen sportswriters were gathered around the big batting cage that was situated beyond the left-field fence; it was completely enclosed in wire, meaning that no baseball could travel more than thirty or forty feet before being trapped in rope; still Mantle and Maris would be swinging, and this, in spring, makes news.

Mantle stepped in first. He wore black gloves to help prevent blisters, He hit right-handed against the pitching of a coach named Vern Benson, and soon Mantle was swinging hard, smashing line drives against the nets, going *ahhh ahhh* as he followed through with his mouth open.

Then Mantle, not wanting to overdo it on his first day, dropped his bat in the dirt and walked out of the batting cage. Roger Maris stepped in. He picked up Mantle's bat.

"This damn thing must be thirty-eight ounces," Maris said. He threw the bat down into the dirt, left the cage, and walked toward the dugout on the other side of the field to get a lighter bat.

DiMaggio stood among the sportswriters behind the cage, then turned when Vern Benson, inside the cage, yelled, "Joe, wanna hit some?"

"No chance," DiMaggio said.

"Com'on, Joe," Benson said.

The reporters waited silently. Then DiMaggio walked slowly into the cage and picked up Mantle's bat. He took his position at the plate, but obviously it was not the classic DiMaggio stance; he was holding the bat about two inches from the knob, his feet were not so far apart, and, when DiMaggio took a cut at Benson's first pitch, fouling it, there was none of that ferocious follow through, the blurred bat did not come whipping all the way around, the No. 5 was not stretched full across his broad back.

DiMaggio fouled Benson's second pitch, then he connected solidly with the third, the fourth, the fifth. He was just meeting the ball easily, however, not smashing it, and Benson called out, "I didn't know you were a choke hitter, Joe."

"I am now," DiMaggio said, getting ready for another pitch.

He hit three more squarely enough, and then he swung again and there was a hollow sound.

"Ohhh," DiMaggio yelled, dropping his bat, his fingers stung, "I was waiting for that one." He left the batting cage rubbing his hands together. The reporters watched him. Nobody said anything. Then DiMaggio said to one of them, not in anger nor in sadness, but merely as a simply stated fact, "There was a time when you couldn't get me out of there."

ARCHITECT OF THE FAIRWAYS
Golf, 1959

EVERYMAN'S PROGRESS IS beset daily by multitudinous little obstacles—the traffic light that turns red at the last moment, the sultry blonde who finally says no, the well-hit golf ball that seems headed for the green, bounces, then skips into the trap. Of course, most of life's obstacles, both real and imaginary, emanate from thousands of diverse sources—except in the game of golf, where many of the obstacles are created by one individual: a small, rather ubiquitous man named Robert Trent Jones. Mr. Jones is ranked by many experts as America's top golf course architect. During the last 25 years he has built or remodeled 250 courses, numerous creeks, and nearly 8000 traps.

To build his famous fairways and traps, Mr. Jones and his employees have had to cut through jungles, dynamite rocks, and stalk across swamps. In so doing they have uprooted alligators in Florida, elks in the Rockies, and snakes nearly everywhere. Once, while shaping a course in Canada, a large bear lumbered into Jones' hut, stole honey, and made a mess of the kitchen. On another occasion, as Jones was studying the contour of a new green at the Broadmoor Country Club, in Colorado Springs, Colorado, he casually turned around to find a huge mountain lion standing in the rough, watching him passively.

One of Jones' engineers was just about to take off, when Jones snapped: "Dammit, don't run!"

"Well, I'm going to walk damned fast!" said the other.

Jones and his engineer both took the longest strides of their lives toward the jeep, looking over their shoulders every second or so to see if they were being followed.

"He's still looking at us, but he hasn't moved," said Jones, as he whirled the jeep around, and sped in the other direction. Nobody back at the motel believed the tale, of course, until it was learned that a lion had escaped from the local zoo. To this day the ninth hole at Broadmoor is known as "Jones' Lion Hole."

Jones, who is as controversial a figure as Frank Lloyd Wright, has often been regarded as a predatory creature by many of golf's chronic complainers and paranoiacs. They have preferred to view him as a sadistic architect who designs tough courses and then settles back gleefully to watch other people swinging futilely in sand traps, flinging their clubs in frustration, and never leaving the hole with less than a double-bogey.

The resentment against Robert Trent Jones' design was never more passionately expressed than at the United States Open in 1951, at the Oakland Hills Country Club, outside Detroit. Before the start of the tournament, it was decided that the old course needed remodeling, that it was no longer a challenge for the pros who, in this age of ultra-powerful equipment, were over-shooting the traps. So Mr. Jones was hired to re-arrange the course. Strategically moving the traps back and arranging them on the flanks of the fairways, he placed them in just the right spots to lure all but the perfect down-the-middle drives. He actually created 75 traps along the fairways and another 75 around the greens. For the tournament pros, it was a weekend of diabolical madness.

With the slightest hook or slice, their drives were being swallowed up by Jones' new traps. And the professionals were infuriated. In the clubhouse afterwards they fussed, fumed, and fretted.

"Did you *ever* see such a damned, stupid golf course in all your life?" asked one. "What's this Jones trying to do? What the hell's that trap doing on the fairway on the fifteenth?"

In one moment of creativity, Robert Trent Jones had placed a trap on the fairway of the remodeled fifteenth hole, a dog-leg that formerly was a pushover par-four. Jones made it an excruciatingly tough par-four. It seemed that nearly the whole field was in that trap at one time or another. In the third round, even Ben Hogan landed there.

During the four rounds of the Open, only two players broke the par of 70—Clayton Heafner, the runner-up, who had a 69; and Ben Hogan, the winner, with a 67, both on the final day. (Hogan played the trap short on the fifteenth in the final round.)

When it was over, Jones was elated. He was elated because the course was an honest test of true golfing skill. Not one golfer among the final field of fifty was a dark-horse; the course had beaten all but the genuinely top-ranked 50 players before the weekend, and during the third and fourth rounds the course was a grand test of skill for the 50 contenders. The course was designed so that on each of the 18 holes the pro had to use every club in his bag, had to try every shot in golf.

"Hogan's 67 saved my face," Jones admitted afterwards. "Hogan proved that, if you played great golf, it could be done at Oakland Hills, too."

Robert Trent Jones is a friendly, moderately tweedy man of fifty-three. He has large, alert eyes; is endlessly articulate; and has a wide, round face that is relatively free of pouches, crevasses or hummocks. He plays a fine game of golf, and rarely becomes irritated—even when he lands in his own traps, which he occasionally does. On his better days he is in the 70's.

While he does not find it necessary to defend himself against his critics, he has long felt that golf courses were getting too soft, and that the modern game, with its lively ball and power-built clubs, did not require the skill that golf required when Bobby Jones and Walter Hagen were in their heyday. Thus, Jones constructed all his traps at distances of 220-or-more yards from the tee—where they would obstruct the long-hitting golfers' imperfect drives but would not punish the Sunday golfer, whose drives would not reach that distance.

As much as anything else, however, Robert Trent Jones strives to design and build courses that are aesthetically pleasing to the eye. By plane, train, rowboat and mule he travels over 150,000 miles a year inspecting dreamy sites upon which to build courses. One of the most gorgeous jobs he has done is the Dorado Beach Golf Club, in Puerto Rico, a picturesque and grand course that cost Laurence Rockefeller $1,000,000 for 18 holes. Currently it is being expanded to a 36-hole course. The third and fifth greens of the latter course are designed to curl around a yacht basin, and it is thus possible for some vacationing plutocrats to chip toward the green from their yachts. This course was especially expensive because it had to be built in swampland. Normally, a Jones-built course would run anywhere from $250,000 to $400,000 these days, and would take close to a year to complete.

Jones' courses are sprawled from Colorado to Connecticut and down to Caracas. Collectively they are designed to be enjoyed by the 90-to-100 golfer, and to provide challenges to the long-hitting, skilled golfers. He believes the toughest hole he ever built is the eleventh at Augusta, a par-four. Until Jones redesigned it five years ago, it was a relatively straight, uncomplicated hole. But Jones moved the tee back 50 yards or so, and then created a formidable lake along the left flank of the green. This hole has been a horrible mess to many tournament professionals since then, and it is general knowledge that, under pressure, some of the nation's leading golfers have taken eights and nines there.

The most scenic courses he has worked on during the last decade are, in addition to Dorado, the Ponte Vedra Club, with its ninth green a small island in a lagoon; the Air Force Academy Golf Course, in Colorado; Coral Ridge Country Club, Fort Lauderdale, Florida; Cotton Bay Club, in Eleuthera, Bahamas; and the Houston Country Club, in Texas. The toughest hole among these six courses, he says, is the fifth hole at Coral Ridge. "It's the only hole of its kind in the world," he says, "because there are 300 ways of playing it. It's horseshoe-shaped from tee to green, and has hills and trees forming the semi-circle between the tee and green. You might try to shoot over the hazards, or might decide to go around them; at any rate, there are dozens of perfectly good (and bad) ways to play that hole."

Robert Trent Jones was born in 1906 to Welsh parents in Ince, England, a long par-five from Liverpool. When he was four years old, his parents emigrated to East Rochester, New York, where, like many youths of his period, he became captivated by Rochester's new golfing hero, Walter Hagen. Jones caddied and played golf after school and, at sixteen he shot a 69 to win an amateur tournament sponsored by the Rochester Journal-American. He certainly seemed well on his way to a successful golf future when, to the surprise of everyone who knew him, he developed a duodenal ulcer. Jones never seemed the worrisome type; on the contrary, he seemed like a somnolent, unambitious youth. At any rate, his tournament hopes for the future were thwarted.

For a while he held down a totally uninspiring job as a draftsman in a Rochester office, but he quit to hunt for something more creative. All the while, he had thoughts of becoming a golf course architect, but getting an education in such a special field was difficult. However, in 1926 he finally talked his way into Cornell where, as a student interested only in golf courses, he studied landscape architecture, horticulture, hydraulics, agronomy, economics and chemistry.

There was nothing America needed less in those days than a golf course architect. It was during the depression. When Jones left Cornell, he nevertheless began to seek his fortune. He got a job as a junior partner with the eminent Canadian golf course architect, the late Stanley Thompson, and his first assignment was in his hometown of Rochester to build the Midvale Golf Club. He plowed the fairways with 32 horses and 200 men. It took him four months to complete the course. He was then twenty-four. He was patted on the head by club members for doing a fine job. They would have loved to pay him for his work, but soon afterwards the club went bankrupt.

Next he took on assignments in Syracuse and Ithaca, but these two clubs also went broke, and it was fortunate for Jones in those days that he was sleeping, and free-loading, at his parents' home in Rochester.

It was only a last-ditch idea that saved Jones in 1935, and got him started as a money-maker. He convinced some Works Progress Administration officials that instead of having unemployed men rake only leaves, why not have them rake golf courses? He convinced them that the construction of public courses would be of durable value; and, with federal funds, he was able to build six public courses within the next four years—two in St. Charles, Illinois; four in New York State.

When the nation was back in the chips, and private courses were again being built, Jones and Thompson broke up their partnership; by mutual agreement, Thompson built his courses in Canada, and Jones stuck to the United States.

Robert Trent Jones, who is one of 15 recognized golf course architects now working in America, preferred building his courses on the linksland; that is, the sandy area along the coast hard by the ocean side. This terrain is ideal for grass and beautiful courses, and it was on such ground that the Scots began the game of golf. Like many purists, Jones regards only seaside courses as "links;" all other golf courses, though generally known as golf links, are strictly courses to Jones.

"The shepherds of Scotland began playing along these big patches of grass and dunes," Jones says. "And the natural bunkers and sand dunes along the linksland were our first traps. Nowadays, when we build a golf course, we're merely duplicating the natural appearance of the linksland."

Duplicating the linksland of Scotland has invariably called for unlimited imagination, since Jones frequently has been asked to build courses on rocky hills, through woodlands, and within deserts. The toughest job he was ever assigned was the course at West Point, New York, which was begun after World War II with the funds generally earned by the Blanchard-Davis football teams. Jones and 200 workers had to work through swampland and timber, removing rocks the size of Cadillacs. Only nine holes have ever been completely finished. Football money ran short.

Jones, who has a staff of three landscape architects, two civil engineers and three draftsmen, follows five steps in building a course. First, he inspects the site on foot. Then he has the area photographed from an airplane, to further examine the topography. Third, he lays out the course on paper. Then he has a clay course, built to scale, made and laid out; by this time he has solved his drainage and irrigation problems. Finally, he starts on the last—and most difficult—phase: the actual construction. His bulldozers and trucks are grinding away from sun-up to sun-set, and soon the whole course begins to take shape. Occasionally some visiting club members will criticize certain holes, claiming perhaps that they are too long for a par-three. On more than one occasion Jones has then gone into his car, fetched a club and ball, and tested the hole. He has executed some of his finest shots under these conditions—once scoring a hole-in-one with skeptical members grouped behind him.

Robert Trent Jones is on the go 250 days a year inspecting land, plotting traps, and supervising the creation of new golf courses. Business has never been better. Currently he is building ten new courses and has plans for fifteen more when he has the time. He does very little advertising. He does not have to.

When he is not traveling, he lives a quiet suburban life in Montclair, New Jersey, with his wife and two sons—Robert Trent, Jr., a 20-year-old Yale sophomore who has a two handicap; and Rees, seventeen, a ten-handicap player on the Montclair High golf team. The Joneses talk golf incessantly to anyone willing to listen.

Robert Trent Jones has rather grandiose plans for the future. He hopes to build a golf mecca in Florida consisting of five courses—each course characteristically different from the other, but all five situated in the same area. One course would possess the subtle plateaus and lawnlike features of Augusta, while a second course would be a mass of sandy traps, like Pine Valley. A third course would have dunes and sandtraps patterned after the Merion Golf Club's course in Ardmore, Pennsylvania, while a fourth would feature tremendously wide and rolling greens like the famous old St. Andrews course in Scotland. The fifth course would have water hazards and hills, but otherwise it would be a real dream. No traps.

ERIC AND BETH HEIDEN: A BOND OF BLOOD ON SKATES

The *New York Times*, 1980

SPEED SKATING IS an esoteric sport that is artfully per-formed in America by only a few dozen frozen fanatics who dwell along the Great Lakes and drive their bent bodies around an oval rink with such power and detached determi-nation that they are not always aware of the blood that some-times oozes out of their feet and stains the inner lining of their boots.

While this bleeding could be reduced or eliminated if the skaters wore heavy wool socks or inserted soft padding around their ankles and toes, most young Spartans of the sport insist on wearing only nylon socks—or no socks at all—because it allows them more intimate contact with the ice, a varying sur-face that they sense through their blades as surely as a violinist feels vibrations through his bow.

Indeed, the long racing blade is a kind of bow, an ancillary instrument that cuts across the ice with angled precision; and, as the various woods of a violin are tempered by the process through which the violin is formed, so is the ice affected by the elements within the water, and this in turn influences the performance of the skaters upon it.

Ice that is created from the pure mountain streams of Northern Europe or the Soviet Union freezes into a smooth fast surface that the skaters cross with relative ease, whereas the ice formed from the polluted waters of the Great Lakes is coarse and slow, forcing Americans to compensate with extra drive and perseverance if they wish to rival the records set on the crystalline rinks of foreign lands. A skater who can excel on the ice of the Great Lakes region can excel on ice anywhere in the world, a fact substantiated by the achievements in recent years of a remarkable young man from Wisconsin named Eric Heiden.

Three years ago, as an obscure 18-year-old premedical student enrolled at the University of Wisconsin, Eric Heiden traveled overseas to test his athletic talent against Scandinavians, Russians, Germans and others who were competing in the world men's speed-skating championship before 18,000 spectators in the Dutch city of Heerenveen. After four grueling races that ranged from the 500-meter sprint (which is less than a third of a mile) to the 10,000-meter marathon (which is more than six miles), Eric Heiden astonished everyone by compiling the best aggregate time in the four events—and he thus became world champion.

It was the first time since 1891 that an American man had been so honored; and as Eric Heiden, a broad-shouldered 6-footer with dazzling dark eyes and casually cut long brown hair, stood in the arena hearing the crowd's applause, and as he later joined other skaters in a Dutch tavern and tilted steins of beer in acknowledging their toasts, he felt that it was all part of a dream, a wondrous fantasy that would fade before dawn.

His self-doubt, however, was dispelled by his success in several subsequent races in other European cities, and in the 1978 competition in Sweden, Heiden again won the world title. In the 1979 world championships in Norway, he gained the title a third time, and his speed and style so impressed the Norwegians—who are possibly more enthusiastic about speed skating than Americans are about football or baseball—that he was adopted as a Nordic folk hero.

His wholesome profile appeared on the front pages of newspapers and the back sides of milk cartons. Recording artists dedicated songs to him; a Norwegian publishing firm distributed a hardcover biography about him; American diplomats overseas, most of whom had never heard of Eric Heiden until reading about him in the foreign press, proclaimed him an Honorary American Ambassador to the Kingdom of Norway and induced President Carter to write Heiden a letter of congratulations.

When touring members of a Soviet wrestling team visited Wisconsin, they identified the city of Madison not as the capital of the state but as the birthplace of Eric Heiden. They were also aware that he had exhibited his skill before Soviet officials in the Soviet Union's elaborate Medeo Sports Center in the mountains of Alma Ata, near the Chinese border. The rarefied water of Alma Ata produces a rink as clear as Baccarat crystal, as smooth as vodka, and its surface is considered the fastest in the world. Heiden shared that opinion after he had taken a few spins around the 400-meter oval at speeds approaching 35 miles an hour, which was more than 10 miles an hour faster than the world's swiftest runners and was nearly as quick as the 40 m.p.h. pace of top thoroughbred race horses.

But Heiden's technique is close to inimitable, relying as it does on his long and muscular legs, developed and strengthened on the resistant Midwestern ice, his powerful heart and lungs, his dancer's sense of balance, his willingness to hurl his 185-pound body into the sharp curves of the oval rink and thus gain speed on the turns that enables him to cover the distance of more than five football fields in less than 40 seconds.

For all his energy and effort, Heiden hardly seems winded at the end of a race, even after the arduous 10,000-meter test. Due primarily to his superior stamina, many Olympic officials and competitors predict that Eric Heiden will win as many as four or even five gold medals at Lake Placid in the next two weeks.

Unlike the rules that obtain in the annual world championships, in which the winner's time is based on his performance in four events—the 500, 1,500, 5,000 and 10,000 meters—the Olympics rules award a gold medal to the fastest skater in each of those four events as well as a fifth race, the 1,000 meters. If Heiden loses any of these five Olympic races at Lake Placid, according to the sport's parka-clad cognoscenti, it will probably be in one of the shorter races—if he slips during one of his derring-do turns. In the longer races, no one in the world should be able to match his drive and audacity on the slippery surface.

But should an unforeseen mishap prevent Heiden from fulfilling this prognosis, the American speed-skating team of 17 skaters, 10 from Wisconsin, will look to the women's squad for the gathering of gold medals. And here, too, the most prominent individual on the list is named Heiden. She is Eric's 20-year-old sister, Beth, a petite green-eyed blonde whose size-6 feet on 16-inch blades carried her to the world overall title for women last year in the Netherlands. Winning all four events, from the 500 to the 3,000 meters, she became the first American woman to do that in 43 years. Last month, she finished second over all.

A foot shorter than the 6-foot-1-inch Eric, and 80 pounds lighter, Beth Heiden is built like a gymnast; and except for those days when awesome winds threaten to sweep her slim figure off the edge of the ice while she is navigating a turn, her lack of weight is never a handicap because she is so superbly conditioned and gifted as an athlete.

Not surprisingly, Beth and Eric Heiden—sometimes refered to by Wisconsin sportswriters as the Donnie and Marie of speed skating—are the progeny of Midwestern health culturists and outdoor enthusiasts. Their parents, Nancy and Jack Heiden, met in Wisconsin during the mid-1950's as members of a local ski club, and they courted on the slopes. In addition to Jack Heiden's proficiency in skiing and skating, bicycling and running, he was an intercollegiate fencing champion at the University of Wisconsin; and after graduating in 1958 from the university's medical school, he became an orthopedic surgeon specializing in sports medicine. Now, in his off-hours, he devotes some of his time to sharpening his children's blades.

Nancy Heiden, the mother of Eric and Beth, who is affectionately regarded by them as a kind of macho feminist who can be as assertive in the kitchen as on an athletic field, is the ruddy, 44-year-old daughter of a robust physical education instructor in Madison named Art Thomsen; and it was this man, along with the skaters' parents, who guided the future world champions onto the ice as infants, watched them toddle and fall on the ponds near the Heiden home, and in time saw them grow into graceful performers who could spin and speed on the ice with a control uncommon even among the agile offspring of Wisconsin's lake people.

In 1972, the young Heidens' development was influenced

further by the arrival in town of a 20-year-old scholarship student at the University of Wisconsin named Dianne Holum, an Olympic speed skating gold medalist earlier that year in Sapporo, Japan. Volunteering to coach a speed-skating club in Madison when she was not preoccupied with her college classes in physical education, Miss Holum gradually became impressed by the talent of Eric and Beth Heiden, who were not yet teen-agers; and they were already impressed with Holum, having seen her skate on television during the Olympics.

Thrilled that they had a television celebrity in their midst, the young Heidens—whose dedication to television watching in those days challenged their devotion to speed skating—suddenly sought Miss Holum's approval, responded to her encouragement, and within four years they had both become members of the United States Olympic team.

While they were perhaps premature participants in the 1976 Olympics at Innsbruck—the 17-year-old Eric finished 19th in the 5,000 meters and seventh in the 1,500, and 16-year-old Beth was 11th in the women's 3,000—neither was discouraged by the experience, and within a year both had sufficiently improved to catch their competitors by surprise.

Last year, they dropped out of college temporarily to concentrate on their skating. Now, as they appear at Lake Placid as world champions, they will hear for the first time the cheering of thousands of spectators in their own language, in their own land.

THE KICK SHE MISSED

The following piece is an excerpt from Talese's 2006 book A
Writer's Life. *In it, Talese recounts his life as a journalist, including writing about sports for various publications. He also details the fits and starts of a writer seeking his next big book. For
a time, he thought his subject would be Liu Ying, a Chinese soccer player who missed an important goal in the 1999 women's
World Cup.*

MR

SINCE THE CHINESE won the coin toss, they were the
first to send a kicker onto the field. She was a round-faced,
ponytailed brunette who wore the number 5 and seemed to be
a bit taller and sturdier than her characteristically petite teammates. She was not, however, as imposing in appearance as the
burly 150-pound black American goalkeeper who stood in
front of her, staring at her, although the Chinese girl paid little
attention as she slowly lowered the ball with both hands and

positioned it on the white grass spot that marked the twelve-yard target site. She was said to be China's most reliable penalty kicker, which was why the coach had assigned her ahead of the others, expecting her to get his team off to a good start. She was also functioning with full energy, since she had not played long in today's heat, having entered the game as a substitute late in the second overtime. After hearing the referee's whistle, she charged the ball and kicked it so swiftly and surely that the American goalie could only watch it sail high over her own right shoulder into the left corner of the net. As the kicker's teammates and the coaches clapped along the sidelines, China took a 1–0 lead.

The first American kicker was the team captain, wearing number 4, a lanky chestnut-haired woman with delicately refined facial features and the reputation for being an indelicate and indefatigable defender. But she would also prove to be a surefooted kicker on this occasion, unhesitatingly attacking the ball and driving it low and hard past China's goalie into the opposite side of the net that the first Chinese kicker had hit. Jubilantly, after watching her ball slam into the cords, the American pumped her fist in the air and then jogged back to the sidelines while most of the stadium's crowd stood cheering and her teammates came forward to embrace her. The score was now 1–1.

The second Chinese kicker was a slender brunette who wore number 15. She had seen action earlier in the game as a substitute and was not a key player on the team except in times like this. She was an excellent penalty kicker. Some of her teammates considered her the equal of their premier penalty converter, the surefire number 5. I had read that there were some fine players among the Chinese—and among the Americans and other teams, as well—who had stage fright when confronting penalty-kick situations. They were more comfortable running

262

and kicking while surrounded by crowds of scrambling opponents than they were when standing alone behind an unmoving ball spotted on the grass and having to boot it twelve yards toward a spacious net that was guarded by a solitary defender in a one-on-one matchup being scrutinized by every fan in the stadium and perhaps millions of watchers on television. There were players who practically begged their coaches not to select them for the penalty spotlight, which could subject them to such vast humiliation should their booted ball be blocked or, worse, should they fail to hit the net.

But the second kicker for China, the reputably unflappable number 15, was known within the team as being a rather narcissistic young woman who welcomed as much attention as she could get and was a very focused performer when all eyes were upon her; and so after she had taken her running start and had struck the ball cleanly to her left, she paused to watch with apparent satisfaction as it glided beyond the goalie's fingertips and went crashing into the cords, bringing smiles from her coach and her teammates, if not from the overwhelmingly pro-American assemblage in the stands. Then she turned around and trotted back to the sidelines in an unhurried stride that suggested to me both self-assurance and a lingering interest in being watched. And so China had regained the lead, 2–1.

The second kicker for the United States was also known for exhibiting poise under pressure, and, while not renowned for being self-absorbed, she acquitted herself well when in center-stage situations. She was a thirty-one-year-old Californian who wore number 14 and had been a U.S. team leader for nearly a decade, having taken leave from the sport only intermittently to bear two children and to recover from a broken right leg suffered while competing in 1995. Although her forte was defense—it was she who singularly stopped the Chinese from scoring during this game's first overtime by leaping into the net to deflect a shot that had sailed over the head of the U.S. goalkeeper—she was also formidable on the attack, having scored the third goal in her team's 3–2 triumph over Germany during the quarter-final round of this World Cup. Now, as a penalty kicker, she approached the ball slowly but with practiced deliberation and deception, freezing the Chinese goalkeeper in a fixed position near the middle of the box while the ball soared into the net yards beyond the goalie's upraised left hand. And so the score was again tied, 2–2.

The third kicker for China was a twenty-five-year-old native of Beijing who had close-cropped black hair and a straight-lined figure, and she wore the number 13. She had been a member of the national squad for six years, and a starting player for the past two, developing into a scoring threat as well as a steadfast defender. Her versatility and diligence meant that, except when she was injured, she was not replaced by a substitute if the score was close, and on this afternoon in the Rose Bowl, she had been active during each and every minute of this long and debilitating test of wills and tenacity.

As she prepared for her penalty kick—the announcer introduced her as Liu Ying, it being one of the few Chinese names I could pronounce—she was being watched by the stout and sturdy American goalkeeper, Briana Scurry, who stood waiting twelve yards in front of her in a crouched and challenging stance. Briana Scurry had been a youth-league football player in her hometown of Minneapolis, and later a high school trackster and basketball player as well as an outstanding performer in this sport of soccer, for which she would win a scholarship to the University of Massachusetts. Beginning in 1994, she would achieve whatever distinction went with being the one black woman on the otherwise all-white starting lineup of the U.S. national team. She once described herself to a reporter as "the fly in the milk." In a *New York Times* article that was published a few weeks *after* this game, she recalled that when the third Chinese kicker, the aforementioned Liu Ying, had positioned herself behind the ball, "Her body language didn't look very positive. It didn't look like she wanted to take it. I looked up at her and said, 'This one is mine.'"

The *Times* article also reported that during this crucial moment, Briana Scurry had decided to try to limit Liu Ying's effectiveness by defending against her improperly, moving forward a couple of steps in front of the net even *before* Liu Ying's foot had touched the ball, reducing the angle of the kick. This was a goalkeeper's ploy that Briana Scurry and other teams' goalies occasionally resorted to, hoping it would offset some of the disadvantage of being on the receiving end of what goalkeepers often compare to Russian roulette. Sometimes the referee's whistle signaled a goalkeeper's unauthorized movement, allowing the shooter a second chance if the ball had not gone into the net. At other times the referees failed to see, or were too uncertain to confidently call, an infraction; it was frequently very difficult to determine if a goalkeeper *had* stepped forward a split second before the kicker's toe had touched the ball. With regard to Briana Scurry in the Rose Bowl, it appeared to some reporters and other onlookers that she had moved forward ahead of time against the *first* Chinese penalty kicker, number 5, but there had been no whistle—and number 5 had made her shot anyway.

But China's third kicker, Liu Ying, was less fortunate. Her shot was not well hit. Her footwork seemed to be tentative during her approach. Perhaps she was distracted by Scurry's movement, if the latter *had* moved too early. There had not been a whistle. Still, Scurry instinctively sensed or rightly guessed that the ball would be coming to her left side, and as it sailed off Liu Ying's right foot, Scurry was already leaping toward it, her outstretched body surging through the air parallel to the ground with both of her arms fully extended and the fingers of her gloved hands elongated and rigid until being bent back by the force of the ball, which was nevertheless deflected and sent bouncing inconsequentially toward the sidelines.

As Scurry fell heavily to the turf—she said later that as she lay in pain she feared she'd chipped a hipbone and mangled a stomach muscle—she was immediately revived by the applause that surrounded her and the sight of far-flung confetti and the enthusiasm of her teammates jumping and hugging one another near the bench. Scurry leaped to her feet and pumped her arms several times while the captain of the U.S. team raised her own index finger above her high-browed forehead, signaling perhaps that the Americans were now alone at the top.

If this was the captain's intention, it was a premature gesture. The game was not over. It was true, however, that if all the remaining shooters (the three Americans and the two Chinese) were successful, the final tally would favor the Americans, 5–4, and the World Cup trophy would become the property of the United States.

Ultimately, this is what happened. China's last two kickers—number 7 and number 9—both aimed accurately beyond Scurry's reach, the first player shooting to the right, the second to the left. But the trio of Americans—which included Mia Hamm, who shot fourth—were also flawless. The American who made the fifth and decisive kick was number 6, Brandi Chastain, a ponytailed blond Californian with a suntanned and gracefully delineated muscular figure that *Gear* magazine had photographed in the nude ("Hey, I ran my ass off for this body" was her response to the media; "I'm proud of it"). After she had blasted her winning shot to the left side of the lunging Chinese goalkeeper, Chastain pulled off her shirt and fell to her knees in front of the net, wearing a black sports bra as she clenched her fists in a triumphant pose that would make the cover of the next issue of *Newsweek* under the headline GIRLS RULE!

I stood in front of my television set without elation as the victorious U.S. team continued to celebrate on the field, and I kept watching as the roving eye of the camera zoomed in on the stadium's multitudes of American revelers with their smiling and patriotically painted faces and their party hats and horns, embracing and kissing—it was a midsummer prelude to New Year's Eve, and overlooking the scene was a big balloon, the Goodyear blimp. But my own thoughts were now concentrated on an individual who had disappeared from the screen, the young woman from China, Liu Ying, who had missed her kick.

I imagined her at this moment sitting tearfully in the locker room. Nothing in the life of this young woman of twenty-five could have prepared her for what she must have been feeling, for never in the history of China had a single person so suddenly been embarrassed in front of *so many* people—including 100 million from her home country. Was she surrounded now in the locker room by sympathetic teammates? Was she sitting in isolation after being rebuked by her coach? Was the coach at fault for selecting her as a kicker when he might have known that she was too physically exhausted and mentally distracted to meet the test? Would the bureaucrats who ruled over the Party's sports apparatus soon replace the coach? If he retained his job, and if Liu Ying were not demoted from the national team, would the coach choose her in the future to take a penalty kick in an important game?

I was asking questions as if I were a born-again sportswriter with access to the locker room, and if I were, *she* would have been my story, she who would probably not sleep tonight and might forever be haunted by the remembrance of her woeful moment in the sun while much of the world was watching. Or was I overdramatizing, overstating the sensibilities of this young athlete? Among the supposed strengths of a successful athlete is the capacity to overcome one's shortcomings and mistakes by not dwelling upon them, by not obsessing over them, by *forgetting* them, and—quoting the tiresome term of the 1990s—moving on. And yet it seemed to me that Liu Ying's failed penalty kick was momentous and heartrending in ways well beyond the blown save by Mariano Rivera of the Yankees, and even the pounding humiliation that I can recall watching decades ago as it was being inflicted by Muhammad Ali upon Floyd Patterson.

Losing the 1999 World Cup soccer title to the Americans when China was simmering with political tension, rivalry, and resentment toward the United States lent significance to this World Cup match that it would not have otherwise warranted, and it brought forth wishful expectations and nationalistic passions within the Chinese population that would not be gratified by the conclusion of this game. I could not imagine a longer and more uncomfortable airplane ride than the one scheduled to transfer this player and her teammates from Los Angeles back to Beijing. In China, where it is acknowledged that most parents lack enthusiasm for the birth of females, what amount of enthusiasm would greet this particular female when she returned to her homeland? What would her family say to her? What would I say were she my daughter? What would be the response from the people who lived in her neigh-

THE SILENT SEASON OF A HERO

borhood, and from the men who headed the regime's sports commission?

The television cameras focused on the Americans receiving their medals. It was now nearly 6:45 P.M. I had been watching television for about five and a half hours. I was restive. My wife was still upstairs reading. Her door was closed. She had called down earlier, requesting that I lower the sound coming from the television. She also suggested that we dine out in a restaurant that night, but not before 8:30. I was about to turn off the program, but hesitated. Usually after a major sporting event—a World Series game, a championship prizefight, tennis from Wimbledon, the Super Bowl—the losing competitors were invited to the microphones to offer their views and explanations concerning the outcome. I was hoping to hear something from the Chinese, especially from Liu Ying. But the network terminated its World Cup broadcast shortly after 6:45 without a word from her and without any information about how she was bearing up.

Why did I care? Why did I quietly think about her throughout dinner while I listened listlessly to my wife and a few of our friends who had joined our table at Elaine's? Why was I so disappointed and displeased the following morning after I had perused several newspaper articles about the game and learned nothing that I wanted to know about Liu Ying? Later in the week when the newsmagazine cover stories that featured the World Cup also failed to include even a brief interview with her, or any information that would satisfy my curiosity about her, I telephoned an important editor I knew named Norman Pearlstine, who oversaw the publication of Time Warner's many periodicals—among them *Sports Illustrated*, *Time*, and *People*— and I asked if he might consider ordering a story in one of his magazines that would describe how the Chinese people had responded to Liu Ying's return, and how she herself had reacted and was reacting to her Rose Bowl experience, and, finally, what if anything this had to say about contempory attitudes and expectations with regard to young women in a changing China.

If I was sounding a bit lofty on the phone as I impersonated being an editor to one of the most savvy and successful editors in New York, it did not greatly concern me. I was sixty-seven. He was maybe fifty. At my advanced age, I have become accustomed to being indulged by younger people, many of them no doubt encouraged by the fact that they will not have to indulge me much longer. And so I let Norman Pearlstine indulge me. I elaborated and digressed without any interruption on his part, and while at no point did he commit himself or even pass judgment on my idea, he also voiced no objection when I volunteered to send him a memo expressing my thoughts in writing.

I faxed him at once.

Dear Norman:

As I was saying on the phone, I believe that last week's single blocked kick of the Chinese World Cup soccer player, Liu Ying, might provide us with a story angle by which we may measure China and the United States in ways well beyond the realm of sports competition.

There's a photo in today's *New York Times* showing President Clinton greeting the triumphant American women in the White House. How did China's officials greet the Chinese women after their return to their homeland? Who was at the airport? . . . the story should be told through this one woman,

Liu Ying, a step-by-step account of how her life has gone since her foot failed her in the Rose Bowl.

Back in the 1950s I began my *Times* career as a sportswriter, and I've always found losers' locker rooms as learning experiences; and I think that the losing effort by the Chinese women last week in California might tell us a lot about our comparative societies.

I'd be happy to assist if you and your other colleagues think I can. I could assist your China-based correspondents with an interview, or sidebar writing, or whatever.

I'd surely be interested in visiting the mainland if you think I'll be a help . . . so after you have had time to think it through, let me know. . . .

After I had faxed the memo, I wished that I had deleted the last two paragraphs. My phone call had been entirely prompted (or so I told myself) by my desire to have my idea accepted by Pearlstine, with the assumption that he would later turn it over to be developed and written by members of his organization. In a sense, I had been doing him a favor. I had come up with an uncommon approach to a story that the rest of the press had apparently overlooked, and I was giving it to him gratis.

But at the end of my fax I had gracelessly insinuated myself into the assignment, promoting the notion that Pearlstine might like to send me halfway around the world (at his expense) so that I might "assist" his China-based correspondents with my story idea. How utterly *stupid* of me to propose that! If his China-based correspondents needed my assistance, they were unqualified for their jobs and should be fired. I was also appalled by the tone of false modesty in my final paragraph and the obviousness of my opportunism in seeking to take professional advantage of my personal relationship with the magazine czar at Time Warner. It is one thing to make a suggestion and quite another to belatedly try to horn in on an assignment or reappropriate a story idea after I had relinquished my proprietary claim to it with my call soliciting Pearlstine's help in publicizing what was of interest to me.

Maybe I was making too much of this, I reasoned, and for all I knew Pearlstine had liked my memo, and had already forwarded it with his approval down to one of his magazines, and soon I would be consulted by the corporation's travel department, asking me how soon I could leave for China.

A few days later I received a call from a high-ranking Time Warner executive who explained that Norman Pearlstine was traveling but that the editors had found my idea very interesting and were grateful that I had contacted them about it. Even though they would not be using it, he assured me that they were sincere in wanting me to continue sending them ideas in the future. I promised that I would.

As I hung up, I was quite disappointed, but also relieved. China was very far away. I had my overdue book to deal with. The World Cup was yesterday's news. Liu Ying had invaded my thoughts for more than a week, and now I could thank the Time Warner people for bringing me to my senses. Who wanted to read anything centered on a little Chinese soccer maiden who could not kick straight? The twenty-first century was upon us, and I had new things to think about.

If this was the case, why did I soon find myself on a jet airplane flying toward China (at my own expense, without an assignment, and without knowing where in that vast country I might find Liu Ying), anticipating my rendezvous with her?

THE GREATEST

EVEN THOUGH HE was entering his mid-sixties, Gay
Talese still reported like a young man, jumping on planes
at the last minute, flying around the world, hanging out with
characters for long stretches. But in the eyes of the New York
magazine world, the alleged inventor of new journalism was
now something of an old man. His instincts to run away from
news, to examine the lives of unknown people, or famous people well into the down slope of their lives, were seen as quaint
relics. The focus now: the celebrity of the moment, the man in
the news, the latest scandal, the "here's the story that matters to
your life right now."

Talese learned this lesson painfully in trying to publish what
he believes is his greatest magazine piece—"Ali in Havana,"
about Muhammad Ali's 1996 trip to Cuba to meet Fidel Castro.
The piece had originally been assigned by the *Nation*, but when
Talese delivered a story that began with an extended scene of
two men haggling over cigars and then moseyed around the island from the point of view of all the characters surrounding

Ali, the magazine backed away. "Over the hill," Talese thought. "I was finished."

Tina Brown at the *New Yorker* took a pass. So did *GQ*. And *Sports Illustrated*. *New York Times Magazine* editors didn't believe the dialogue between Ali's entourage and Castro. "Castro doesn't talk like that," the editors told him. Talese knew Castro did talk like that, and to be sure he had writen the dialogue verbatim, having gone to a CBS studio to review tape of the meeting, which *60 Minutes* had filmed. The *Times* passed anyway. *Rolling Stone* balked. *Commentary* turned it down. *Esquire,* his old home, was interested, but they wanted to delete the opening scene. Talese pronounced that ridiculous. "I was very upset about all this and I was surprised but in retrospect it was an awakening that whatever reputation I had in journalism schools or magazine writing courses was based on the past," Talese says.

Eventually, *Esquire*'s editors printed the story as Talese had written it. The piece was buried in the back of the September 1996 issue, likely missed by many readers, but interest in the piece was revived, and its virtues celebrated, when the following year it was included in an annual anthology of the nation's best nonfiction writing. "I love the scenes in this piece," Talese says. "I love the cigars, the streets in Cuba, the colors, the scenes with Castro. But maybe I like it so much because it reaffirmed my sense of worth as a published author."

It is fitting that the story that reaffirmed for Talese his worth as a writer concerned an old fighter, a man who can no longer speak, a champion no more, an outsider—the sort of character Talese has always revered and depicted so elegantly in his stories.

MR

ALI IN HAVANA

Esquire, 1996

IT IS A warm, breezy, palm-flapping winter evening in Havana, and the leading restaurants are crowded with tourists from Europe, Asia, and South America being serenaded by guitarists relentlessly singing *"Guan-tan-a-mera . . . guajira . . . Guan-tan-a-mera";* and at the Café Cantante there are clamorous salsa dancers, mambo kings, grunting, bare-chested male performers lifting tables with their teeth, and turbaned women swathed in hip-hugging skirts, blowing whistles while gyrating their glistening bodies into an erotic frenzy. In the café's audience as well as in the restaurants, hotels, and other public places throughout the island, cigarettes and cigars are smoked without restraint or restriction. Two prostitutes are smoking and talking privately on the corner of a dimly lit street bordering the manicured lawns of Havana's five-star Hotel Nacional. They are copper-colored women in their early twenties wearing faded miniskirts and halters, and as they chat, they are watching attentively while two men—one white, the other black—huddle over the raised trunk of a parked red Toyota, arguing about the prices of the boxes of black-market Havana cigars that are stacked within.

The white man is a square-jawed Hungarian in his midthirties, wearing a beige tropical suit and a wide yellow tie, and he is one of Havana's leading entrepreneurs in the thriving illegal business of selling top-quality hand-rolled Cuban cigars below the local and international market price. The black man behind the car is a well-built, baldish, gray-bearded individual in his midfifties from Los Angeles named Howard Bingham; and no matter what price the Hungarian quotes, Bingham shakes his head and says, "No, no—that's too much!"

"You're crazy!" cries the Hungarian in slightly accented English, taking one of the boxes from the trunk and waving it in Howard Bingham's face. "These are Cohiba Esplendidos! The best in the world! You will pay one thousand dollars for a box like this in the States."

"Not me," says Bingham, who wears a Hawaiian shirt with a camera strapped around his neck. He is a professional photographer, and he is staying at the Hotel Nacional with his friend Muhammad Ali. "I wouldn't give you more than fifty dollars."

"You really are crazy," says the Hungarian, slicing through the box's paper seal with his fingernail, opening the lid to reveal a gleaming row of labeled Esplendidos.

"Fifty dollars," says Bingham.

"A hundred dollars," insists the Hungarian. "And hurry! The police could be driving around." The Hungarian straightens up and stares over the car toward the palm-lined lawn and stanchioned lights that glow in the distance along the road leading to the hotel's ornate portico, which is now jammed with people and vehicles; then he turns and flings a glance back toward the nearby public street, where he notices that the prostitutes are now blowing smoke in his direction. He frowns.

"Quick, quick," he says to Bingham, handing him the box. "One hundred dollars."

Howard Bingham does not smoke. He and Muhammad Ali and their traveling companions are leaving Havana tomorrow, after participating in a five-day American humanitarian-aid mission that brought a planeload of medical supplies to hospitals and clinics depleted by the United States's embargo, and Bingham would like to return home with some fine contraband cigars for his friends. But, on the other hand, one hundred is still too much.

"Fifty dollars," says Bingham determinedly, looking at his watch. He begins to walk away.

"Okay, okay," the Hungarian says petulantly. "Fifty."

Bingham reaches into his pocket for the money, and the Hungarian grabs it and gives him the Esplendidos before driving off in the Toyota. One of the prostitutes takes a few steps toward Bingham, but the photographer hurries on to the hotel. Fidel Castro is having a reception tonight for Muhammad Ali, and Bingham has only a half hour to change and be at the portico to catch the chartered bus that will take them to the government's headquarters. He will be bringing one of his photographs to the Cuban leader: an enlarged, framed portrait showing Muhammad Ali and Malcolm X walking together along a Harlem sidewalk in 1963. Malcolm X was thirty-seven at the time, two years away from an assassin's bullet; the twenty-one-year-old Ali was about to win the heavyweight title in a remarkable upset over Sonny Liston in Miami. Bingham's photograph is inscribed, "To President Fidel Castro, from Muhammad Ali." Under his signature, the former champion has sketched a little heart.

*   *   *

Although Muhammad Ali is now fifty-four and has been retired from boxing for more than fifteen years, he is still one of the most famous men in the world, being identifiable throughout five continents; and as he walks through the lobby of the Hotel Nacional toward the bus, wearing a gray sharkskin suit and a white cotton shirt buttoned at the neck without a tie, several guests approach him and request his autograph. It takes him about thirty seconds to write "Muhammad Ali," so shaky are his hands from the effects of Parkinson's syndrome; and though he walks without support, his movements are quite slow, and Howard Bingham and Ali's fourth wife, Yolanda, are following nearby.

Bingham met Ali thirty-five years ago in Los Angeles, shortly after the fighter had turned professional and before he discarded his "slave name" (Cassius Marcellus Clay) and joined the Black Muslims. Bingham subsequently became his closest male friend and has photographed every aspect of Ali's life: his rise and fall three times as the heavyweight champion; his three-year expulsion from boxing, beginning in 1967, for refusing to serve in the U.S. military during the Vietnam War ("I ain't got no quarrel with them Vietcong"); his four marriages; his fatherhood of nine children (one adopted, two out of wedlock); his endless public appearances in all parts of the world—Germany, England, Egypt (sailing on the Nile with a son of Elijah Muhammad's), Sweden, Libya, Pakistan (hugging refugees from Afghanistan), Japan, Indonesia, Ghana (wearing a dashiki and posing with President Kwame Nkrumah), Zaire (beating George Foreman), Manila (beating Joe Frazier) . . . and now, on the final night of his 1996 visit to Cuba, he is en route to a social encounter with an aging contender he has long admired—one who has survived at the top for nearly forty years despite the ill will of nine American presidents, the CIA, the Mafia, and various militant Cuban-Americans.

Bingham waits for Ali near the open door of the charter bus that is blocking the hotel's entrance; but Ali lingers within the crowd in the lobby, and Yolanda steps aside to let some people get closer to her husband.

She is a large and pretty woman of thirty-eight, with a radiant smile and a freckled, fair complexion that reflects her interracial ancestry. A scarf is loosely draped over her head and shoulders, her arms are covered by long sleeves, and her well-designed dress in vivid hues hangs below her knees. She converted to Islam from Catholicism when she married Ali, a man sixteen years her senior but one with whom she shared a familial bond dating back to her girlhood in their native Louisville, where her mother and Ali's mother were sisterly soul mates who traveled together to attend his fights. Yolanda had occasionally joined Ali's entourage, becoming acquainted not only with the boxing element but with Ali's female contemporaries who were his lovers, his wives, the mothers of his children; and she remained in touch with Ali throughout the 1970s, while she majored in psychology at Vanderbilt and later earned her master's degree in business at UCLA. Then—with the end of Ali's boxing career, his third marriage, and his vibrant health—Yolanda intimately entered his life as casually and naturally as she now stands waiting to reclaim her place at his side.

She knows that he is enjoying himself. There is a slight twinkle in his eyes, not much expression on his face, and no words forthcoming from this once most talkative of champions. But the mind behind his Parkinson's mask is functioning normally, and he is characteristically committed to what he is doing: He is spelling out his full name on whatever cards or scraps of paper his admirers are handing him. "Muhammad Ali." He does not settle for a time-saving "Ali" or his mere initials. He has never shortchanged his audience.

And in this audience tonight are people from Latin America, Canada, Africa, Russia, China, Germany, France. There are 200 French travel agents staying at the hotel in conjunction with the Cuban government's campaign to increase its growing tourist trade (which last year saw about 745,000 visitors spending an estimated $1 billion on the island). There is also on hand an Italian movie producer and his lady friend from Rome and a onetime Japanese wrestler, Antonio Inoki, who injured Ali's legs during a 1976 exhibition in Tokyo (but who warmly embraced him two nights ago in the hotel's lounge as they sat listening to Cuban pianist Chucho Valdes playing jazz on a Russian-made Moskva baby grand); and there is also in the crowd, standing taller than the rest, the forty-three-year-old, six-foot five-inch Cuban heavyweight hero Teófilo Stevenson, who was a three-time Olympic gold medalist, in 1972, 1976, and 1980, and who, on this island at least, is every bit as renowned as Ali or Castro.

Though part of Stevenson's reputation derives from his erstwhile power and skill in the ring (although he never fought Ali), it is also attributable to his not having succumbed to the offers of professional boxing promoters, stubbornly resisting the Yankee dollar—although Stevenson hardly seems deprived. He dwells among his countrymen like a towering Cuban peacock, occupying high positions within the government's athletic programs and gaining sufficient attention from the island's women to have garnered four wives so far, who are testimony to his eclectic taste.

His first wife was a dance instructor. His second was an industrial engineer. His third was a medical doctor. His fourth and present wife is a criminal attorney. Her name is Fraymari, and she is a girlishly petite olive-skinned woman of twenty-three who, standing next to her husband in the lobby, rises barely higher than the midsection of his embroidered guayabera—a tightly tailored, short-sleeved shirt that accentuates his tapered torso, his broad shoulders, and the length of his dark, muscular arms, which once prevented his opponents from doing any injustice to his winning Latin looks.

Stevenson always fought from an upright position, and he maintains that posture today. When people talk to him, his eyes look downward, but his head remains high. The firm jaw of his oval-shaped head seems to be locked at a right angle to his straight-spined back. He is a proud man who exhibits all of his height. But he does listen, especially when the words being directed up at him are coming from the perky little attorney who is his wife. Fraymari is now reminding him that it is getting late—everyone should be on the bus; Fidel may be waiting.

Stevenson lowers his eyes toward her and winks. He has gotten the message. He has been Ali's principal escort throughout this visit. He was also Ali's guest in the United States during the fall of 1995; and though he knows only a few words of English, and Ali no Spanish, they are brotherly in their body language.

Stevenson edges himself into the crowd and gently places his right arm around the shoulders of his fellow champion. And then, slowly but firmly, he guides Ali toward the bus.

The road to Fidel Castro's Palace of the Revolution leads through a memory lane of old American automobiles chugging along at about twenty-five miles an hour—springless, pre-embargo Ford coupes and Plymouth sedans, DeSotos and LaSalles, Nashes and Studebakers, and various vehicular collages created out of

Cadillac grilles and Oldsmobile axles and Buick fenders patched with pieces of oil-drum metal and powered by engines inter-linked with kitchen utensils and pre-Batista lawn mowers and other gadgets that have elevated the craft of tinkering in Cuba to the status of high art.

The relatively newer forms of transportation seen on the road are, of course, non-American products: Polish Fiats, Russian Ladas, German motor scooters, Chinese bicycles, and the glistening, newly imported, air-conditioned Japanese bus from which Muhammad Ali is now gazing through a closed window out toward the street. At times, he raises a hand in response to one of the waving pedestrians or cyclists or motorists who recognize the bus, which has been shown repeatedly on the local TV news conveying Ali and his companions to the medical centers and tourist sites that have been part of the busy itinerary.

On the bus, as always, Ali is sitting alone, spread out across the two front seats in the left aisle directly behind the Cuban driver. Yolanda sits a few feet ahead of him to the right; she is adjacent to the driver and within inches of the windshield. The seats behind her are occupied by Teófilo Stevenson, Fraymari, and the photographer Bingham. Seated behind Ali, and also occupying two seats, is an American screenwriter named Greg Howard, who weighs more than 300 pounds. Although he has traveled with Ali for only a few months while researching a film on the fighter's life, Greg Howard has firmly established himself as an intimate sidekick, and as such is among the very few on the trip who have heard Ali's voice. Ali speaks so softly that it is impossible to hear him in a crowd, and as a result whatever public comments or sentiments he is expected to, or chooses to, express are verbalized by Yolanda, or Bingham, or

Teófilo Stevenson, or even at times by this stout young screen-writer.

"Ali is in his Zen period," Greg Howard has said more than once, in reference to Ali's quiescence. Like Ali, he admires what he has seen so far in Cuba—"There's no racism here"—and as a black man he has long identified with many of Ali's frustrations and confrontations. His student thesis at Princeton analyzed the Newark race riots of 1967, and the Hollywood script he most recently completed focuses on the Negro baseball leagues of the pre-World War II years. He envisions his new work on Ali in the genre of *Gandhi*.

The two-dozen bus seats behind those tacitly reserved for Ali's inner circle are occupied by the secretary-general of the Cuban Red Cross and the American humanitarian personnel who have entrusted him with $500,000 worth of donated medical supplies; and there are also the two Cuban interpreters and a dozen members of the American media, including the CBS-TV commentator Ed Bradley and his producers and camera crew from *60 Minutes*.

Ed Bradley is a gracious but reserved individualist who has appeared on television for a decade with his left earlobe pierced by a small circular ring—which, after some unfavorable comment initially expressed by his colleagues Mike Wallace and Andy Rooney, prompted Bradley's explanation: "It's *my* ear." Bradley also indulges in his identity as a cigar smoker; and as he sits in the midsection of the bus next to his Haitian lady friend, he is taking full advantage of the Communist regime's laissez-faire attitude toward tobacco, puffing away on a Cohiba Robusto, for which he paid full price at the Nacional's tobacco shop—and which now exudes a costly cloud of fragrance that appeals to his friend (who occasionally also smokes cigars) but is not appreciated by the two California women who are seated two rows back and are affiliated with a humanitarian-aid agency.

Indeed, the women have been commenting about the smoking habits of countless people they have encountered in Havana, being especially disappointed to discover earlier this very day that the pediatric hospital they visited (and to which they committed donations) is under the supervision of three tobacco-loving family physicians. When one of the American women, a blonde from Santa Barbara, reproached one of the cigarette-smoking doctors indirectly for setting such a poor example, she was told in effect that the island's health statistics regarding longevity, infant mortality, and general fitness compared favorably with those in the United States and were probably better than those of Americans residing in the capital city of Washington. On the other hand, the doctor made it clear that he did not believe that smoking was good for one's health—after all, Fidel himself had given it up; but unfortunately, the doctor added, in a classic understatement, "some people have not followed him."

Nothing the doctor said appeased the woman from Santa Barbara. She did not, however, wish to appear confrontational at the hospital's news conference, which was covered by the press; nor during her many bus rides with Ed Bradley did she ever request that he discard his cigar. "Mr. Bradley intimidates me," she confided to her California coworker. But he was of course living within the law on this island that the doctor had called "the cradle of the best tobacco in the world." In Cuba, the most available American periodical on the newsstands is *Cigar Aficionado*.

*　　*　　*

The bus passes through the Plaza de la Revolución and comes to a halt at a security checkpoint near the large glass doors that open onto the marble-floored foyer of a 1950s modern building that is the center of communism's only stronghold in the Western Hemisphere.

As the bus door swings open, Greg Howard moves forward in his seat and grabs the 235-pound Muhammad Ali by the arms and shoulders and helps him to his feet; and after Ali has made his way down to the metal step, he turns and stretches back into the bus to take hold of the extended hands and forearms of the 300-pound screenwriter and pulls him to a standing position. This routine, repeated at each and every bus stop throughout the week, is never accompanied by either man's acknowledging that he has received any assistance, although Ali is aware that some passengers find the pas de deux quite amusing, and he is not reluctant to use his friend to further comic effect. After the bus had made an earlier stop in front of the sixteenth-century Morro Castle—where Ali had followed Teófilo Stevenson up a 117-step spiral staircase for a rooftop view of Havana Harbor—he spotted the solitary figure of Greg Howard standing below in the courtyard. Knowing that there was no way the narrow staircase could accommodate Howard's wide body, Ali suddenly began to wave his arms, summoning Howard to come up and join him.

Castro's security guards, who know in advance the names of all the bus passengers, guide Ali and the others through the glass doors and then into a pair of waiting elevators for a brief ride, which is followed by a short walk through a corridor and finally into a large white-walled reception room, where it is announced that Fidel Castro will soon join them. The room has high ceilings and potted palms in every corner and is sparsely furnished with modern tan leather furniture. Next to a sofa is a table with two telephones, one gray and the other red. Overlooking the sofa is an oil painting of the Viñales Valley, which lies west of Havana; and among the primitive art displayed on a circular table in front of the sofa is a grotesque tribal figure similar to the one Ali had examined earlier in the week at a trinket stand while touring with the group in Havana's Old Square. Ali had then whispered into the ear of Howard Bingham, and Bingham had repeated aloud what Ali had said: "Joe Frazier."

Ali now stands in the middle of the room, next to Bingham, who carries under his arm the framed photograph he plans to give Castro. Teófilo Stevenson and Fraymari stand facing them. The diminutive and delicate-boned Fraymari has painted her lips scarlet and has pulled back her hair in a matronly manner, hoping no doubt to appear more mature than her twenty-three years suggest, but standing next to the three much older and heavier and taller men transforms her image closer to that of an anorexic teenager. Ali's wife and Greg Howard are wandering about within the group that is exchanging comments in muted tones, either in English or Spanish, sometimes assisted by the interpreters. Ali's hands are shaking uncontrollably at his sides; but since his companions have witnessed this all week, the only people who are now paying attention are the security guards posted near the door.

Also waiting near the door for Castro is the four-man CBS camera team, and chatting with them and his two producers is Ed Bradley, without his cigar. There are no ashtrays in this room! This is a most uncommon sight in Cuba. Its implications might be political. Perhaps the sensibilities of the blonde woman from Santa Barbara were taken into account by the doctors at the hospital and communicated to Castro's under-lings, who are now making a conciliatory gesture toward their American benefactress.

Since the security guards have not invited the guests to be seated, everybody remains standing—for ten minutes, for twenty minutes, and then for a full half hour. Teófilo Stevenson shifts his weight from foot to foot and gazes over the heads of the crowd toward the upper level of the portal through which Castro is expected to enter—if he shows up. Stevenson knows from experience that Castro's schedule is unpredictable. There is always a crisis of some sort in Cuba, and it has long been rumored on the island that Castro constantly changes the location of where he sleeps. The identity of his bed partners is, of course, a state secret. Two nights ago, Stevenson and Ali and the rest were kept waiting until midnight for an expected meeting with Castro at the Hotel Biocaribe (to which Bingham had brought his gift photograph). But Castro never appeared. And no explanation was offered.

Now in this reception room, it was already 9 P.M. Ali continues to shake. No one has had dinner. The small talk is getting smaller. A few people would like to smoke. The regime is not assuaging anyone in this crowd with a bartender. It is a cocktail party without cocktails. There are not even canapés or soft drinks. Everyone is becoming increasingly restless—and then suddenly there is a collective sigh. The very familiar man with the beard strides into the room, dressed for guerrilla combat; and in a cheerful, high-pitched voice that soars beyond his whiskers, he announces, "*Buenas noches!*"

In an even higher tone, he repeats, "*Buenas noches,*" this time with a few waves to the group while hastening toward the guest of honor; and then, with his arms extended, the seventy-year-old Fidel Castro immediately obscures the lower half of Ali's expressionless face with a gentle embrace and his flowing gray beard.

"I am glad to see you," Castro says to Ali, via the interpreter who followed him into the room, a comely, fair-skinned woman with a refined English accent. "I am very, very glad to see you," Castro continues, backing up to look into Ali's eyes while holding on to his trembling arms, "and I am thankful for your visit." Castro then releases his grip and awaits a possible reply. Ali says nothing. His expression remains characteristically fixed and benign, and his eyes do not blink despite the flashbulbs of several surrounding photographers. As the silence persists, Castro turns toward his old friend Teófilo Stevenson, feigning a jab. The Cuban boxing champion lowers his eyes and, with widened lips and cheeks, registers a smile. Castro then notices the tiny brunette standing beside Stevenson.

"Stevenson, who is this young woman?" Castro asks aloud in a tone of obvious approval. But before Stevenson can reply, Fraymari steps forward with a hint of lawyerly indignation: "You mean you don't remember me?"

Castro seems stunned. He smiles feebly, trying to conceal his confusion. He turns inquiringly toward his boxing hero, but Stevenson's eyes only roll upward. Stevenson knows that Castro has met Fraymari socially on earlier occasions, but unfortunately the Cuban leader has forgotten, and it is equally unfortunate that Fraymari is now behaving like a prosecutor.

"You held my son in your arms before he was one year old!" she reminds him while Castro continues to ponder. The crowd is attentive; the television cameras are rolling.

"At a volleyball game?" Castro asks tentatively.

"No, no," Stevenson interrupts, before Fraymari can say anything more, "that was my former wife. The doctor."

Castro slowly shakes his head in mock disapproval. Then he

abruptly turns away from the couple, but not before reminding Stevenson, "You should get name tags."

Castro redirects his attention to Muhammad Ali. He studies Ali's face.

"Where is your wife?" he asks softly. Ali says nothing. There is more silence and turning of heads in the group until Howard Bingham spots Yolanda standing near the back and waves her to Castro's side.

Before she arrives, Bingham steps forward and presents Castro with the photograph of Ali and Malcolm X in Harlem in 1963. Castro holds it up level with his eyes and studies it silently for several seconds. When this picture was taken, Castro had been in control of Cuba for nearly four years. He was then thirty-seven. In 1959, he defeated the U.S.-backed dictator Fulgencio Batista, overcoming odds greater than Ali's subsequent victory over the supposedly unbeatable Sonny Liston. Batista had actually announced Castro's death back in 1956. Castro, then hiding in a secret outpost, thirty years old and beardless, was a disgruntled Jesuit-trained lawyer who was born into a landowning family and who craved Batista's job. At thirty-two, he had it. Batista was forced to flee to the Dominican Republic.

During this period, Muhammad Ali was only an amateur. His greatest achievement would come in 1960, when he received a gold medal in Rome as a member of the U.S. Olympic boxing team. But later in the sixties, he and Castro would share the world stage as figures moving against the American establishment—and now, in the twilight of their lives, on this winter's night in Havana, they meet for the first time: Ali silent and Castro isolated on his island.

"*Que bien!*" Castro says to Howard Bingham before showing the photograph to his interpreter. Then Castro is introduced by Bingham to Ali's wife. After they exchange greetings through the interpreter, he asks her, as if surprised, "You don't speak Spanish?"

"No," she says softly. She begins to caress her husband's left wrist, on which he wears a $250 silver Swiss Army watch she bought him. It is the only jewelry Ali wears.

"But I thought I saw you speaking Spanish on the TV news this week," Castro continues wonderingly before acknowledging that her voice had obviously been dubbed.

"Do you live in New York?"

"No, we live in Michigan."

"Cold," says Castro.

"Very cold," she repeats.

"In Michigan, don't you find many people that speak Spanish?"

"No, not many," she says. "Mostly in California, New York"—and, after a pause—"Florida."

Castro nods. It takes him a few seconds to think up another question. Small talk has never been the forte of this man who specializes in nonstop haranguing monologues that can last for hours; and yet here he is, in a room crowded with camera crews and news photographers—a talk-show host with a guest of honor who is speechless. But Fidel Castro plods on, asking Ali's wife if she has a favorite sport.

"I play a little tennis," Yolanda says, and then asks him, "Do you play tennis?"

"Ping-Pong," he replies, quickly adding that during his youth he had been active in the ring. "I spent hours boxing . . ." He begins to reminisce, but before he finishes his sentence, he sees the slowly rising right fist of Muhammad Ali moving toward his chin! Exuberant cheering and hand clapping resound through the room, and Castro jumps sideways toward Stevenson, shouting, *"Asesorame!"*—"Help me!"

Stevenson's long arms land upon Ali's shoulders from behind, squeezing him gently; and then, after he releases him, the two ex-champions face each other and begin to act out in slow motion the postures of competing prizefighters—bobbing, weaving, swinging, ducking—all of it done without touching and all of it accompanied by three minutes of ongoing applause and the clicking of cameras, and also some feelings of relief from Ali's friends because, in his own way, he has decided to join them. Ali still says nothing, his face still inscrutable, but he is less remote, less alone, and he does not pull away from Stevenson's embrace as the latter eagerly tells Castro about a boxing exhibition that he and Ali had staged earlier in the week at the Balado gym, in front of hundreds of fans and some of the island's up-and-coming contenders.

Stevenson did not actually explain that it had been merely another photo opportunity, one in which they sparred open-handed in the ring, wearing their street clothes and barely touching each other's bodies and faces; but then Stevenson had climbed out of the ring, leaving Ali to the more taxing test of withstanding two abbreviated rounds against one and then another young bully of grade-school age who clearly had not come to participate in a kiddie show. They had come to floor the champ. Their bellicose little bodies and hot-gloved hands and helmeted hell-bent heads were consumed with fury and ambition; and as they charged ahead, swinging wildly and swaggering to the roars of their teenage friends and relatives at ringside, one could imagine their future boastings to their grandchildren: On one fine day back in the winter of '96, I whacked Muhammad Ali! Except, in truth, on this particular day, Ali was still too fast for them. He backpedaled and shifted and swayed, stood on the toes of his black woven-leather pointed shoes, and showed that his body was made for motion—his

Parkinson's problems were lost in his shuffle, in the thrusts of his butterfly sting what whistled two feet above the heads of his aspiring assailants, in the dazzling dips of his rope-a-dope that had confounded George Foreman in Zaire, in his ever-memorable style, which in this Cuban gym moistened the eyes of his ever-observant photographer friend and provoked the overweight screenwriter to cry out in a voice that few in this noisy Spanish crowd could understand, "Ali's on a high! Ali's on a high!"

Teófilo Stevenson raises Ali's right arm above the head of Castro, and the news photographers spend several minutes posing the three of them together in flashing light. Castro then sees Fraymari watching alone at some distance. She is not smiling. Castro nods toward her. He summons a photographer to take a picture of Fraymari and himself. But she relaxes only after her husband comes over to join her in the conversation, which Castro immediately directs to the health and growth of their son, who is not yet two years old.

"Will he be as tall as his father?" Castro asks.

"I assume so," Fraymari says, glancing up toward her husband. She also has to look up when talking to Fidel Castro, for the Cuban leader is taller than six feet and his posture is nearly as erect as her husband's. Only the six-foot three-inch Muhammad Ali, who is standing with Bingham on the far side of her husband—and whose skin coloring, oval-shaped head, and burr-style haircut are very similar to her husband's—betrays his height with the slope-shouldered forward slouch he has developed since his illness.

"How much does your son weigh?" Castro continues.

"When he was one year old, he was already twenty-six

pounds," Fraymari says. "This is three above normal. He was walking at nine months."

"She still breast-feeds him," Teófilo Stevenson says, seeming pleased.

"Oh, that's very nourishing," agrees Castro.

"Sometimes the kid becomes confused and thinks my chest is his mother's breast," Stevenson says, and he could have added that his son is also confused by Ali's sunglasses. The little boy engraved teeth marks all over the plastic frames while chewing on them during the days he accompanied his parents on Ali's bus tour.

As a CBS boom pole swoops down closer to catch the conversation, Castro reaches out to touch Stevenson's belly and asks, "How much do you weigh?"

"Two hundred thirty-eight pounds, more or less."

"That's thirty-eight more than me," Castro says, but he complains, "I eat very little. Very little. The diet advice I get is never accurate. I eat around fifteen hundred calories—less than thirty grams of protein, less than that."

Castro slaps a hand against his own midsection, which is relatively flat. If he does have a potbelly, it is concealed within his well-tailored uniform. Indeed, for a man of seventy, he seems in fine health. His facial skin is florid and unsagging, his dark eyes dart around the room with ever-alert intensity, and he has a full head of lustrous gray hair not thinning at the crown. The attention he pays to himself might be measured from his manicured fingernails down to his square-toed boots, which are unscuffed and smoothly buffed without the burnish of a lackey's spit shine. But his beard seems to belong to another man and another time. It is excessively long and scraggly. Wispy white hairs mix with the faded black and dangle down the front of his uniform like an old shroud, weatherworn and drying out. It is the beard from the hills. Castro strokes it constantly, as if trying to revive the vitality of its fiber.

Castro now looks at Ali.

"How's your appetite?" he asks, forgetting that Ali is not speaking.

"Where's your wife?" he then asks aloud, and Howard Bingham calls out to her. Yolanda has once more drifted back into the group.

When she arrives, Castro hesitates before speaking to her. It is as if he is not absolutely sure who she is. He has met so many people since arriving, and with the group rotating constantly due to the jostling of the photographers, Castro cannot be certain whether the woman at his side is Muhammad Ali's wife or Ed Bradley's friend or some other woman he met moments ago who left him with an unlasting impression. Having already committed a faux pas regarding one of the wives of the two multimarried ex-champions standing nearby, Castro waits for some hint from his interpreter. None is offered. Fortunately, he does not have to worry in this country about the women's vote—or any vote, for that matter—but he does sigh in mild relief when Yolanda reintroduces herself as Ali's wife and does so by name.

"Ah, Yolanda," Castro repeats, "what a beautiful name. That's the name of a queen somewhere."

"In our household," she says.

"And how is your husband's appetite?"

"Good, but he likes sweets."

"We can send you some of our ice cream to Michigan," Castro says. Without waiting for her to comment, he asks, "Michigan is very cold?"

"Oh, yes," she replies, not indicating that they already discussed Michigan's winter weather.

"How much snow?"

"We didn't get hit with the blizzard," Yolanda says, referring to a storm in January, "but it can get three, four feet—"

Teófilo Stevenson interrupts to say that he had been in Michigan during the previous October.

"Oh," Castro says, raising an eyebrow. He mentions that during the same month he had also been in the United States (attending the United Nations' fiftieth-anniversary tribute). He asks Stevenson the length of his American visit.

"I was there for nineteen days," says Stevenson.

"Nineteen days!" Castro repeats. "Longer than I was."

Castro complains that he was limited to five days and prohibited from traveling beyond New York.

"Well, *comandante*," Stevenson responds offhandedly, in a slightly superior tone, "if you like, I will sometime show you my video."

Stevenson appears to be very comfortable in the presence of the Cuban leader, and perhaps the latter has habitually encouraged this; but at this moment, Castro may well be finding his boxing hero a bit condescending and worthy of a retaliatory jab. He knows how to deliver it.

"When you visited the United States," Castro asks pointedly, "did you bring your wife, the lawyer?"

Stevenson stiffens. He directs his eyes toward his wife. She turns away.

"No," Stevenson answers quietly. "I went alone."

Castro abruptly shifts his attention to the other side of the room, where the CBS camera crew is positioned, and he asks Ed Bradley, "What do you do?"

"We're making a documentary on Ali," Bradley explains, "and we followed him to Cuba to see what he was doing in Cuba and . . ."

Bradley's voice is suddenly overwhelmed by the sounds of laughter and hand clapping. Bradley and Castro turn to discover that Muhammad Ali is now reclaiming everyone's attention. He is holding his shaky left fist in the air; but instead of assuming a boxer's pose, as he did earlier, he is beginning to pull out from the top of his upraised fist, slowly and with dramatic delicacy, the tip of a red silk handkerchief that is pinched between his right index finger and thumb.

After he pulls out the entire handkerchief, he dangles it in the air for a few seconds, waving it closer and closer to the forehead of the wide-eyed Fidel Castro. Ali seems bewitched. He continues to stare stagnantly at Castro and the others, surrounded by applause that he gives no indication he hears. Then he proceeds to place the handkerchief back into the top of his cupped left hand—packing with the pinched fingers of his right—and then quickly opens his palms toward his audience and reveals that the handkerchief has disappeared.

"Where is it?" cries Castro, who seems to be genuinely surprised and delighted. He approaches Ali and examines his hands, repeating, "Where is it? Where have you put it?"

Everyone who has traveled on Ali's bus during the week knows where he hid it. They saw him perform the trick repeatedly in front of some of the patients and doctors at the hospitals and clinics as well as before countless tourists who recognized him in his hotel lobby or during his strolls through the town square. They also saw him follow up each performance with a demonstration that exposed his method. He keeps hidden in his fist a flesh-colored rubber thumb that contains the handkerchief that he will eventually pull out with the fingers of his other hand; and when he is reinserting the handkerchief, he is actually shoving the material back into the concealed rubber thumb, into which he then inserts his own right thumb. When he opens his hands, the uninformed among his onlookers are seeing his empty palms and missing the fact that the handkerchief is tucked within the rubber thumb that is covering his outstretched right thumb. Sharing with his audience the mystery of his magic always earns him additional applause.

After Ali performs and explains the trick to Castro, he gives Castro the rubber thumb to examine—and, with more zest than he has shown all evening, Castro says, "Oh, let me try it; I want to try—it's the first time I have seen such a wonderful thing!" And after a few minutes of coaching from Howard Bingham, who long ago learned how to do it from Ali, the Cuban leader performs with sufficient dexterity and panache to satisfy his magical ambitions and to arouse another round of applause from the guests.

Meanwhile, more than ten minutes have passed since Ali began his comic routine. It is already after 9:30 P.M., and the commentator Ed Bradley, whose conversation with Castro was interrupted, is concerned that the Cuban leader might leave the room without responding to the questions Bradley prepared for his show. Bradley edges close to Castro's interpreter, saying in a voice that is sure to be heard, "Would you ask him if he followed . . . was able to follow Ali when he was boxing professionally?"

The question is relayed and repeated until Castro, facing the CBS camera, replies, "Yes, I recall the days when they were discussing the possibilities of a match between the two of them"—he nods toward Stevenson and Ali—"and I remember when he went to Africa."

"In Zaire," Bradley clarifies, referring to Ali's victory in 1974 over George Foreman. And he follows up: "What kind of impact did he have in this country, because he was a revolutionary as well as . . . ?"

"It was great," Castro says. "He was very much admired as a sportsman, as a boxer, as a person. There was always a high opinion of him. But I never guessed one day we would meet here, with this kind gesture of bringing medicine, seeing our children, visiting our polyclinics. I am very glad, I am thrilled, to have the opportunity to meet him personally, to appreciate his kindness. I see he is strong. I see he has a very kind face."

Castro is speaking as if Ali were not in the room, standing a few feet away. Ali maintains his fixed facade even as Stevenson whispers into his ear, asking in English, "Muhammad, Muhammad, why you no speak?" Stevenson then turns to tell the journalist who stands behind him, "Muhammad does speak. He speaks to me." Stevenson says nothing more because Castro is now looking at him while continuing to tell Bradley, "I am very glad that he and Stevenson have met." After a pause, Castro adds, "And I am glad that they never fought."

"He's not so sure," Bradley interjects, smiling in the direction of Stevenson.

"I find in that friendship something beautiful," Castro insists softly.

"There is a tie between the two of them," Bradley says.

"Yes," says Castro. "It is true." He again looks at Ali, then at Stevenson, as if searching for something more profound to say.

"And how's the documentary?" he finally asks Bradley.

"It'll be on *60 Minutes*."

"When?"

"Maybe one month," Bradley says, reminding Castro's interpreter, "This is the program on which the *comandante* has been interviewed by Dan Rather a number of times in the past, when Dan Rather was on *60 Minutes*."

"And who's there now?" Castro wants to know.

"I am," Bradley answers.

"You," Castro repeats, with a quick glance at Bradley's earring. "So you are there—the boss now?"

Bradley responds as a media star without illusions: "I'm a worker."

Trays containing coffee, tea, and orange juice finally arrive, but only in amounts sufficient for Ali and Yolanda, Howard Bingham, Greg Howard, the Stevensons, and Castro—although Castro tells the waiters he wants nothing.

Castro motions for Ali and the others to join him across the room, around the circular table. The camera crews and the rest of the guests follow, standing as near to the principals as they can. But throughout the group there is a discernible restlessness. They have been standing for more than an hour and a half. It is now approaching 10 P.M. There has been no food. And for the vast majority, it is clear that there will also be nothing to drink. Even among the special guests, seated and sipping from chilled glasses or hot cups, there is a waning level of fascination with the evening. Indeed, Muhammad Ali's eyes were closed. He is sleeping.

Yolanda sits next to him on the sofa, pretending not to notice. Castro also ignores it, although he sits directly across the table, with the interpreter and the Stevensons.

"How large is Michigan?" Castro begins a new round of questioning with Yolanda, returning for the third time to a subject they explored beyond the interest of anyone in the room except Castro himself.

"I don't know how big the state is as far as demographics,"

Yolanda says. "We live in a very small village [Barrien Springs] with about two thousand people."

"Are you going back to Michigan tomorrow?"

"Yes."

"What time?"

"Two-thirty."

"Via Miami?" Castro asks.

"Yes."

"From Miami, where do you fly?"

"We're flying to Michigan."

"How many hours' flight?"

"We have to change at Cincinnati—about two and a half hours."

"Flying time?" asks Castro.

Muhammad Ali opens his eyes, then closes them.

"Flying time," Yolanda repeats.

"From Miami to Michigan?" Castro continues.

"No," she again explains, but still with patience, "we have to go to Cincinnati. There are no direct flights."

"So you have to take two planes?" Castro asks.

"Yes," she says, adding for clarification, "Miami to Cincinnati—and then Cincinnati to South Bend, Indiana."

"From Cincinnati . . . ?"

"To South Bend," she says. "That's the closest airport."

"So," Fidel goes on, "it is on the outskirts of the city?"

"Yes."

"You have a farm?"

"No," Yolanda says, "just land. We let someone else do the growing."

She mentions that Teófilo Stevenson traveled through this part of the Midwest. The mention of his name gains Stevenson's attention.

"I was in Chicago," Stevenson tells Castro.

"You were at their home?" Castro asks.

"No," Yolanda corrects Stevenson, "you were in Michigan."

"I was in the countryside," Stevenson says. Unable to resist, he adds, "I have a video of that visit. I'll show it to you sometime."

Castro seems not to hear him. He directs his attention back to Yolanda, asking her where she was born, where she was educated, when she became married, and how many years separate her age from that of her husband, Muhammad Ali.

After Yolanda acknowledges being sixteen years younger than Ali, Castro turns toward Fraymari and with affected sympathy says that she married a man who is twenty years her senior.

"*Comandante!*" Stevenson intercedes, "I am in shape. Sports keep you healthy. Sports add years to your life and life to your years!"

"Oh, what conflict she has," Castro goes on, ignoring Stevenson and catering to Fraymari—and to the CBS cameraman who steps forward for a closer view of Castro's face. "She is a lawyer, and she does not put this husband in jail." Castro is enjoying much more than Fraymari the attention this topic is now getting from the group. Castro had lost his audience and now has it back and seemingly wants to retain it, no matter at what cost to Stevenson's harmony with Fraymari. Yes, Castro continues, Fraymari had the misfortune to select a husband "who can never settle down. . . . Jail would be an appropriate place for him."

"*Comandante*," Stevenson interrupts in a jocular manner that seems intended to placate both the lawyer who is his spouse and the lawyer who rules the country, "I might as well be locked up!" He implies that should he deviate from marital fidelity, his lawyer wife "will surely put me in a place where she is the only woman who can visit me!"

Everyone around the table and within the circling group laughs. Ali is now awake. The banter between Castro and Stevenson resumes until Yolanda, all but rising in her chair, tells Castro, "We have to pack."

"You're going to have dinner now?" he asks.

"Yes, sir," she says. Ali stands, along with Howard Bingham. Yolanda thanks Castro's interpreter directly, saying, "Be sure to tell him, 'You're always welcome in our home.'" The interpreter quotes Castro as again complaining that when he visits America, he is usually restricted to New York, but he adds, "Things change."

The group watches as Yolanda and Ali pass through, and Castro follows them into the hallway. The elevator arrives, and its door is held open by a security guard. Castro extends his final farewell with handshakes—and only then does he discover that he holds Ali's rubber thumb in his hand. Apologizing, he tries to hand it back to Ali, but Bingham politely protests. "No, no," Bingham says, "Ali wants you to have it."

Castro's interpretor at first fails to understand what Bingham is saying.

"He wants you to keep it," Bingham repeats.

Bingham enters the elevator with Ali and Yolanda. Before the door closes, Castro smiles, waves good-bye, and stares with curiosity at the rubber thumb. Then he puts it in his pocket.

OVERTIME

SWAN SONG FOR GAY TALESE

Ocean City Sentinel-Ledger, 1949

A LL GOOD THINGS come to an end, some time or another, and so does my relationship with the *Sentinel-Ledger*.

It has been more than two years since I first began to cover the sports front for this newspaper. Now, as I look back over those years, I realize that I enjoyed every hour of it and am now sorry to call it quits.

I consider myself lucky to have had an opportunity to contribute to such a fine weekly and come in contact with such swell people around the office. There could have been no better experience for a teen-ager interested in this business than to work for a small town newspaper like this one.

Now, however, myself and thousands of other ex-high school seniors begin a life on a college campus. For me, it'll be the University of Alabama, and a real Southerner is I gonna be! Away down there, in the deep South, with a rat cap to wear and a button to display on my lapel. No BMOC yet, but only a Freshman, the lowest living thing in creation.

But I'll really miss writing for this paper, no kidding. I will also miss seeing the football season, for the first time since I knew the difference between a pigskin and a milk bottle.

I'm going to miss reporting on basketball, my favorite sport to cover. It gave me a thrill to write about it, especially last year when I wrote about a winner. And besides, I prefer to take notes inside, instead of freezing my fingers stiff on a frozen football field.

I cannot say I got started in a blaze of glory in this business. I was no Don Parker, believe me. My main trouble at the start was spelling easy words. Mostly carelessness. The poor copy reader had a miserable time of it. As a reporter, I was as green as Mrs. Murphy on St. Pat's Day.

My first assignment was to report on the progress of the girls in Home Economics class. A great topic! It took me an hour to pound out a few paragraphs, but as time passed I improved, or so the editor said.

I should say something about this Editor, just about the greatest guy that ever corrected a misspelled word. Lorin D. Angevine, (Mr. Angevine to me) is a great teacher of the field and a wonderful person to work for. You just don't want to let a person like him down.

He still says that I'm the "World's Worst" when it comes to spelling the easy words, but whenever he heckles me, I always come back with, "Well, whatta ya want for a dime an inch—Walter WINDchell?" That holds him.

This good-natured ribbing goes on and on and never ceases. Everyone seems happy around the office.

My successor is one whom I believe will do a fine job as sports writer and school reporter. He is Bob Halleran, now a senior, and the favorite son of Ocean City's gift to literature—Mr. Eugene (Who Dun It?) Halleran; among other things, a teacher of American History at the local high school. Maybe Junior will be a chip off the ol' block when it comes to writing. Mr. Angevine hopes so.

When I first began, I thought this job of writing sports was about as easy as easy could be. I thought of the metropolitan sports writers—Red Smith, Jimmy Powers, Jimmy Cannon, et al. Whatta racket it was, I thought to myself.

The guys get into the ball parks, fights, races, etc., for nothing, and they have the nerve to take a salary, besides! This was the field for me.

Then, when I started to hear complaints about everything from typographical errors to "I didn't like what you wrote, take this—Ouch!"

And when I began getting the "cold treatment" from some of the two-bit "athletes" around here (and I don't mean Toni cold wave) for writing about their flubbing a play that lost a game, then I got my taste of what sports writers have to go through.

Invariably it's the "bench warmers" who give you the most trouble, the guys who'll never make Varsity with their skill, but only with their lip. You never hear a thank you for writing some glowing report about "Joseph V. Holeteam," but let there come a time when you have to say something non-flattering. Then you are labeled persona non grata!

But I'm finished with it. Now I'd better get ready and not miss the Southern Express.

Maybe Sportopics will be continued in the Crimson Tide of Alabamee, pertaining to the 'Bama boys instead of the Red

Raiders. This University, I am told and have read, has one of the most beautiful campuses and co-eds (Ooo la la!) in the U. S. Never cold there.

Yes, it'll be hard to take, listenin' to those Suth'rn femmes with that cute drawl.

Oh, well, if you gotta go, guess ya' just gotta go. Merry Christmas, yo' Yankees, yo'! This is Gaylord signing off.

A NOTE ON THE AUTHOR

Gay Talese is an internationally acclaimed and bestselling author whose works include *Unto the Sons, Honor Thy Father, Thy Neighbor's Wife, A Writer's Life, The Kingdom and the Power, The Bridge,* and *The Gay Talese Reader.* He lives in New York City and Ocean City, New Jersey.

A NOTE ON THE EDITOR

Michael Rosenwald is a staff writer at the *Washington Post* and has written for the *New Yorker, Esquire,* and *GQ.*